An Alley in Chicago

The Ministry of a City Priest

by
Margery Frisbie

Sheed & Ward

Sheed & Ward™ is a service of National Catholic Reporter Publishing Company, Inc.

Library of Congress Cataloging-in-Publication Data

Frisbie, Margery.
      An alley in Chicago : the ministry of a city priest / by Margery Frisbie.
          p.   cm.
      Includes index.
      ISBN: 1-55612-463-5 (pbk. : alk. paper)
      1. Egan, John J.   2. Catholic Church—United States—Clergy—Biography.   I. Title
      BX4705.E17F75 1991
      282'.092—dc20   91-61105
      [B]   CIP

Published by: Sheed & Ward
                115 E. Armour Blvd. P.O. Box 419492
                Kansas City, MO 64141-6492

To order, call: (800) 333-7373

Cover painting of Holy Name Cathedral, Chicago, by Franklin McMahon.

Contents

For Richard

Acknowledgments

This book is based largely on a series of interviews with Monsignor John Joseph Egan, about one hundred hours in all. I am in debt to him and to his administrative assistant, Peggy Roach, for their overwhelming willingness to further the cause of the book in any way they could. There was nothing they could do that they were not willing to do.

Author/columnist Georgie Anne Geyer, long-time friend of Monsignor Egan, showed her devotion to him by taking the manuscript on flights to several continents, meticulously editing as she flew. Her suggestions to add here, rip out there, dramatize in places, all seemed on target to the grateful author. People willing to contribute interesting sidelights on Monsignor Egan's life are too numerous to mention, but those who were willing to interrupt their busy lives for lengthy interviews must be thanked: Rev. Arthur Brazier, Rev. James Burtchaell, Richard Conklin, Patty Crowley, Mary Dowling, Harry Fagan, Tom Foran, Tom Gaudette, Rev. Joseph Gremillion, Rev. Theodore Hesburgh, John Hill, Patricia Hollahan Judge, Bishop Timothy Lyne, Edward Marciniak, Rabbi Robert Marx, Nina Polcyn Moore, Kathy Pelletier Moriarity, Rev. Philip Murnion, David Ramage, Mary Louise Schniedwind, Evelyn and James Whitehead.

In an interesting reversal of role, my husband Richard to whom this book is dedicated did much of the basic drudge work: editing, spellchecking, printing out endless revisions, and holding the author's hand both literally and figuratively when it was necessary.

"Writing," Graham Greene once said, "is for the most part a lonely and unsatisfying occupation. One is tied to a table, a chair, a stack of paper." When one has a chance to work with Monsignor Egan and those who have shared his life, writing has its compensations. It is a more satisfying and less lonely occupation.

When I shall be dead,
tell the kingdom of the earth
that I loved it much more
than I ever dared to say.

—Georges Bernanos

Preface

Monsignor John Joseph Egan has two great loves: his Church and his city. Like all good priests, he brings the sacraments to his people. Like the best of Chicago politicians, with whom he has a lot in common, he's forever working the angles to improve his people's lives. Like every gifted preacher, Monsignor Egan also likes a good story when he hears one, especially a story that strikes close to his heart like one of his favorites about the famous, perhaps notorious, Monsignor Patrick J. Molloy.

The then-Father Molloy functioned in the 1920s as the trusted go-between between two gangs warring for Chicago's profitable bootlegging trade. Al Capone, the most powerful gang boss of his day, had a weekly payroll of $300,000. He could brag, "I own the police," because half the police in the county were on his payroll. He also "owned" aldermen, state's attorneys, mayors, legislators, and even congresspersons. The only major force in Capone's way in 1927 was the brash Bugsy Moran who served three prison sentences before he was twenty-one for twenty-six known robberies. The leader of the North Side gang hated Capone and tried to assassinate him. Between them, Capone and Moran gave Chicago a reputation it has never shaken.

What Father Molloy was trusted to carry back and forth between the gangs is no longer known, but when $600,000 was "misplaced" between one gang and the other, a friendly phone caller let George Cardinal Mundelein know that if Molloy wasn't out of town by midnight, he'd be at the bottom of the Chicago River by daylight. Father Molloy was transferred fast and far away—to Argentina.

As Father Molloy grew familiar with the Southern Cross, Chicago's gang wars moderated. The Bugs Moran gang was whittled down by the famous St. Valentine's Day Massacre. Then the Depression slicing into drinkers' disposable income cut Capone's profits. He could no longer pay off the police and the politicians. In 1931 he was sent to prison for income tax invasion. The gang wars had mowed down a thousand people, but they were over. It was safe for Father Patrick Molloy to come back to Chicago, to Annunciation Church, and then to St. Leo the Great Church at Seventy-eighth and Emerald Avenue on Chicago's South Side.

On the fortieth anniversary of his ordination, Father Molloy was invested as a Domestic Prelate with the title Right Reverend Monsignor. The party was grand. Samuel Cardinal Stritch was present, as was Monsignor Molloy's good friend, Mayor Richard J. Daley. Molloy circulated happily among family members, politicians, policemen, parishioners, trusted clergy, "and probably a few old time members of the mobs," according to Monsignor Egan.

When it was Monsignor Molloy's turn at the podium it was clear to all how happy he was to be home. "I have seen the great boulevards of the world," he told friends gathered in his church basement. "The boulevards of Rome. The boulevards of Paris. The boulevards of Rio de Janeiro. The boulevards of Tokyo. They are all grand." His voice had risen dramatically. His audience was in his hands where he liked to have them. He paused only briefly before he acknowledged his devotion to his native city. "But I would rather have an alley in Chicago than any one of them."

Monsignor Egan, faithful attendee at wakes, Forty Hours, and priests' anniversary celebrations, heard Monsignor Molloy's avowal with a full heart. That self-same song made a path through his heart when he thought about the great city, the great people of the city, the great possibilities of the city. His spirits lifted at the thought of the vital, demanding, electrifying energy symbolized by Chicago's alleys. He'd loved alleys since he was a kid in Ravenswood because they meant city to him. He knew he would never forget that evening because, "I felt exactly the way that Pat did. He loved Chicago and so did I. Chicago is my life."

It was in that moment Monsignor Egan made up his mind that if ever a book should be written about him, he wanted it to be called *An Alley in Chicago*.

Foreword

Monsignor John Egan is a name I have heard all my life as a priest. We were ordained within two months and 100 miles of each other during May and June of 1943. More important than name recognition is the fact that our lives have crossed on many occasions, but mainly during three time periods.

The first period covers roughly the quarter of a century following our ordinations. We intersected in the early years because we were both involved in Catholic Action when it was quite avant-garde to do so. Young Catholic Students really began at Notre Dame under Father Louis Putz. Young Catholic Workers were midwifed into being by Monsignor Reynold Hillenbrand and his phalanx of eager young priests like Jack Egan. My doctoral thesis in 1945 on the theology of Catholic Action made me part of the scene.

My first assignment as President of Notre Dame in 1952 was to address the first conference of the Christian Family Movement on campus. All of the lay leadership for CFM in those days came out of Chicago, with Pat and Patty Crowley.

Jack Egan was a pioneer. As the chairman of our Theology Department, Father Dick McBrien, puts it, Jack was "a pioneer in the marriage and family apostolate, a pioneer in the urban ministry apostolate, a pioneer in the lay apostolate, a pioneer in the building of priests' associations, a pioneer in inner city (minority) ministry, a pioneer in community organization, a pioneer in priestly ministry as a ministry to the whole Church and to the whole of society."

This fascinating book by Margery Frisbie is the story of Jack Egan's pioneering work in these apostolates, all rather unusual and innovative in the Pre-Vatican II Church. In fact, he and other Chicago priests laid the groundwork for much that was later outlined in the Council regarding ministry.

The second phase of my relationship with Jack Egan began when I met him one day in the Chicago airport. He looked awful: wan, drawn and pale. "Jack," I said, "you look like my father's colorful expression 'hell hit with a shovel.'" He admitted things were going pretty badly so I came up with a radical suggestion: "Why don't you come down to

ix

Notre Dame for a sabbatical year (a year off)? You can take some theology courses, read a lot of good books, enjoy the exhilarating atmosphere of a front line university, and get generally renewed in spirit."

He asked, "You mean it?" I answered, "I mean it." He cleared it with Cardinal Cody. I wrote, too, and the cardinal said okay. He was probably glad to get Jack off center stage in all the racial problems then afflicting Chicago. The second stage began quietly and lasted thirteen years. Great years for Jack and great years for Notre Dame, too. The first year was really rehabilitation, spiritually and humanly.

As the year drew to a close, it was evident to me that Jack could contribute more to making Notre Dame a vital leader in the new Church apostolates than he could contribute to the work of the Church in a fairly hostile Chicago environment. Again, Jack and I wrote Cardinal Cody and received permission for Jack to stay at Notre Dame. This book chronicles all that happened as Jack became my assistant for Notre Dame's role in all Church affairs, the director of a new Institute of Pastoral and Social Ministry, the national leader of the Catholic Committee on Urban Ministry with summer school each year at Notre Dame, and other meaningful endeavors (like a summer school for new bishops) that made the university so much more relevant for the Church. Blessed years, great work on the part of Jack and his indomitable assistant, Peggy Roach. Like my secretary of thirty-eight years, Peggy Roach doubled and tripled Jack's effectiveness in his national apostolates. Someone said, cynically, that Peggy did all the organizing and Jack got all the credit. It really wasn't that way. Each had a very important and different role to play. Together, they made it work. It's called symbiosis.

All good things come to an end. Chicago finally had a wonderful new cardinal, Joseph Bernardin, so it was time for Jack to return to his home city and archdiocese, and to help the new cardinal with his urban and ecumenical challenges. Jack is doing superbly during this third part of his life, still in progress.

In a day when many stories about priests are not all that illuminating and edifying, here is a story of a diocesan priest who started with fairly ordinary talents and by the work of the Holy Spirit built them into an extraordinary priestly life. Jack is very close to thousands of souls he has served unstintingly. He has been support and inspiration to many, especially other priests, always far beyond the call of duty, answering the higher call of love, justice, and social concern.

Father Egan—you'll be a better Christian for knowing him, and a better human being after learning of the broad sweep of his humanity.

Jack Egan—a priest for all seasons. May his tribe increase.

Theodore Hesburgh, C.S.C.
President Emeritus, University of Notre Dame
Notre Dame, Indiana
7 March 1991

1

"I Was a Very Friendly Little Guy"

Monsignor John Joseph Egan got his start in public life hawking the Chicago Tribune the big news night in 1927 when Gene Tunney beat Jack Dempsey for the second time in the "battle of the long count." It was a fitting beginning for Monsignor Egan's career, for he would spend much of it helping people "on the ropes" as he worked in St. Justin Martyr Parish, in the Cana Conference, in urban neighborhoods, at the University of Notre Dame, and in community organizations.

Jack Egan sold a lot of papers his first night in business. He'd already learned, at eleven, to compensate for his bantam size with a wide smile and a friendly manner. Some people who came out when he shouted, "Extra, Extra," gave him as much as a quarter or a fifty cent piece for the three cent paper.

For people in Chicago's Ravenswood neighborhood two years before the stock market crash of 1929, that newspaper peddled at their doors by newsboys like Jack Egan was the equivalent of television's ten o'clock news a generation later. They happily overtipped to be on top of the news.

There was no way Jack Egan could have known that night in 1927 that thirty years later he would be the big news of the day himself or that the *Chicago Tribune* would be one of his opponents as he took on many of Chicago's powerful vested interests in a battle about the city's future. Like Jack Dempsey, Jack Egan would not win his fight. Against his powerful adversaries, he didn't have a chance. But with the characteristic spunk of a bantamweight, Jack Egan would give his fight his best shot in what might be called his battle of the long shot.

In 1958 the headline news was urban renewal in Hyde Park-Kenwood on Chicago's near South Side. The federal government was making funds available to the city, but those funds were limited. From

1

Monsignor Egan's point of view, University of Chicago officials wanted to use the federal money to build a moat around their ivy-covered campus. City Hall supported them. That was all right with Monsignor Egan so long as they provided housing alternatives for the poor blacks and whites presently living in the quarters about to be demolished.

On behalf of the Archdiocese of Chicago, Monsignor Egan pleaded at City Hall the case of those about to be dislodged. Like a log cabin trying to overshadow the Sears Tower, the earnest young priest made his case that the poor in Boss Daley's great city by the lake had the same right to benefit from the city's urban renewal funds as the great university.

Opposing Monsignor Egan was the array of Goliaths that had been working out the Hyde Park-Kenwood plan for three years. They were Mayor Richard J. Daley: president-maker, hizzoner, "Boss," "the guy who got things done," and the Chicago City Council: clout-kingdom, a body strong enough to unmake a lesser mayor. Monsignor Egan was also up against the University of Chicago: one of the world's powerhouse educational forces, supplied by Rockefeller millions, birthplace of the atom bomb, and the *Chicago Tribune*: "the world's greatest newspaper," a bastion of conservatism in its Gothic tower on Michigan Avenue.

Monsignor Egan confronted the city's power centers pretty much alone, as the archdiocese's front man, its agent. There were many official manifestoes to support him. Popes as far back as Leo XIII in 1891 had written encyclical letters urging Catholics to concern themselves about the plight of the poor and the rights of working people. American bishops had published letters of their own, specific to the United States, on the problems of the powerless. American theologians linked the teachings of Jesus on the poor to the condition of the poor in twentieth century United States. All those brave words meant nothing unless there were brave souls to take the Church's brave teachings into the streets.

Who might be expected to verbalize the Church's tilt toward the poor? Was the task too political for Chicago's sweetly permissive Cardinal who could look out innocently from his red moire camouflage and ask a street-savvy, hard-nosed, community organizer, "Now, sonny, tell me what is happening?" Would it have been inappropriate for the brilliant, charismatic rector of the archdiocesan seminary who encouraged men like Jack Egan to take a stand for the poor and then held back on support when their stand was too public?

In the end, it took a Jack Egan backed by the carefully progressive Samuel Cardinal Stritch and trained by that inspiring but repressive seminary rector, Monsignor Reynold Hillenbrand, whose long Teutonic visage shared the measured gravity of Grant Wood's *American Gothic*. It took a Jack Egan, one of "Rynie Hillenbrand's young men," part of a group of young priests upon whom the influential Hillenbrand placed his stamp. As an English contemporary described Jack Egan's circle of seminarians, "When they emerged from the seminary, they had already had a kind of formation that no priests in the U.S. had. There had never been a seminary like this." Those young priests, maybe a dozen of them, were part of a group of priests and lay people who created what Jack Egan looks back on as a Golden Age in the Chicago Church. That was the decade before John Cardinal Cody arrived. It was the decade when Chicago led the Church in the United States.

Rynie's young men were a phenomenon. No matter what parish they were sent to after their ordination, what jobs they were given, they made daring, not always popular, breakthroughs in liturgy, in social questions, in their relations with the people in the pew. They were farsighted. Their ministries were fresh.

Jack Egan with his leprechaun zest, silver-tongued like early Irish labor organizers of the same heritage, ingratiating, and convinced the Church's place was beside the poor, took the most public positions. He stood, as early Catholic Action chaplain Father Gerard Weber (another of Rynie's young men) said of himself and Egan, "with one foot in the Church and one foot outside." Several cardinal archbishops of Chicago supported Jack's initiatives. Yet over the years Monsignor Jack Egan stood basically alone. As a self-designated connector, he was a lynchpin extraordinaire, linking the Church to the city, ideas to action, people to people, organizations to leaders.

In one sense, Jack Egan was an unlikely slingshooter in the contest with the University of Chicago. He could have been, and for a brief interval later on admits he was, a typical Irish pastor, a "boss" in his own way. Much in his background fit him to be a priest of the old school, not the new: an Irish heritage, training with the Sisters, a fiercely authoritarian father, and a devout Irish mother.

Like most of the Catholics of their day, Jack's parents were immigrants. Nellie (Helen) Curry and John Egan left poor Irish families in thatch-roofed cottages spiked with the lingering pungency of burning peat to emigrate to New York. Helen came from the hilly farm area of County Fermanagh in what is now Northern Ireland, and John from the gently rolling countryside of County Offaly about sixty miles west from Dublin. Dressmaker Helen met Fifth Avenue bus driver John about two years after she debarked, a winsome Irish colleen, in the daunting metropolis on Manhattan Island. "With all sincerity," Jack relates, "I think mother left home because there was no place for her in a family with ten children. The easiest thing to do was to come to the United States where her sister had preceded her."

Jack remembers hearing that his parents met at an Irish Fellowship dinner or dance. "It may have been his (John's) brother Mike who introduced him to my mother. It may have been her sister Annie, her sister Rose. But anyway they fell in love. A rich love. A typically Irish love. Fidelity was unquestioned." They had a good marriage. Jack doesn't remember their acts of affection as visible. "Yet he confided everything to her. He knew of her good common sense. She knew everything about him. They had a life apart from the children. They had a relationship."

The second child, after his sister Helen, Jack was born October 9, 1916, on New York's 134th Street, now part of Harlem. The family lived in typically Irish St. Aloysius Parish, a grounding point for newcomers like his parents. Jack was six when the Fifth Avenue Motor Coach Company, having bought out the Chicago Motor Coach Company, transferred his father to Chicago. "Dad had a good education and a good mind for figures. While he was ambitious, he was cautious. He had the title of Chief Clerk in the Transportation Department."

The Egans left St. Aloysius where Jack, got up as a resplendent page boy, first experienced the Church's panoply at Forty Hours Devotion (or, maybe, Confirmation), and Central Park, where he got a nasty scratch and a scolding he never forgot for teasing an organ grinder's monkey. The family rode the New York Central to Chicago, nine-month-old Jimmy on Nellie Egan's lap, Helen and Jack watching at the train windows for their first glimpse of Chicago, the city with which Jack would deeply identify and which would in time identify with him.

Like most Chicago apartment-dwellers of the twenties, the Egans joined annual May moving-day throngs in their early years in the city.

They ricocheted from their first Uptown flat further north to a basement apartment below Alerdice Plumbers in the 5400 block of North Broadway, kitty-corner from the imposing French Gothic church Father John Crowe was building for St. Ita parishioners. Briefly, they enjoyed their mutual Irish roots (Father Crowe was imbedding a black rock in his cornerstone from the ruins of St. Ita's monastic school in his native County Limerick). The Egans next moved to St. Mel's on the West Side, and, finally, to a series of apartments on North Paulina and Hermitage in Our Lady of Lourdes parish where two more children, Kathleen and Pat, were born. "My life sort of began at Lourdes," Jack says.

It was in that North Side Ravenswood neighborhood that Jack Egan settled into the Church. There he first served at the altar, learning to respond, "*Ad Deum qui laetificat juventutem meum*," to Father James Scanlan's, "*Introibo ad altare Dei*." Jack would have nipped two blocks through the pre-dawn cold to meet the priest in the sacristy. Together they would walk out onto the altar. It was Jack's duty to ring the bells, carry the missal from one side of the altar to the other, and hold the paten under the chins of the dark figures who came forward out of the recesses of the huge Spanish-style interior for Communion. Jack never forgot the morning the venerable old priest put his arm around his young server and told him, "I hope I don't die before I see you a bishop."

Organized in 1892 to serve the English-speaking Catholics in Ravenswood, this originally "suburban" parish had a church modeled after a cathedral in Valladolid in northern Spain (where Columbus died in 1506). The parish was largely Irish until World War I. By the time Jack Egan's family moved in, the installation of the Ravenswood elevated line and the construction of apartment buildings to supercede the roomy mansions of the original parishioners had created more of a United Nations. "Japanese, Swedish, Norwegian, German, Polish, and Italian, as well as Irish," Jack recalls from the days when he delivered his neighbors' *Chicago Tribunes*, their *Herald Americans*, their *Chicago Daily Newses*, and their *Abendposts*.

Grateful now for that neighborhood melange, Jack credits the mix for his ability to empathize with a wide variety of human beings. He got into the homes of the people on his route. "I talked to them. I was a very friendly little guy. They liked me." Jack learned the world is made up of people other than Irish. "We weren't part of the West Side Irish

or the South Side Irish. I didn't have to work through that tribalism."
The Swedish clerks at Signe Carlson's Bakery on Winnemac rewarded
him at the end of his daily paper route with a bag of day-old buns for a
dime, and his only neighborhood nickname—"Stale Buns Egan." He
got to know the firemen of Hook and Ladder Number 22 on Winnemac
Street, Protestant ministers and their wives, people in the meat market
and the grocery store. He felt he got "a love and appreciation of people,
an understanding of them."

It wasn't that Jack didn't identify with his Irish roots or share the
sustaining pride of the Irish in the University of Notre Dame long
before his brother Jimmy went to school there and Jack served as assistant to the president, Father Theodore Hesburgh. Jack remembers
crying as he delivered the newspapers headlining Notre Dame coach
Knute Rockne's death in a plane crash in 1931. He still grins when he
recollects the 120,000 fans—"I think it is still the largest crowd that
ever watched a football game"—exulting as Notre Dame's Four Horse-
men led their team to victory over Army at Chicago's Soldier Field in
1924. To this day he rues the hours he was forced to listen to Father
Charles Coughlin from six to seven o'clock p.m. CST on Sunday
evenings, another Irish tribal ritual.

Father Coughlin's popular demagoguery was supported by the lower
middle class and upper-working-class Irish and German Catholics, according to sociologist Father Andrew Greeley. (Three months after joining CBS, Coughlin got an average of 80,000 letters a week enclosing
more than $20,000, William Manchester noted in *The Glory and the
Dream.* As his popularity grew, Father Coughlin might receive a million
letters after some broadcasts. It could take 150 clerks to sort out the
bills and stack the change.)

In 1928 Jack's empathy was already wider than Father Coughlin's
anti-Semitism or Chicago's bias against its increasing black population
even though he had little opportunity to meet blacks in the Ravenswood
area of an increasingly segregated Chicago. In those days black runner
Ralph Metcalfe training for the 1936 Olympics in Chase Park across
from Our Lady of Lourdes was an exotic sight to Jack and his friends.
However, Jack came to know his first black not only in the bosom of
his family, but also at a time when the Egan family was at its most
vulnerable. During a time when Mrs. Egan was hospitalized, Jimmy
Egan struggled to breathe in a darkened bedroom, his life threatened by
pneumonia. The darkness reaching out from that room touched the

Egans' every waking moment. Through the long weeks of Jimmy's crisis, and then convalescence, the only light came from the black housekeeper. "Mrs. Bishop was a mother to us," Jack remembers gratefully. "What a lovely woman, the soul of kindness, gracious, quiet, helpful, generous, cheerful. I can't say enough about her."

Jack recalls confiding in his father one morning when it seemed life would never be normal again, "Gee, Daddy, I'm glad you and I are well." By this time, his mother had been hospitalized more than a month with her tumor surgery. His brother still lay rasping in his dark room. Medical bills that would overshadow their lives for years were accumulating. But the family never regretted what had gone to Mrs. Bishop. Her nurturing presence had sustained them. "How we loved her," Jack recalls. "How we cried when she left."

Jack believes it was Mrs. Bishop who influenced his response to an early "funding experience" (in the phrase of Chicago writer Father Jack Shea) that burned into Jack's mind and "may have marked my later interest in civil rights." It concerned an incident involving a black man riding a streetcar.

In those days a kid paid three cents on the streetcar, and an adult seven. This fare included a "transfer" to allow riders to change cars for complicated routes. One day after Jack's mother agreed a twelve-year-old was old enough to negotiate a solo trip to Chicago's downtown "Loop," a scared Jack witnessed a conductor's refusal of a black man's transfer. He said it was over the time limit. The streetcar had rattled halfway down the block "fairly rapidly" when the "conductor came over and took the old black man and threw him off the streetcar. I remember being absolutely terrified. I looked back at the poor man lying in the street and people beginning to gather."

Jack's terror increased when the conductor turned to him. "Whether he said, 'Did you see him pull a knife on me?' or hit me, or whatever it was, I insisted, 'I did not,' ran through the streetcar and got off at the next stop."

Tremendously agitated, not knowing where he was, Jack had known enough to vacate that dangerous scene. "This was the first time I had a sense of a person of another race being so cruelly treated. The fact that the old man was black affected me very deeply." That experience followed Jack Egan through his life, just as his experience on his paper route would do.

It was in Our Lady of Lourdes days that Jack Egan hawked those papers for the Dempsey-Tunney fight. A friend of Jack's who knew there'd be fight-result editions of the *Chicago Tribune* and *Herald-Examiner* asked Jack along to peddle the Extras. Jack's first experience excited him. "You would go up and down the streets yelling, 'Extra, Extra,' and someone would lean out the window and ask what was happening."

By first peddling the newspapers and then taking on a regular paper route for A. H. Gridley, who had the franchise from Foster Avenue to Irving Park, and from Clark to Ravenswood (the area occupied by Our Lady of Lourdes parish), Jack played directly into his father's two paramount cachets, a demanding work ethic ("he was a very hard worker; to my mind, too hard") and dogged loyalty ("he was loyal to his company to a fault"). Jack stuck with Mr. Gridley from the time he was ten until he went to work part-time at Sears at seventeen. At times his sister Kathleen helped with the route. Even Mr. Egan took a turn pulling the wagon on cold January mornings. Jimmy, already "an ideal young man" according to his brother, had his own route with Mr. Gridley.

His father's single-mindedness deeply affected Jack's childhood. "For example, we never took a vacation," he recalls. "Dad was always going to bring us to the Wisconsin Dells. But when the time came, he never thought the Ford would get that far. So we never got there." His father's drives also dominated Jack's adult life.

They were burned into Jack. Working hard was so ingrained that even a major, death-threatening, heart attack in his early forties couldn't tip Jack off his father-imposed treadmill. His father's will to work and his father's obsessive obedience to authority shaped Jack's life. "To jump ahead sixty years," Jack says, as he ruminates about his father's influence, "when I went to see Cardinal Cody about going to Notre Dame in 1970, if he had said, 'John, I want you to stay here,' I'd have stayed. But he didn't say that." Jack would have stayed because his father had imbued Jack with the loyalty that kept his father at Chicago Motor Coach for forty-five years.

Hard on himself, Mr. Egan kept a goad at his sons' backs from their earliest days. "I guess I was a great crybaby," Jack says, recalling a family story of his waking in the night and crying. His father, an early riser who didn't want his night's sleep interrupted, ordered, "Nellie, that child has cried enough." He spanked his son efficiently enough to stop that crying bout and all subsequent outbursts. From that moment

Jack's father had only to warn his toddler, "Sh-h-h-h. Keep quiet," and "I would swallow any crying I wanted to do." Obedience became as routine as oatmeal.

A few years later when Jack or his siblings were out playing baseball in the empty lot across the street, his father would whistle when he wanted them in. "He didn't want to whistle twice. We came."

This demand for inflexible obedience was still a problem when Jack was a student at DePaul Academy. By now the issue was the familiar familial battleground, use of the family conveyance. "I wouldn't know until about six o'clock on the night of a dance whether my father would let me use the car. That created a lot of tension and stress and anger."

When Jack's father finally gave his permission, he also imposed an eleven o'clock curfew. Sometimes, in those days when the archdiocese included the Joliet diocese, Jack couldn't make it sixty or seventy miles home from an inter-school basketball game. On occasion that meant someone else had to return his date to her door. Other times, Jack leaned against a locked front door until his mother got permission to come and say, "Jack, come on in."

Jack conformed with his father's notions of obedience and discipline. "You studied hard." His father tore up any homework he didn't approve. "You worked hard." Any time Jack finished his homework before bed, his father would set him to practicing Palmer method. "You brought in enough to pay for your tuition and your clothes." Jack paid his way at DePaul just as his sister Helen earned her tuition for Immaculata High School clerking at the local National Tea Store on Saturdays.

Looking back, Jack assesses the usefulness of his father's penchant for instant obedience. "My father lacked understanding, and lacked forgiveness, and was very, very strict," Jack says. But in at least one way the father's rigidity stood both sons in good stead. "I will never forget my brother telling that Navy discipline was nothing after what we went through with our father." While it's true that Jimmy's light-hearted nature ("he always had my father laughing") bore up better under the father's strictures, he, too, felt the paternal pressure.

Jack's father prepared him for life in the seminary. "Some of my classmates chafed under the discipline, but it was duck soup for me." Meticulously as he conformed, however, Jack reserved a portion of his soul from his father's domination. He didn't have the chutzpa at twelve or thirteen to take off for the Oblates of Mary seminary against his father's wishes, although he was very attracted to their life. However, when he decided about that time to learn to swim, he saved money from his paper route to join the local YMCA without parental permission. He regularly turned up for lessons until his father discovered Jack's insubordination. Shocked at the deception—and the male nudity in the pool—Jack's father decreed that swimming was too dangerous. "But it was too late. I had already learned to swim." Jack never told his father that he was right about the peril, for on one occasion Jack was pulled unconscious from the pool after he slipped on the concrete floor and rolled, helpless and comatose, into the water.

The paper routes that provided funds for the swimming lessons and for tuition for DePaul Academy also isolated Jack. "I didn't belong to any gang or crowd," Jack recalls. He wasn't a loner. He had friends. But he "didn't mind being alone." Later in life, he regretted that his work routine kept him from reading the classics, "the books every young person should read when he or she is in grammar school and high school."

Jack has an easy explanation: "My father didn't read. He worked. He expected us to do what he did." That's exactly what Mr. Egan's children did.

2

"I Think the Only Thing I Was Good At Was Working"

Although he came when the whistle blew, Jack Egan hearkened to other calls than the voice of rote obedience. In that part of himself he'd kept protected from his father's domination, Jack made a life-career decision against his father's express wishes in 1935. Instead of continuing at DePaul University where he had just completed his first year and going on to law school, Jack made up his mind to enter the seminary. He'd decided to be a priest of the Archdiocese of Chicago.

This decision was harder than learning the Australian crawl at the YMCA. When Jack boarded the Chicago Motor Coach bus for the minor seminary, his father's disappointment rode with him. "I'd fallen out of my father's favor. That made a very severe mark on me. It was the first time I went against any authority."

Considering how urgently most Irish parents geared their sons for God's service, it's surprising how determinedly Jack's father fought to keep him out of the religious life. Why was Mr. Egan different from the norm? When Jack had first been attracted to the life of an Oblate of Mary as an eighth grader, his father's arguments against the decision to rush off to Texas made sense. Jack was young and untried. Texas was very distant for a young teen. As much as the Oblate life appealed to Jack, his father "put his foot down. 'You don't know your own mind. Wait until you are old enough.' Of course I didn't go," Jack recalls now. In 1930 Jack accepted instead the scholarship to DePaul Academy offered to a youngster from one of the North Side parishes.

Five years later, however, Jack disregarded his father's ultimatum. After four good years at DePaul Academy and a year at the university following his father's blueprint for a career as a lawyer, Jack wasn't happy with himself. He always felt the need to be someone else, some-

11

one more competent, smarter, better at athletics, better at speaking, better looking. Although he made good friends among the students and faculty, he never felt in solid with a group. "Remember that line from *Death of a Salesman*," he says, "'He was liked, but not well liked.' I think that was me. I had only a few friends growing up. I didn't think people would like me. I didn't think I had enough stuff for people to like me."

It wasn't that Jack didn't make the effort. He worked for acceptance. Looking back, he sees that as both a strength and a weakness, because "you do things in life when you want people to like you that you probably shouldn't do, that can be vicious and dangerous." Psychiatrist Anthony Storr explains in *Solitude* that children not certain that their parents' love for them is unconditional feel that they have to be compliant. They have to partially deny or repress their true natures because they are relying on external sources for the maintenance of their self esteem. Such children are vulnerable. They develop into adults who continue to feel that they have to be successful, or good, or approved of by everyone to retain their sense of value.

Jack was stymied by his father's devaluation. Because he couldn't please his father, Jack thought he didn't please anyone. That made him compliant, in Storr's sense. Typically, he feared rejection. Untypically, he recognized that he had a strong point. He was an excellent worker. "I think the only thing I was good at was working," Jack laments ruefully. "What I remember about my youth is that I was working all the time."

For Mr. Egan that very quality was Jack's ticket to the law career he'd mapped out for his son. "A lot of damned nonsense. Somebody has twisted your mind," he announced impatiently when Jack crossed his father and announced he was going to study for the priesthood in August 1935.

Mr. Egan persisted in treating Jack's notion as an idle fancy past the day after Labor Day when Jack boarded the bus for what would be a daily trip to Quigley Preparatory Seminary at Rush and Chestnut Streets. At this Gothic minor seminary, its chapel copied after Sainte Chapelle in Paris (renowned worldwide for its beauty) and paid for by the pennies of Chicago's Catholic schoolchildren, Jack was to learn the Greek and Latin he needed to enter the major seminary at Mundelein. In the third year Latin class and first year Greek class he was assigned to, Jack found that his student strategy of rote memorizing was not nearly as useful in the seminary as his filial virtue of rote obedience. At first he "didn't know what the hell was going on."

What supported Jack was the strong pull of the priesthood. He didn't want to fail. "A lot of things came together for me that summer after my freshman year at DePaul. That black man I saw pushed from the streetcar. Working with people. Having the Depression behind us. Seeing people suffer. Observing how the priests in the parish operated, especially a group of young priests at Our Lady of Lourdes for the summer. When I saw what they were doing, I thought the priesthood was just a wonderful way to be a help to people and to serve people."

Jack had developed some autonomy through his own diligent industry, his mother's unflagging support, and that father-inculcated loyalty. He'd learned to swim when he saw it as necessary for his development. Now he caught that bus with his books under his arm every morning in spite of the fact that his father would not speak to him. "To stand up against my father allowed me not to accept authority without question, even as I continued obedient to authority."

His father's intransigence was not Jack's only trial as he walked five days a week into the buildings Cardinal Mundelein considered "unquestionably the most beautiful here in Chicago, not excluding the University of Chicago." Even in this inspiring environment, Jack Egan found the study of classical languages very intimidating. "That study knocked a lot of conceit out of me. However, standing up to my father strengthened me and, in a sense, enabled me to get through. I was determined. Nothing was going to stop me from getting through Quigley except my own inability." They were tough years, some of the hardest Jack would experience in his life.

For six months Mr. Egan did not address a word to his son. "What a tension there was at the dinner table with five children there and my dear mother trying to keep the peace and my father absolutely ignoring me." Years later his mother recalled how she had laid in bed and asked her husband, "Why are you so hard on Jack? It's so difficult for him."

Jack would not know the answer to his mother's poignant question—"I don't want the same thing to happen to him that happened to me"—until the night his father was buried. Even then it was an inadvertent query that revealed the wound in Mr. Egan's spirit that made him fight his son's vocation. As the family gathered to mourn, to console, and to reflect on family concerns after Mr. Egan's funeral, Jack put an idle question to his Uncle Mike. He had no advance notion of the jolt he was about to receive. Reminded by the funeral notice that his father's middle name was Gerard, inclined to focus on family questions by the nature of the occasion, Jack idly inquired where his father got his middle name. "Was that from Confirmation?"

His Uncle Mike laughed as if to pass off the importance of the revelation he was about to make to his priest-nephew. "That was your father's name when he was a Christian Brother."

Jack was totally taken aback at this incredible disclosure of a paternal past he had never suspected. "I was just shocked. I had been a priest for eight years." This was the first time Jack had heard that he wasn't the first in the family to choose the religious life. He began rapidly sorting out the cues he might have picked up on. Pieces of the family puzzle fell together for him: his father's unusually accurate knowledge of Gander, Newfoundland, at the time Charles Lindbergh took off for Paris; his father's fierce resistance to Jack's vocation, and his father's puzzling attachment to a little black box he often riffled through in the basement.

Now that Jack thought about it, he could picture his father kneeling on a kitchen chair, saying his prayers for as much as ten minutes at a stretch, unaware of his young son watching from the bedroom door. Only when he started going to work with his father did Jack observe that part of his father's daily routine was a climb up the stairs of the baroquely elegant St. Hyacinth Church for six o'clock Mass every day of the week.

Over tea, after the family had left, Jack probed with his mother this stunning gap in the family story, this catalyst for Mr. Egan's strenuous opposition to Jack's career choice. "Now, Mom, you better tell me the whole story," he gently begged his mother. At last she was willing. "I promised your father that I would never tell a living soul. But now that he's dead. . . ."

She told Jack she'd always thought he should know how his father had trained to be an Irish Christian Brother, but changed his mind before he took any vows. His father hadn't agreed with her view. "I don't want to be kidded by the boys," he would say. His father's resistance, she admitted to Jack, was fueled by a panic that his son would fail as he had done. The other factor was Mr. Egan's Irish phobia about "spoiled priests" (men who left the seminary before being ordained).

Jack could remember times when his father had lingered in the basement after helping his mother with the laundry. When the kids would ask what was going on downstairs, she'd put them off with excuses. Some strain in her voice and tenseness in her manner alerted the kids to the significance of the little black box their father pored over. Now that they could investigate family mysteries without causing pain, Jack and his brother Jim broke into their father's talisman and found the pathetic remnants of his novitiate days at Gander, Newfoundland, the links that connected him to a life he'd aspired to: some compositions, letters from Brothers, a picture of Mr. Egan in the Christian Brothers habit, memorial cards for former companions who had died. They were only shadows of a dream deferred, but they could have blocked a less determined son than Jack Egan and changed the history of the Church in Chicago.

Had Jack understood in 1935 when he opened the books on two of the hardest years of his life that his father's silence flowed from his father's pain, he could have lived more peacefully with his own decision. As it was, he resolutely applied himself to learning the Latin and Greek requisite for the major seminary burdened by the knowledge he was creating disquiet in his home.

He didn't need that additional burden. Quigley Preparatory Seminary was hard enough. What with the necessity of earning his tuition and expenses from the time he was ten, Jack had never learned good study habits. He knew "the value of a dollar, and not to waste, and to work hard," as he likes to say. But these skills didn't transfer to translating Virgil. What kept him going was his determination to be a priest, not his success at his studies. Jack pored over the texts, but he couldn't get his grades up. He remembers the kindness of his third-year Latin professor, particularly on a day when Father Peter Cameron had his prefect hand out the corrected papers to the class. He kept Jack's. He personally carried it down the aisle to the struggling seminarian. "He put the paper on my desk and on top of it was the test score, a 16."

Then, as Jack says, "In the understatement of my life, Father Cameron suggested hesitantly, 'Johnny, I think you'll have to do better.'"

Father Cameron was only one of the priests at Quigley convinced that the talents of this young seminarian were not for dead languages but for live people. Another was Father George Beemsterboer, a professor at Quigley for twenty-two years who remembered Jack from Our Lady of Lourdes. Jack describes Beemsterboer as the "final filter. If you didn't get through him, you didn't get to Mundelein."

Knowing how hard Jack was trying, Father Beemsterboer called him in a few days before the end of school. "Egan," he said to Jack, "you didn't quite make it, but I am going to give you a few points." He was giving him a chance, he told Jack, "because we need priests who are kind more than we need priests who know Latin." Lest Jack be overly hopeful, Father Beemsterboer added a caveat. Five times before he had taken this chance on a young seminarian, "but never did any man to whom I gave points become ordained."

The rector at Quigley, Monsignor Malachy Foley, wasn't any more sanguine, "Egan," he said to Jack, "we're giving you a chance. We're letting you go to Mundelein, but we don't think you'll make it."

"So I got through Quigley," Jack says, "not by the skin of my teeth but by the kindness of other people."

3

"To Serve God and Be of Some Use to People"

That wasn't the end of his troubles with Latin, Jack admits. At the major seminary all the courses were taught in Latin. "Our textbooks were in Latin, the lectures were in Latin, examinations were in Latin." When Jack didn't fare well his first semester, the professor of his most important class identified Latin as the pothole on Jack's road to learning. Taking Jack aside, he tactfully adverted to his inauspicious grades.

"Mr. Egan," he said, "I would like to recommend that you think about going to a seminary where they teach philosophy and theology in English instead of Latin."

Having established himself at Mundelein in spite of his difficulties at Quigley, Jack wasn't going to be dismissed that easily. Casting about for an alternate solution, he studied fellow seminarians who were successful, who could do what he couldn't do, who could learn the theology based on the Council of Trent (when the Catholic Church defined its doctrines in the late sixteenth century) and the philosophy based on Thomas Aquinas (thirteenth century scholastic philosopher, also definitive) in the language of the Caesars. He asked a couple of them to tutor him in their skills. He picked the right pair.

Jack's knack for picking the right people went back to his high school days when he chose the staff for the DePaul Academy newspaper he edited. It was then he began developing "an ability which stood me in good stead through the years." When he had a position of authority, he seized instinctively on appropriate confederates. Part of the skill may have been inborn, but Jack developed it deliberately. Later on, he would intuitively scan gatherings for recruits the way retirees scour suburban parkways with metal detectors. As a result, he remembers his good friend Father Kevin Conway telling him on a street in Baltimore,

"You may not be very bright, Jack, but you certainly know how to pick good people."

All Jack had ever learned to do was memorize. "George Drury and John O'Connell showed me how to think of an entire thesis instead of simply memorizing the proofs. It was then, in my first year at the major seminary when I was twenty-one years of age, that I finally learned to study." Drury and O'Connell made it possible for Jack to stay at St. Mary of the Lake. Jack's contribution to his own advancement was finding the right people. That knack for descrying tutelary geniuses— and, in time, becoming one—was as natural to Jack Egan as greeting Sunday morning Mass-goers with a smile.

Like Jack, his classmates were Depression kids. Born during the war to end all wars, they'd spent their early years in a world of illusory stability and fragile prosperity. Even during what are looked back on as the boom years of the twenties, Jack's family seemed poor to him, although his father always had a steady job. A basement apartment under a north Broadway plumbing establishment in the early twenties was not palatial accommodation. Sleeping with his brother in a Murphy bed they pulled out of its wall cupboard each night was not luxury living, nor was sharing a bed on a sun porch until he went to the seminary.

Jack was ten when his father said, "When are you going to go out and get a job?" and launched his career, "if you can call it such," of some ten years of rolling out of his bed at four in the morning to cart the *Chicago Tribune* and *Herald Examiner* to the parents of his classmates still abed. Later on, Jack added an afternoon route and tossed copies of the afternoon papers, the *Chicago Daily News* and the *Abendpost*, up on porches and front steps while his classmates tossed softballs in the neighborhood's empty lots.

On the morning after the presidential inauguration in March, 1929, when Herbert Hoover told Americans that they had "reached a higher degree of comfort and security than has ever existed before in the history of the world," Jack Egan was up as usual at four in the morning delivering the newspaper which quoted the new president's unfortunate—and unprescient—claim. Jack's family, like most of the working class, had not got a fair shake in the evanescent boomtime of the twenties. Although there was more wealth than ever before in the country, the working classes were not getting their share, a factor in the trouble brewing. Their purchasing power—if they had had a fair shake—could have kept U.S. production increasing and possibly staved off the world-wide shutdown.

Jack saw this close at hand the summer of 1934 when he was working with his father at the Chicago Motor Coach. The drivers went out on strike. On the midnight to eight a.m. shift, Jack got all the reports on "what the goons were doing to the motor coach drivers, shooting ball-bearings with slingshots through windshields of the busses of the drivers who were joining the union, breaking their legs on the curb with baseball bats—cheery things like that."

"There was a lot of bloodshed and finally (the goons) broke the attempt of the union to organize the drivers which turned me against company unions and made me see that they would always be a tool of the company. The independence of the workers in choosing representatives to truly represent them was just ignored. That was 1933-34. It made me realize the absolute necessity for labor unions and the labor movement in the U.S."

Even though Jack's father counseled patience, "Don't knock it, son, because that is the company that is putting bread on the table," Jack turned against the management and decried the Motor Coach management ads in the *Chicago Tribune* arguing the company should not be organized. "They really detested, hated Franklin Roosevelt, and they felt the unions were a tremendous attack on the whole free enterprise system."

In some ways, the Depression years were more democratic than the boom times. Few families totally escaped hardship when men and machines lay idle everywhere in the Western world. The entrenched poor and the suddenly poor tramped the streets searching for buttons to maintain their sanity, queued in soup kitchens, sold apples and pencils, got a night's sleep in municipal lodging houses. Beggars marked the back doors of housewives found willing to share a sandwich and a cup of coffee.

The young seminarians at Mundelein coming out of a babushka, nine-day-novena and vigil-light-in-the-parlor Church knew personally of Depression conditions even if they had never personally gone to bed hungry or stuffed cardboard into their shoes to keep out winter's slush. They had seen the Depression overwhelm families. Many of them were sensitized to the plight of the poor and, like Jack Egan, were ready to take a more intense interest in the role of labor unions and the condition of the working man than they might have in more prosperous times.

By 1937 when Jack's class came to St. Mary of the Lake, the nation was coping under President Franklin Roosevelt's administration although suffering was still widespread. At Mundelein the new seminarians found unaccustomed amenities in what was considered the crown jewel of American seminaries. They passed copies of seventeenth and eighteenth century masterpieces in their marble halls. They looked down on flower gardens in American flag designs. They stared up at a library interior modeled after the Barberini Palace in Rome, in a building with an Early Georgian exterior. Even if they hadn't heard tales of Cardinal Mundelein tramping the site with his architect Joseph McCarthy, planning the unlikely blend of Roman interiors and Early American exteriors to link the Church's long history to the country's, the seminarians felt ennobled—as the United States' first American cardinal west of the Alleghenies meant they should—by their new environment. Being at Mundelein, they shared an eminence with His Eminence.

Their homes away from home were the Early American dormitories of the Cardinal's dream seminary. His home away from his stately mansion on north State Street in Chicago duplicated Mount Vernon. The main chapel at the seminary was a double of the Congregational Church in Old Lyme, Connecticut. Its chandeliers were replicas of the enormous brass and crystal chandeliers in the White House. Other buildings were also ambitiously Georgian. What Cardinal Mundelein had conceived as a melting pot for archdiocesan seminarians had inflated into a sacred vessel of dramatic proportion.

From its inception, Cardinal Mundelein insisted on an austere regime at the seminary, an almost monastic schedule of exercises, classes and study periods. There were no magazines to read, no novels, no radios. Seminarians were discouraged from banding in groups. They couldn't visit in each others' rooms or speak in the corridors. They couldn't go home for Christmas. If the regulations and scheduling were austere, however, the accommodations were first class. Each seminarian had his private room and bath, his own desk and bed. Facilities for sports—which were encouraged—were lavish for the times: a swimming pool, a superb gymnasium, and ball fields far more satisfactory than the vacant lots where most of the seminarians had played piggy-bounce-out as kids.

Cardinal Mundelein would have been gratified at Jack Egan's reaction to his university of the west. "There wasn't an unhappy day. Were there tough days? Yes. I loved it. It was the first time I had my own room, my own bathroom. It was the first seminary in the world where every room had its own facilities. The food was good. The professors were good, I thought. The studies were exciting."

Jack took in stride the discipline fearsome to young men not conditioned by authoritarian fathers. He liked the orderliness of the day, the pressure of the studies, and the companionship of the other seminarians. He felt respected by his classmates, although "I wasn't one of the favorite guys in the class," he says.

A great, wide, stimulating world was opening up for Jack and his peers. They'd had some exposure to the ferment germinated in the Church during their high school years. Jack ·had visited the Catholic Worker house and, as an old hand at hawking papers, had peddled *The Catholic Worker* during a rally to oppose *El Caudillo* Franco in the Spanish civil war along with Ed Marciniak, a friend from CISCA (Chicago Inter-Student Catholic Action). Other seminarians had been exposed to the Church's teaching on race relations, social justice, and labor unions at CISCA where Father Martin Carrabine, S.J., presided in the ascetic and gentle aloofness that belied the fire in his belly, or at Summer Schools of Catholic Action at the Morrison Hotel. Like hundreds of other students, some of the seminarians had come under the influence of the affable and inspiring Father Daniel Lord of the *The Queen's Work*, a publication for students in Catholic Action, and Father Edward Dowling, S.J., an early spiritual influence on the evolution of Alcoholics Anonymous. These were men with tremendous power to inspire generous action in young persons.

Some CISCA messages conflicted with the status quo messages the seminarians heard in the tight enclaves of their home parishes. There, parishioners sometimes fought to keep out the outlanders—even if they were fellow Roman Catholics. Peggy Roach, Jack Egan's long-time associate who shared his ministry after 1966, remembers her mother mimicking the German pastor at St. Henry's Church who excoriated "you damn Irishers" for attending the Luxemburgers' church even if they lived within parish boundaries. "Go to St. Tim's, the Irish parish," the pastor thundered from the pulpit. "That's where you belong on Sunday."

The strength of the Church in Chicago was that blood-bond of people who had left an old country for a new. Once they were established and had built their ethnic churches, they wanted to control them, like the Lithuanian women at Providence of God Church who used their hatpins to drive off the police trying to protect their pastor from them. The dispute was over control of parish finances. According to a contemporary account in the *Chicago Inter-Ocean* in February, 1906: "Confused by showers of bricks and paving blocks, menaced by flying bullets, and suffering keenly from wounds made by the hatpins wielded by the women, the police were at last compelled to fire over the heads of the mob."

Jack Egan's classmates were tied by blood and sweat to those fiercely protective pastors and parishioners. They shared their passions and their prejudices. Those ordained as late as 1957 "were most of us out of lower economic class families—many of us with immigrant parents who had no formal schooling," according to Father Patrick O'Malley, pastor of St. Celestine's in Elmwood Park in 1990. They had come to Mundelein hankering for a greater vision, for expanded horizons, for goals on which to hang their youthful ideals. At Mundelein Jack's fellow seminarians found a rector to inform and quicken those ideals, a charismatic intellectual to expand their horizons, to throw open windows on the world thirty years in advance of Pope John XXIII's aggiornamento of the 1960s.

That rector of the seminary, Monsignor Reynold J. Hillenbrand, was an original. Not banked with the warm fire within of a Pope John, Hillenbrand was a firebrand, not a comfortable hearth. He was intense, cerebral, driven, and indefatigable. Where John XXIII would draw people to him, Monsignor Hillenbrand's severe mien held them at a distance. The rigidity of his face betrayed the care with which he repressed any perfidious emotion.

Nonetheless, this stubbornly unbending rector was capable of crystallizing all that was inchoate in the groping idealism of young seminarians. He was "the first major intellectual influence in my life," Jack said. That was true for many of Jack's classmates. "Monsignor Hillenbrand opened up a whole new world for us."

No one else had ever told them that lay people participated in the priesthood of Christ by virtue of their baptism and confirmation. Seminarians sat rapt under the great crystal chandeleirs, mesmerized like members of the Christian Family Movement would be in another ten years, by preaching that some members of Hillenbrand's own faculty found radical. Most seminarians and priests assumed down deep that they were the Church. Now it appeared that they "had a deficient sense of church as a living, organic oneness of its members" if they thought that priests had a corner on leadership, initiative and responsibility.

Monsignor Hillenbrand's like has not been seen again in the archdiocese. A brilliant student, he was sent to Rome for further study two years after his ordination. There the seeds were planted that would blossom in the fields of Mundelein. During Hillenbrand's Roman year, Pius XI published the encyclical which would become the handbook of socially active priests, *Quadragesimo Anno*. In 1891, Pope Leo XIII had published the first papal encyclical describing an equitable society in which working people had rights of their own. *Quadragesimo Anno* (meaning "forty years later") brought Leo's teaching up to date. To Hillenbrand this concentration on the plights and rights of the working man was fresh material. He hadn't studied anything like this in his seminary days.

During his Roman year Hillenbrand also came in contact with a Catholic Action movement spreading in Europe. Young Christian Workers were groups of individuals who worked together to Christianize society and bring its institutions in line with Jesus' teachings. Hillenbrand told Cardinal Mundelein's biographer Edward R. Kantowicz that he "didn't get far in his thinking about social reform at this time." It was only after he was assigned to the seminary that Hillenbrand had a chance to focus on the potential of the Young Christian Workers founded by Belgian Canon Joseph Cardijn in 1925 in Brussels. Hillenbrand was impressed by the simple strength and effectiveness of Cardijn's formula. What Young Christian Workers did was straightforwardly analyze the conditions they saw around them in their daily lives according to the values they found in the Gospels they studied. They set themselves to Observe (conditions), Judge (their morality against Gospel values), and Act (to change society). They met weekly or biweekly and reported at every gathering.

Until Canon Cardijn devised this formula for turning talkers into activists, committed Catholics had generally been content to organize study groups, hunch over coffee cups, and discourse on new and improved social arrangments in terms of, say, the encyclicals. Cardinal Cardijn was impatient with that approach. For him, as for Jack Egan later on, to fix upon a stand was to take action. His Observe, Judge, Act

model was formulated to get study group participants out of their co-
coons and into flight. Workers had grievances against society. First,
they identified them. Then they solved them. His strategy worked.
Father John Fitzsimons of Liverpool, an early Young Christian Worker
chaplain and associate of Canon Cardijn, reports that presently the political establishments in Belgium, the Netherlands, France, and other
European countries are staffed with former YCW members. Once
Cardijn's movement gained papal approval, it spread across Europe.

But it didn't affect Hillenbrand until he was back in the United
States. On his return to Chicago, Hillenbrand taught one year at
Quigley Preparatory Seminary before Cardinal Mundelein hand-picked
the bright young scholar to preach in the newly formed Archdiocesan
Mission Band and to teach at Rosary College. During that year, 1933,
Hillenbrand told Kantowicz, he synthesized a theology of Catholic Action. It was grounded in the vision of Christian solidarity in the doctrine of the Mystical Body of Christ. According to the papal encyclical
Mystici Corporis, the Roman Catholic Church was made up of Christ
(the head) and Church members (the body). Together, they created the
Church. Together, they created the liturgy. Christ was in the worship-
ping assembly just as he was in the priest who celebrated the liturgy. It
was a doctrine that would develop thirty years later at the Second Vatican Council into an understanding that Church members were the "people of God" in pilgrimage. In Hillenbrand's mind, in 1933, the concept
of the Mystical Body enlarged the whole notion of Church and gave
power and dignity to lay people. Using it, he could call them to share
the work of the hierarchy in doing the work of Catholic Action.

Hillenbrand used well the unusual study opportunities Cardinal
Mundelein gave him, creating a watershed in his own life and, as rector
of the seminary, a watershed for the archdiocese. When he was appointed rector at Mundelein in 1935 (at thirty-one!), Hillenbrand
brought riches with him. The range of his interest in, and knowledge of,
art, poetry, literature, theology, and liturgy electrified the pious young
men in his care reared in homes and schools largely barren of intellectual delights and wide-ranging interests.

Like Jack Egan, the bulk of the seminarians had come to Mundelein
to "serve God and be of some help to people." Here was a rector who
could make them see how exciting and provocative and daring that
helping could be. They would not be ordained to hide behind rectory
doors, wondering, as Dorothy Parker once said in another connection,

"what fresh hell" was announced by every ring of the doorbell. They were going to be out on the streets, like the Rosary College students Hillenbrand inspired to street-preach in Oklahoma. The seminarians were to bring the life of the Church into the lives of the people. They'd have the tools, the techniques, to mobilize their parishioners. For seminarians begging "more meat for the mind," like Oliver Twist begging "more gruel, please," Hillenbrand was filling a need apparent to them—and to him.

The Roman collars these young men would wear would be an entrée into real power. They would have the chance to make a difference in society. Hillenbrand worked to prepare them for that opportunity.

Hillenbrand drew on other sources besides the encyclicals: American forerunners. As far back as 1908, early social activist Monsignor John Ryan was deploring the condition of the working man in the U.S. He followed up his doctoral dissertation on the living wage with a synthesis of moral principles called *Distributive Justice: The Right and Wrong of our Present Distribution of Wealth* in 1916. He based it on the encyclical *Rerum Novarum* which J. P. Dolan in *The American Catholic Experience* called "the Magna Carta of Catholic social thought." As head of the social action department of the National Catholic Welfare Conference, Ryan organized social action congresses and labor schools to bring the Church's social gospel as outlined in the two major social encyclicals, *Rerum Novarum* and *Quadragesimo Anno*, to Catholic priests and lay persons.

Although most priests in the country adhered to the novena-rosary-parochial school model, restricting themselves pretty much to local parish concerns, John Ryan and his associate Father Raymond McGowan managed to influence an impressive cadre of "labor priests" into serious study of the social encyclicals and their practical applications to American conditions. The principles Ryan and McGowan expounded at their Social Action Summer Programs were not lost on Monsignor Hillenbrand and "Rynie's young men" at St. Mary of the Lake Seminary, one of the summer school sites.

Ryan and McGowan stressed the dignity of work and the dignity of the working man, principles out of the social encyclicals that played into the insights of Pope Pius XII's encyclical on the Mystical Body published in 1943 which also stressed the importance of individual persons, however humble. These encyclicals were the agents of change used by the small groups of factory workers and teachers and students in Europe who were reading Scripture, observing the inadequacies of their schools or workplaces, and fixing on actions needed to bring the practices of the workplace more in line with the Gospel and Catholic social doctrine.

Not content to draw on secondary sources to reach the seminarians' minds, Hillenbrand brought in the innovators themselves, people living by these theological insights. Among them was Dorothy Day, one of the first women to speak at the seminary. In 1933, Dorothy Day and Peter Maurin put flesh on the church's social teaching when they started *The Catholic Worker* newspaper and the Catholic Worker movement to make the Catholic Church "the dominant social dynamic force in the United States." Radical in their pursuit of Christian perfection, they opened houses of hospitality for the poor, homeless, and unemployed. They joined the struggles of labor. They published their tremendously influential penny paper. They bought up farmland for communes. The Baroness Catherine de Hueck Doherty, the founder of Friendship House, as dedicated to the integration of the races as Dorothy Day was to the poor, was also invited to Mundelein. Already in awe of Hillenbrand's deep spirituality and thirsty for these new words of eternal life, seminarians like Jack Egan, men about to make the Chicago Archdiocese the liveliest in the country, found nectar, nurture and a week's inspiration in this access to the best thinking on the Church in the United States and in Europe.

Jack Egan says that the beginning of interest in Catholic Action cells came in the summer of 1938 when Oklahoman Father Donald Kanaly, who had known Canon Joseph Cardijn in Louvain, described Cardijn's organization of small groups of like-minded people for action at the clergy Summer School of Catholic Action.

"Hillenbrand got interested. He got Father Jake Killgallon interested, and some other people—Father Marhoefer."

Jack describes how the young seminarians were readied for take-off. "Everything was happening in those years. The liturgical movement was beginning to find its way from Europe over here—I remember going to the first liturgical conference at Holy Name Cathedral. The Catholic Worker. Friendship House. The beginnings of Catholic Action. The seminarians' study weeks. *Commonweal, America.* The social action movement."

As Hillenbrand's skilled typist, Jack had a special relationship with the rector. Hillenbrand asked Jack to transcribe the talks from the Summer School of Catholic Action. Jack remembers it was such men as "Monsignor John Ryan, Bishop Haas, John Cronin and all those men who were the founders of Catholic social action theory and teaching. All intellectuals. It was four weeks in the summer of both 1938 and 1939. To be able to sit and listen to those men and to type out their talks—just a great experience." As prefect of the deacon building in 1942-43, Jack went over the week's activities with Monsignor Hillenbrand every Saturday night. "When we got finished with the business, we would sit and talk. That was better than any class I ever had. He and I became very close."

Through person-to-person contact like this, the speakers he invited in, his Saturday night seminars on papal social thought, his Sunday homilies when he preached—"really preached," Jack Egan says admiringly—to the seminarians, his selection of diocesan priests to augment the Jesuit faculty, Monsignor Hillenbrand plumbed the roots of Catholic social thinking and liturgical practice. He was energizing his seminarians to change—Christianize—the world, "preferably by noon tomorrow," as one of those early Catholic Action advocates remembers. Some of them really tried to do it.

4

"I Had Disappointed My Father"

Mundelein seminarians did not often get home. At most twice a year. There was a vacation right after Christmas (not for Christmas—after exams), and two weeks in the summertime. Two hours were set aside for visiting once a month. Parents on hard chairs and good behavior sat with their seminarian sons, also on their good behavior. Ranged around the audience room were another fifteen or sixteen similar groups painfully simulating social ease. "Those visits were the most boring things," Jack recalls. "After the first half hour what was there to talk about?"

The inhibiting setting was designed to prevent real communication. After the formalities, there wasn't supposed to be anything to talk about. "That was another part of the strictness. You weren't supposed to be connected with the outside world." Even your own family. "That clerical culture was so rigid that lay people didn't get into it and we didn't get out of it, so there was a great distance between the lay people and ourselves. I think this is one of the things, thank God, that Monsignor Hillenbrand helped me with," Jack says.

There was an additional complication for Jack. His father still frowned on his son's vocation. "Every time my father put me on the train to Mundelein after a vacation at home he would say, 'Now, son, don't forget there's a place at home for you if you decide. . . .'" A compliant, eager young man with an ingrained need to please his father, Jack suffered from his father's reproachful attitude. In choosing the religious life, "I had disappointed my father for the first time in my life."

Yet that very ritual of breaking with his father to become his own man charged Jack with the stamina to struggle through Quigley in spite of his teachers' misgivings and to stick at Mundelein when his philosophy professor counseled a switch. As Jack puts it, "To use a bad word, it prevented me from being a wimp." The father/son rift fueled Jack's ingrained determination to succeed, itself fueled by his father's pressure

28

on Jack. That lack of approval also fueled Jack's need to be liked. "I liked to be liked," Jack admits. "That didn't make me unusual. But I think I liked to be liked to an unusual degree. I was also ambitious for recognition. That was a weakness because it turned people away from me." Perhaps in trying to please, he tried too hard.

Jack ascribes that trait not only to the fact that he could never please his father. It was also "because I was small for my age, and I was never good at athletics even though I played them. I was always the last player chosen for a team and I always got roughed up."

In the end Jack Egan prevailed. He was ordained on "a beautiful May day" in 1943, "and I still have some pictures of me giving my blessing to my mother and father." He still did not know why his father had opposed his vocation. He seemed proud enough of him today. In his formal photographs the new Father John J. Egan retained the fresh-faced look of a polite altar boy. This was the day the Lord had made for Jack and his classmates. "You had just lived for this, worked for it. *Ordination.* It was your 'marriage' day. You never forget, you know where you were and you know everything that happened, who came. . . ."

Jack's father, who had done all he could to thwart this day, described his son's first Mass for his "dear Sister and Brother" in Ireland as a glorious sight. "The High Mass which was, of course, sung by your little nephew, was one of the grandest sights I have seen for a long time. The crowd was enormous, and when the Mass was finished, the people surged out, and down the steps of the Church to the sidewalk. It took at least one hour to clear the entrance of the Church, the steps, and the grounds around the Church." Describing the banquet after the Mass, Mr. Egan revealed his deep feelings about the day. "In Jack's reply to the speeches made regarding him, and which was very touching, many of the people were rubbing their eyes with their handkerchiefs, and trying to refrain from shedding tears." As he promises pictures, and more pictures, and "more news in my next letter regarding the whole affair," Mr. Egan exposes his pride in the vocation he opposed: "It was a grand spectacle to see the high dignitaries of the Church kneeling in the green meadows, receiving the blessing of the new priests. The head prefect (Jack) had a circle of clergy and laity around him for full two hours while he imparted the blessing."

The young seminarians were now priests. They would wear Roman collars on the street and sacred vestments for Mass. Never again would they usher at local theaters or stock groceries at the National Tea Company for twenty-five cents an hour.

Parishioners, whether they wore hairbows, baseball caps or hearing aids, would call them Father. Mid-twentieth century, most ordinary fish-on-Friday, Sid-Caesar-on-Saturday, and Mass-on-Sunday Catholics in Chicago put a lot of stock in the priest's word as God's word. When Father said yes, it was yes. When Father said no, it was no. Father's word was law to the faithful, mostly sons and daughters, grandsons and granddaughters of immigrants, as they were.

The day he was ordained, May 1, 1943, Jack Egan upended that accepted order. He'd joined the priesthood to serve the faithful, not to lay down the law to them. On his great day, Jack made a solemn promise, "something close to a vow, that two things would have precedence in my life. I would try to work for the enhancement of the lay role in the Church and, wisely or not, I would never say no to anyone." It was a promise to God and himself to be open to the people he was ordained to serve. "Now that has caused a lot of difficulty in my life. However, if you will accept the double negative, it has also produced a tremendous number of positives, and great benefits."

Some months prior to his ordination, Jack had heard community organizer Saul Alinsky advise a group of seminarians, "On the day you're ordained, make up your mind whether you want to be a priest or a bishop. Everything else will follow." Jack had no way of knowing that day how profoundly his life would be entwined with Alinsky's. Nevertheless, with his vow to serve lay people he had made the choice Alinsky described, knowingly or unknowingly. Some clerics look for clerical preferment; Cardinal Cody of Chicago was known for carrying sacks of gold to Rome. Jack Egan looked for lay preferment, in the sense that he meant to listen to the people in order to serve their needs.

As Pat Hollahan Judge, lured to Young Christian Students by seminarian Jack Egan, says, "He was an artist at listening. He recognized that every act of listening demands a follow-up, a completion. That's partly why he's always writing notes to people." She's reminded of the *Finian's Rainbow* lyric, "When I'm not near the girl I love, I love the girl I'm near." That's Jack's knack, she suggests, focusing on the person in front of him as, at that moment, the most important person in the world. And the one with the exact information he needs. She sees this as the aspect of Jack Egan that is never replicated, to his long-standing distress. "He took the *priest* pattern, the way all his peers were doing, on his ordination day but then he superimposed the additional dimension of listener/responder." As soon as he began asking questions and offering to help, Jack Egan moved into arenas many Catholics—and many priests—considered off bounds for ordained ministers. He became citizen priest. Nina Polcyn Moore, another early witness, stresses how unusual it was in 1943 for a priest to work at enhancing the lay role.

Was the controversial role of citizen priest an appropriate posture for a priest attached to the archdiocese? Throughout his life, Jack would never be comforted by a sustaining consensus. Bold voices supported him. Disaffected voices, sometimes bitter, castigated him. Jack Egan heard them all as he plunged on, faithful to his early and powerful vision, trying to submerge his need to be liked and admired to the needs of the people he served.

Jack Egan would say that he was only carrying the implications of the doctrine of the Mystical Body to their logical conclusion. Ordained to be a "foot-washer of the world," that's what he'd be. For Jack in 1943 the hierarchical model of the Church was already outmoded and irrelevant. "At our very best we are to be servants of the servants of God. That means we have to put ourselves at the disposal of lay people."

That service should be enhanced by kindness, the "big, rough and tumble, lovable Jesuit who taught Moral Theology" had preached to Jack's classmates. "The day you are unkind in the confessional will be a day you will always regret," Father Jim Mahoney told the young men preparing for Saturdays in the box. Once the penitent vanishes, the priest/professor warned, "you can do nothing about it. You do not know the person to whom you were unkind and you cannot apologize or do anything to rectify the unkindness." That advice Jack never forgot.

Not all the young men ordained in the United States in that decade would ease smoothly onto the fast track leading the Roman Catholic Church world-wide to the second Vatican Council. But the lessons Monsignor Hillenbrand taught of devotion to the liturgy, commitment to social justice based on the encyclicals, and faith in the laity as the Mystical Body of Christ did prepare his seminarians. Once they were ordained to minister to the laity under the astutely permissive Samuel Cardinal Stritch, Archbishop of Chicago, they began to strike out in new directions, pulling along segments of the Chicago Church, people who had been sensitized by Hillenbrand himself or Father Carrabine,

CISCA, the Queen's Work, Father Daniel Lord, Father Edward Dowling, Father John Ryan, Dorothy Day, and the Baroness de Hueck.

Like a shift in tectonic plates that opens up the earth and lets its molten innards erupt in a volcano, Monsignor Hillenbrand had opened the vein in the church that allowed the pent strength of visionaries, contemporary and historical, to affect his students, "Rynie's young men." A powerful force flowed through them into the lay persons they affected, and from those lay people into the national Church. Together, they all shared something of the invigorating exhilaration of the first Pentecost and all those times in the Church's history when Jesus' message is rediscovered, reformulated.

When Rynie's group implemented the theory of the laity as equal members of the Body of Christ, they threatened the Church's authoritarianism. They were forging new pathways, destination unknown. The idea of the Mystical Body seemed fresh as a morning in May in 1943. Few people remembered that Archbishop John England had grounded his teaching in the Pauline image of the Body of Christ, a response to his American experience of Church, a hundred years before. To these young priests, far closer to the mind of their immigrant forebears than they were to the insights of an Archbishop England, it was a giant step to embrace this image without losing touch with the Church they were raised in, the Church of their pious first or second-generation immigrant families.

For the Church they were ordained to serve in Chicago was still suffering the friction of an immigrant Church into the 1930s and 1940s in spite of Cardinal Mundelein's vigorous efforts to introduce discipline, uniformity and centralization. The archdiocese was not nearly so unruly and stormy as Chicago's fourth archbishop found it when he arrived on his special train from New York in 1916. Cardinal Mundelein had been effective. Building a seminary to train young priests from different cultures together was an impressive advance. But, more than that, the dean of American Catholic church historians, Monsignor John Tracy Ellis, credits the Archdiocese of Chicago for a half century of leadership in the American Catholic community before 1965. "It was there that national progressive movements relating to youth, family life, social justice, etc., took their rise during the administrations of Cardinals Mundelein, Stritch, and Meyer."

In a review in *Catholic New York*, Tracy Ellis traced this national leadership "to an impetus given by the bishops of the Middle West that dated from the Third Plenary Council of Baltimore, a gathering that the Middle Western prelates were mainly responsible for bringing into being in 1884, and which has influenced American Catholic life down to our own day."

The Hillenbrand priests had a sense of serving not only their Church, but also their city. The city was their tabula rasa, their drawing board, their action center. A young couple who couldn't save the one-third downpayment necessary to buy a home within the Chicago city limits remember a very young Father Egan aghast that they would leave the hub of life, the site of the ultimate contests, the playing field of the real contenders. They bought the tract house in the suburbs with the ten percent down they could afford. But they always thought of it as second best.

Jack was like a subterranean bulb that summer of 1943, poised to burst forth at the first sunshine. He'd spent six years readying himself for his first parish, his first contact with the people he longed to serve. With no mortgage, no family ties, no money worries to concern him, he could freely belong to the people.

How to be a priest was no mystery to him. Monsignor Hillenbrand had anticipated for "Rynie's young men" the kind of ministry Father Richard McBrien, later chairperson of the theology department at the University of Notre Dame, would describe in *Catholicism*. "Every ministry has something to do with advancing the work of the Church. Every ministry has something to do with building up the Body of Christ and somehow fulfilling the Church's responsibility in the world to live out the Lordship of Jesus, to be a sign of the Gospel, to be an agent of social change, to serve the community as advocate."

All the new Father Egan needed was the fateful letter assigning him to his first parish. For Jack Egan it was St. Justin Martyr at Seventy-first and Honore Streets in Chicago, founded in 1916 to serve Irish Catholics. There the young Father Egan would find his sunshine. By the time Jack arrived, shortly after the celebration of the parish's twenty-fifth anniversary, the ethnic composition of the neighborhood had widened to include an Italian contingent, but it was still largely Irish who watched the host raised over the altar of Connemara marble each Sunday.

Before his assignment, Jack had never heard of St. Justin Martyr. "I remember taking the Ashland Avenue streetcar out there and walking down the street with my suitcase past all the houses with blue and gold stars in the windows. The new priest!" The pastor, Father James G. Halleran, like St. Justin Martyr parish, had recently celebrated his twenty-fifth anniversary. "I thought he was old," Jack says. "He was grey-haired." Father Halleran showed Jack his room, "a lovely room," showed him "the nice rectory, brought me over to the church, the school."

"Jack," Father Halleran said to his new assistant, "your job, yours and (the other associate) Frank Spellman's, is to take care of the people. I'll take care of the administration of the parish." That's all that Jack needed to hear. Like the red rocket streetcar that carried him down Ashland Avenue, Jack's throttle was at full speed ahead. He plunged into parish work. Some new priests would have been content to take over the Sodality and the young people's club as Jack did immediately, and be content. But Jack meant to "take care of the people." That's why he'd come. To him they were the "fair field full of folk" described by Piers Plowman, a fair field for him to care for, to cultivate for the Lord.

To take care of the people the two young curates alerted Sunday Mass-goers that they were going to ring every doorbell for a parish census. Ringing *every* doorbell was their exact intent. With that runaway eagerness of Maria in *The Sound of Music*, they would have climbed every mountain, forded every stream, followed every rainbow, to ring every doorbell, to follow their dream of service.

The first response to their efforts surprised them. Not having had any contact with the housewife's life since they'd left home, the young priests were taken aback by the agitation their announcement provoked. To the women of the parish, a priestly visit meant a priestly checkup on their housekeeping skills. The homemakers in the congregation dashed home to scour their small frame houses. The husbands, delighted, reported to the priests that their homes were tidy for the first time in months. The wives were offended at their husbands' insensitive teasing.

Oops, the young priests realized, consternation and heavy cleaning were not what they had in mind. Clearly, it was unkind to keep all the women poised with their mops. At their next Sunday Masses they gave precise information about the streets they intended to cover, suggesting they didn't expect special treatment nor did they hope to be urged to dine with the family. That would keep the mother busy in the kitchen. What we're interested in, they insisted, is chatting, "getting to know you."

Jack felt visiting in the morning or afternoon was a waste. He wanted the whole family ranged around him while he engaged first the father in conversation about his job as postal worker or patrolman or streetcar motorman working out of the carbarns at Sixty-ninth and Ashland. "How are you getting on at work?" "What's going on in the neighborhood?" "Are you happy with the parish operation?" "Is there any way I can help you?" Then he'd pursue the mother's viewpoint. Before he left he would work down the family, drawing out the kids on their interests and plans. He found they all opened up, even the smart-aleck teen-agers. "Their life, what they're doing, is important to every person."

For some young priests, these forays into parishioners' homes might have been dismaying. But Jack was genuinely interested in the particulars of the parishioners' lives. "I have a great curiosity about people," he says, "what they think, their ideas." Nina Polcyn Moore, who came to Chicago as assistant director of Sheil School the year that Jack Egan was ordained, would agree. She recalls the young curate, "already a rising star, giving lectures on the social encyclicals at the Sheil School," as vastly curious about every aspect of the school, the city, and the Church. She remembers him trudging up four flights of stairs to the Marshall Field Town and Garden apartment she shared with Katie Murphy, the woman who would later be Jack's secretary, at 404 North Evergreen. Even then Jack was a "notorious stopper-inner, being in the neighborhood, don't you know." He would come "in need of a meal, a ham sandwich, and a kind word." He brought the same inquisitiveness to the little frame houses on South Wood and West Seventy-first Street that he brought to North Evergreen.

St. Justin Martyr was a small parish, 800 families. "A lot of those people were bashful, especially people from the Old Country, They considered it a great compliment when a priest visited their home." With a friendly, relaxed young "Father" in their living room, parishioners felt free to bring up minor irritations or disappointments with the parish.

Here at St. Justin Martyr Jack reaped another benefit of his father's withholding of unconditional acceptance besides his ability to accommodate to harsh discipline. Anthony Storr analyzes in *Solitude* how hard children who don't have their parents' unconditional acceptance work to please. That early unhappiness also develops in them a capacity for empathy. Jack's wary appraisal of the feelings of his father as he was growing up gave rise to an unusual capacity to identify with others. What Storr said of Rudyard Kipling in this context was true of Jack at his first parish: "People found themselves telling him their troubles in the assurance that he would not betray them."

For fear that non-Catholic neighbors seeing the priests coming down the street might feel slighted if overlooked, Jack and Frank Spellman rapped at every door within the parish boundaries, "not to proselytize, to pay our respects." Disarmed by the attention to the children, the appropriate nods and cluckings their confidences elicited, the families in the area responded with affection for the young assistant priests with their ready smiles and their serious eyes. That affection stood Jack in good stead when he returned to the area fifteen years later advocating Alinsky-inspired community organization.

According to Andrew Greeley, "a priest in a parish he likes and where he is liked is very much like a man in love." That was Jack Egan at St. Justin Martyr. It was here for the first time in his life that Jack Egan felt he could be loved. Until that time he had always felt shy. "I wanted to be liked; I didn't want to be rejected. I didn't think I had enough stuff for people to like me." In grammar school he'd felt on the social fringe; he worked while the other kids hung out. At Mundelein he felt respected, but, in his own words, "I wasn't one of the favorite guys in the class." At St. Justin Martyr, "I find out for the first time in my life that people can really love me. And I'm very close to them. I fall in love with them and they fall in love with me. It was really great."

Out of that small parish 700 men were serving in World War II when Jack arrived in 1943. As it had done when he noted the gold stars marking the homes of men who'd given their lives for their country, Jack's heart went out to frightened families as they described their sons' suffering, and their own. Jack pondered ways the parish family could communicate its affection and concern for the men serving their country? As St. Justin Martyr parishioner Kay Fox wrote Jack about those days, "It was wartime. Most of the young men in our lives and in the parish were overseas. We needed to stay together and you made it happen. You came up with the great idea of sending a monthly newsletter to the boys of St. Justin's."

When he found the thread to tie those farflung servicemen to the parish back home, Jack had found another key life-long operating technique, one that supplemented his gift for finding the right person: finding the right linkage. With the pastor's permission, he called the newsletter *Just-in-Passing*. For the parish it was an innovation. In Jack Egan it begot a lifetime partiality for the printed tie that binds. Every month each of St. Justin's service men and women got mail from home, a compendium of news collected and collated by Jack Egan, signed by the priests of the parish, and mimeographed and mailed by a crew of young women in their twenties, including Kay Fox, whom Jack recruited. The newsletter "had a tremendous effect on their lives and their relationship with the Church," Jack says.

What the young women remember is, "You wrote the letter and made the mailing of that wonderful letter very important and fun. The boys looked forward to receiving it and we loved sending it." After they'd posted the monthly mailing, the mailing team would regroup at Kay Rodney's house across the alley from the rectory. "You always made time to stop by. You listened to our problems and kept our spirits up. We loved you for the attention you gave us," Kay Fox later wrote Jack Egan.

The essential Father Egan was already forming up in the young curate. The young women, whose loneliness he observed and then mitigated to some extent by organizing an activity for them, saw him as always happy, "even at early morning Mass," as bubbly, and very religious. He was their good friend who drew them out by listening absorbedly to what they had to say.

As the young working women watched their new curate develop, they assumed that someday he would be a bishop. "He was involved in so much, had so much stored in his head that he had to take care of," Kay Fox says. They appreciated his enthusiasm for young and old, how he remembered everyone's name. Grateful for his attention, the young women were understanding, not miffed, when he interrupted every gathering "to make a few phone calls," another Jack Egan hallmark. They felt privileged to garner the attention they got from this busy, involved curate.

That impulse to reach out to those lonely young women, to those in pain, to servicemen who felt out of touch, to the families of the seventeen parishioners who died in World War II, to young men making postwar adjustments, to the young women who married the young men making post-war adjustments, forced Jack to evaluate his counseling skills. Had he been sufficiently prepared in the seminary to respond to the unquiet misery he found around him? Jack thought not. "I felt very inadequate." That inadequacy drew him to the University of Chicago where he experienced another of the great formational "funding"—in the Jack Shea phrase he's adopted—experiences of his life. "I studied with the great Carl Rogers for a year."

Once again Jack Egan showed his genius for ferreting out the person precisely tuned to the service required. At the great university just east of the parish border where he went to learn counseling, Jack encountered a legendary counselor. In Carl Rogers' classroom this young curate who had been reared by an authoritarian father, educated in an authoritarian system, formed for an authoritarian role, learned the Rogerian concept of non-directive counseling: people change from within, at their own pace, when they are fully respected, not when they are ordered or advised, however kindly, to change.

Carl Rogers' principles fit Jack like a cap fits a salt shaker. Monsignor Hillenbrand had showed his young men how people function as parts and parcels of the Mystical Body. Not lesser parts, each was a different part of the Mystical Body. Rogers supplied a psychological principle to undergird the theological principle. He taught Jack that if he, as counselor, accepted people as they were, listened intuitively to their stories, and made his own regard and support palpable, that those who came for counseling would find their own answers. They would also discover within themselves the faith and courage to act on what they saw as right and necessary.

"Out of the experience with Carl Rogers which had an enormous effect on my life," Jack recalls, "I was able to develop an interest in counseling which has perdured all my life." He sees how it's helped him in the confessional, in preparing homilies, in working with the people in distress—those very persons he studied with Carl Rogers to help. At his final conference with Rogers, the therapist advised Jack, "Father, I want you to remember all through your life that you are only responsible for the things that you are responsible for . . ." Acknowledging the "good spirituality" in those words helped Jack over the years although he admits that, humanly, he's violated it, and occasionally "tried to butt into other people's business."

Carl Rogers' insights carried over into the marriage education Jack did during his St. Justin Martyr days. As he'd ask the young marrieds, "How are things going?" he'd hear, "Not so well." The young people had many difficulties adjusting, all of them exacerbated by the shortage of housing right after the war.

Having anticipated some tension and stress, Jack had done marriage preparation with the young women. "We might have had the first marriage preparation for young women planning a wedding as soon as the war was over and the fellows came back." When Monsignor Edward Burke, chancellor of the archdiocese, who would figure later as one of Jack's strongest champions, heard about the marriage preparation sessions sometime in 1945, he asked Jack to develop a marriage course for high school students.

By this time Jack was working on his days off with Catholic Action cells. Never one to play golf or meet cronies regularly for dinner, Jack had eagerly agreed to be chaplain to the Catholic Action cell at Chicago Teachers' College when Monsignor Hillenbrand approached him. Together with two high school students in one of the early CA cells, Mary Lou Genova Wolff and Jeanne Skepnik, Jack planned a marriage manual ("maybe fifty mimeographed pages, maybe in outline form," he recalls), printed it, and promoted it in the schools. It related directly to the kids' needs because Jack used the occasion, and his new counseling skills, to draw information from high school girls about the problems they faced in their homes and with their boyfriends.

At that point Jack Egan could have had no idea how largely marriage education was going to figure in his future and in his ministry. Or how the archdiocesan politics that made him a pioneer in the field would bypass—and embitter—the teacher at Quigley who had done the groundwork for the Cana phenomenon about to burst over the archdiocese.

5

"What Would Jesus Do in This Situation?"

Father Halleran at St. Justin Martyr had the good sense to insist that his young associates get out of the parish on their one day a week off. Young Father Egan didn't have the good sense to listen to his pastor. Once he was involved in Catholic Action groups, he arranged their meetings on his free day. Peg Burke, a member of a CA teachers' group, recalls their coming to the St. Justin Martyr rectory every Wednesday afternoon.

When cell members asked for Father Egan at the door, the housekeeper always demurred. "Father's not in. It's his day off." Their standard rejoinder was, "Father told us we could use his office," and in they'd go. "Father Egan had told us that the pastor was very firm about when it's your day off you are not around, but Father always managed to sneak in each week for our meeting."

Later on, in a Christian Family Movement group chaplained by Father Egan, Peg Burke experienced the adamant aspect of the amiable curate. Supportive and encouraging as Jack Egan was, he expected performance from the people he put his faith in and gave his time to. When he suggested to Burke's CFM group after about six months of meetings that now was the acceptable time for each of the couples to set up CFM sections in their home parishes, the couples balked. "There was a unanimous feeling that we very much needed each other and we felt such support from the group that we just couldn't split up into other groups." Jack Egan reacted by showing what some call "his fierce side."

It's Peg Burke's recollection that, "Father was most displeased with us and somehow I think he gave up on us and we just continued even though he didn't come any more." Nonetheless, Burke assesses the

CFM experience as positive. "Most everyone that was a member of the CFM movement remained active in the Church and became a leader."

The movements did ask a great deal of inexperienced participants. Pat Hollahan Judge was a vibrant, personable, fifteen-year-old (who, like Jack, had eluded the cookie cutter Catholic mold) when Father Egan recruited her at Immaculata High School where his sister Kay was also a student. Jack was still a seminarian when Pat first heard his pitch in the rectory at Our Lady of Lourdes. "He told us what the cell movement meant for the Church, how young people like us could improve our corner of the world.

"He was so young, so excited, so sure, *so sure*. And he had a flattering trust in us. He made us see that if we didn't do this thing he was talking about, the good news wouldn't get out. You got a sense of responsibility for this exciting plan he built up."

Like Jaime Escalante who convinced eighteen Hispanic students in a poor Los Angeles high school that they could pass an advanced placement calculus test (and was memorialized in the movie *Stand and Deliver*), Father Egan plugged his faith into young people's energy sources. He made it possible for them to say, "Of course I can do that." He'd picked the right age group. When he assured Pat she had power, she says, "he tapped right into that idealism we had when we were young. 'You can reach students better than anyone, better than priests, better than the Sisters,' he'd say."

His confidence in them evoked self-confidence in his recruits. "I was told to find a chaplain for a North Side group and recruit from four to six leaders from my high school to commit themselves to this new work of the Church," Pat Judge remembers. She could do it because "Father Egan had communicated the urgency he felt to me. He really believed in the laity. He believed in me. He took risks on people."

He functioned as spiritual director for all the participants, tonic, coach, therapist, model, bracer-upper, teacher. Sometimes, career counselor. It was at Jack's insistence that cell member Jacqueline Krump studied for a Ph.D. "You know," she wrote Jack in later years, "that I attribute my career to you." At base, Jack Egan acted through his identification with Jesus. He looked at people and said, "You I want. You are called to do the work of the Lord."

When the individual groups met—workers, students, teachers—they followed the Observe/Judge/Act formula that Canon Cardijn had worked out. They gathered facts about their small corners of the world. They judged the facts against the Gospel reading prepared with the chaplain. Then they asked themselves, "What would Jesus do in this situation?" Part of their power was their very mandate to act in the name of the Church. No one had ever said before that lay people were important. Now here were these dynamic, engaging, young priests like Jack Egan saying, "Jesus is helpless to bind the world's wounds without your hands, your hearts, your willingness." He'd learned very well from Monsignor Hillenbrand.

That confidence of the priests in the laity was a potent elixir. In Europe, Canon Cardijn, who preached the dignity of the young worker in season and out of season, could gather 100,000 Young Christian Workers in Heyssel Stadium in Brussels. Young Americans wanted to effect changes in the workplace and in politics, as European Young Christian Workers were doing. In 1945, immediately after the war's end, the Europeans invited Catholic Action members from the United States to an international YCW meeting in Brussels. If they could get there, Chicago's cell members realized, they could see first hand the sources of YCW power and élan. But how could they get there? The obstacles seemed insurmountable to the members of the struggling organization. No one was traveling in that postwar world who didn't have important business overseas. According to Nina Polcyn Moore, Jack Egan refused to see the obstacles as insurmountable. Just as he scoured St. Benet Library and Book Shop regularly for books to focus cell members' minds, he prescribed travel and European contacts to broaden their viewpoints and sharpen their perspectives.

With a little help from this pushy friend, the "senior working girls" made a quixotic decision to send two delegates.

They were up against such insuperable odds that only professionally visionary enthusiasts like Jack Egan could believe that they could ever marshal the resources: money, reservations, passports and visas. As Edwina Hearn Froelich remembers it, "TWA, the only airline flying overseas commercially at that particular time, laughed at our request to book a round trip to Belgium. They made it very clear that they considered it highly unlikely that two seats would become available for a year or more." The embassies were more intractable than TWA. "They each let us know they were not just letting anybody in." Besides, as Edwina recalls, she didn't have a penny in the bank.

Cell members sold silk stockings—hard-to-get items—because there wouldn't be any financial aid from the archdiocese for whom Catholic Action cells were definitely a peripheral concern. Cell groups were suffered, not honored. While it was true that the archdiocese provided space in the derelict schoolhouse at Three East Chicago Avenue, the priests who hung around there too much could get in trouble for doing it. Most pastors frowned upon Catholic Action. It threatened their absolute rule.

Moreover, it took up time and energy young curates might spend organizing the Sodalities and other controllable containers for young people that didn't promise participants a say in what goes on in the Church.

Edwina Hearn Froelich remembers screwing her nerve to the sticking place to address a small group with the unusual (for its day, threatening) salutation: "Your Eminence, Honored Monsignori, and *laity*." She blanched when Cardinal Stritch commented pointedly on the "new language we had here." A gentle man, he would never have excoriated Edwina for brashness. Yet he couldn't let pass her temerity in assigning the laity what might be construed as equal status. Edwina had added the word laity in the full knowledge that no one ever addressed the laity as if they actually existed in a mixed priest/laity group. She couldn't have done it before her Catholic Action chaplain, Father Romeo Blanchette, urged Catholic Action members to think for themselves. In the lexicon of the 1940s (outside of Catholic Action circles) members of the *laity* didn't figure in salutations. Nor did they think for themselves. "Holy Mother Church (in the person of the pastor) took care of that obligation," according to Edwina.

The unsettling practice of laypersons taking themselves seriously as thinking religious persons was taking hold only marginally in the postwar Church. It takes a vigorous leap of imagination to capture mentally a time when a young woman's daring use of the word *laity* in the sacred circle of those addressed at an intimate, enclosed meeting could create a situation. But that illustrates the measure of Monsignor Hillenbrand's achievement in tilting at the clerical windmill of, "Father says."

However, Hillenbrand was not the first American cleric to acknowledge the baptismal priesthood of the laity. Along with its triumphalist authoritarian lineage, the U.S. Catholic Church had consistently harbored a more democratic strain back to its first bishop, John Carroll.

As Jack Egan was to do later, Bishop Carroll took part in the civic life of his country, contributing to a letter congratulating George Washington on his unanimous election and asking that Catholics share "equal rights of citizenship, as the price of our blood as spilt under your eyes, and of our common exertions for her defence, under your auspicious conduct—rights rendered more dear to us by the remembrance of former hardships." When Washington died, Bishop Carroll issued a pastoral letter, asking pastors to observe on February 22 "the departed Spirit of the first of Heroes."

Later explosions of immigrant populations diluted such liberal expressions of solidarity with the body politic. Conservatism, however, could never completely suppress the emergence of an Orestes Brownson or Bishop John England of Charleston, or Isaac Hecker, founder of the Paulists, to restore the balance as such restoration was needed.

When Jack Egan was introduced as chaplain of Edwina Hearn Froelich's Catholic Action cell, her first thought was, "Oh, my God, he's not dry behind the ears." Slight, round-faced, he looked like an altar boy, not a great believer in laity thinking for themselves and a natural heir to Bishop John Carroll. How could she tell that Jack Egan was as likely as Bishop Carroll to write congratulations to newly elected city officials and make himself useful to them, to a point that one day he'd be invited to serve on a mayor's "kitchen cabinet?" Before Edwina met him at the second string CA hangout, Yonkers Restaurant on Chicago Avenue, Jack Egan had already begun to move out of the restricted culture of clerical life into the civic life of the community. But only marginally. His real initiation was yet to come when his concern for the housing needs of his St. Justin Martyr people sent him to testifying at City Hall. But that was later. When Edwina met him, she didn't guess how wide his interests would grow, what a "marvelous listener this peppy interesting priest" would be, and how he would make things happen.

Through the sale of the silk stockings and the good offices of Jack Egan and the other chaplains and cell members, checks—"many from people none of us knew personally"—appeared in the mail for the plane trip to the international Catholic Action gathering in Belgium. Edwina and Mary Irene Caplice Zotti, the chosen delegates, made all their preparations in absolute reliance that if God wanted them to go to Europe, tickets and money and reservations would fall into place. And so they did. Embassy clearances were obtained, and rationed seats found on

Trans World Airlines. The two women enplaned, not knowing where they would lay their heads or eat in a Europe where food was still scarce and rationed. Edwina lost fifteen pounds before she returned. If they'd had enough money, they still would have had difficulties.

Father Egan said a last Mass for the two women representing all of the Catholic Action cells in the United States at St. Justin Martyr Church before they took off from Midway Airport for an apostolic adventure that would change their lives, and change the direction of Catholic Action in the United States. In the three months it took to get clearance back to the United States, they quit their jobs to become full-time YCW organizers, having learned, as they said on their return, that "we're doing YCW all wrong in the United States." To identify with the Europeans, American Catholic Action groups would now be called, variously, Young Christian Workers and Young Christian Students.

Although Edwina remembers hearing that in some places clergy dominated the cell movements, "it was never the case in the Chicago area." No dependency on the chaplain existed "in my relationship with Father Egan, or any of the other YCW women with their spiritual directors. The clergy had a great influence on us, but we ran our own show." Edwina acknowledges that the group did not change the world, as they had hoped, "by noon tomorrow." But the women themselves were changed, permanently. "It was a time of tremendous growth for any who participated. The kind of spiritual nurturing we received through our activity in YCW was not available to the average young Catholic." She capsulized the experience as doing for her, "and for many like me, what the recent George Gallup survey is recommending that the present Church should be doing. It helped us to find God in ordinary experiences. Somehow when that happens everything else falls into place."

These two young women, Edwina Hearn Froelich and Mary Irene Caplice Zotti, who wanted to be holy without being goody-goody, gained a strong sense of their own power as women, lay women, in the YCW group Father Egan chaplained. Dedicated to the group's spiritual development, he planned regular study days, celebratory Masses, and retreats. On occasion, Mary Irene and Edwina had their own private retreats with Father Egan at the Cenacle Convent on Fullerton Avenue. They responded by becoming strong leaders. "All through those years," Mary Irene notes, "we were totally convinced that we were doing something important, largely because of your complete and unmitigated faith in us."

The education went two ways. Jack Egan was educated by cell members (in a way that prepared him for archdiocesan marriage work) even as he educated them. "I think it was from Viola Brennan and Edwina Hearn Froelich (along with Msgr. Hillenbrand, of course) that I learned the most about the meaning of priesthood; the relationship of priesthood to married people, courtship and marriage, and the psychology of women and men."

That confession sounds strange to him now because he'd been some years ordained. Nonetheless, it was they who "taught me about the dignity of the individual. I got a deep appreciation of the meaning of women in the world. Since these were working women and we were having inquiries about the working conditions that women had to face—everything from unequal pay to intellectual and sexual abuse and harrassment, the psychological problems women faced in the work force—(their perceptions) had a very deep effect on my life."

For Edwina Hearn Froelich the cell movement presented "the first time in all my years of Catholic education I had the opportunity to talk to dedicated, caring young priests. The Roman collar was very much there, but the barrier of the pulpit and the confessional were not there at these enlightening and enjoyable times. With these priests I could set aside the don't-bother-Father-he's-too-busy attitude I had grown up with. They were there, they cared about my spiritual growth, they were interesting and knowledgeable and caring. Moreover, I could even have my very own spiritual director, a priest who was really accessible to me personally."

For Jack, the YCW inquiries were stepping stones to the feminist revolution, a revolution he considers "the most important revolution that has happened in our century, in its implications far greater than the civil rights movement" because "it's going to affect half the population of the world."

Jack Egan finds it strange to walk by the Chicago Athletic Association on Michigan Avenue today and recall the time when women couldn't use the main entrance. "When Bob Cronin (who structured the Pre-Cana organization as it still exists) and Mary Cronin would take me to dinner there, Mary had to go through a side entrance."

Jack vividly recalls community activist Saul Alinsky ranging his organizers across from the University Club, up the avenue from the CAA. He'd have them stand across Monroe Street and gaze up at the magnificent Gothic exterior. "Look at that," he'd snort. "That is the University Club. In order to get into it as a member, you not only have to have a university degree. You have to be recommended and voted on. Then you have to be admitted and pay heavy dues. They say they are dignified, that they represent the scholarship of the world. But they will not admit a Jew, a black or a woman. Never forget that."

This exclusionary policy bothered Saul Alinsky who shared Jack Egan's belief that "there should be absolutely no division between people. The dignity of every human person, which Canon Cardijn used to talk about, which Dr. Martin Luther King spoke about, is in the Gospel. Every single solitary individual is of infinite worth," Jack insists. Dating back to early sessions with the Young Christian Worker women, Jack has acted on principles he learned from Monsignor Hillenbrand. Never seeing women as inferior, he insists he loves "to work with women who are more competent than I. I have never shied away from that." He credits his early training in YCW "where I had very bright and wonderful persons to instruct me, guide me, suppport me, interpret for me, build bridges for me, and help me to understand the meaning of the world."

He recalls that the people who were "closest to Christ in his life in many respects were women," and questions the contemporary role assigned women in the Church. "This is one of the reasons why I feel the Church is making a serious mistake, which we will pay for as the years and decades go on, by not taking the lead and assuming that women would have a full role in any part of the function of the Church, the administration of the Church."

As the Church approaches the second millenium of its founding tempered by the emanicipating free play of Vatican II, Jack's stand for women is no more amazing than Mary Cronin's taking the main entrance into the Chicago Athletic Association. In the triumphalist Church of the 1950s, however, when pastors could flag down police cars for police escorts to Comiskey Park and an occasional new mother was still being "churched" (cleansed) after childbirth, a priest admitting he'd learned something from a woman was like a priest permitting a girl to serve Mass.

Unheard-of.

It was excellent preparation, however, for the responsibilities that would soon be Jack's.

6

"Selling God, He Got Us"

On his birthday, October 9, 1947, Jack Egan had been on his St. Justin Martyr honeymoon for three and one-half years. With one phone call, his ministry was going to widen from one parish to the whole archdiocese. Dan Ryan, Cardinal Stritch's secretary, rang up. The cardinal archbishop of Chicago wished to see Father Egan at eleven that morning.

"What's it about, Dan?" Jack asked. Ryan didn't know. At least, he said he didn't.

Three priests sat with Father Egan in the cardinal's waiting room at the appointed hour, all summoned that morning and equally in the dark about the reason they were there. Father Bill Quinn, ordained several years before Jack, was working with Catholic Action groups. Fathers James Voss and Charles (Jules) Marhoefer were distinguished doctors of theology and professors at Quigley Preparatory Seminary, the impressive French Gothic complex built by Cardinal Mundelein at Rush and Chestnut.

Fathers Egan and Quinn were ushered first into the presence of Cardinal Stritch, only the second cardinal to head the Chicago archdiocese when he'd received the red hat in ceremonies in St. Peter's Basilica in Rome the year before.

Stritch was a sweet man, liberal, astute, but seemingly vague. Chauffered to a formal engagement at which he'd agreed to preside, he would stage-whisper to the Sister hurrying him into the auditorium, "Mother, Mother, where am I? Is this Rosary College?" if he was at Mundelein College, and probably "Mundelein, Sister?" if he was at the west suburban Rosary. This morning he did not look up at the two young priests ushered in by his secretary Dan Ryan. "I'm not sure he knew which one was Quinn and which one was Egan," Jack says.

48

Murmuring into the papers before him, Cardinal Stritch allowed that Catholic Action was developing to such an extent in the archdiocese that it was thought by him and his associates (in response to petitions from Catholic Action activists and the Cana lay panel) that the movements should have permanent directors. He was appointing Father Quinn to take charge of the Catholic Action movements. Then he said, "Father Egan, I'm appointing you the director of the Cana and Pre-Cana programs." Only after he'd made the appointments did the cardinal look up at the two eager young priests standing before his desk. "I am not too fully informed as to the extent of this work," he admitted, "and I'm sure you will keep me informed from time to time both by visiting me and in writing. You can begin immediately. See Monsignor Burke, the chancellor, to be removed from your present assignments and then I am sure you will be able to work out appropriate places to live." He was orderly, but casual, according to Egan's recollection, about these important assignments.

Jack Egan was familiar with Cana and Pre-Cana as innovative marriage education programs, Cana for the married and Pre-Cana for those about to be married in the archdiocese. Father Egan's reflective successor, Father Walter Imbiorski, would later define Cana's function as "restoring the poetry which is the Divine idea of man and woman and marriage." The programs were tentative in 1947. Jack was appointed to organize them across the archdiocese.

Unaware of the damaging rebukes awaiting their fellow priests, Quinn and Egan waved goodbye to Fathers Marhoefer and Voss as they passed through the waiting room and went off to Yonker's Restaurant on Chicago Avenue for the first of four decades of lunches on the anniversary of their momentous appointments. Their lives had just taken a sharp turn. October 9 would also change the course of the lives of Marhoefer and Voss in a very different, and for them, devastating, way.

Marhoefer and Voss had good reason to believe that they were the natural heirs to the appointments that had just gone to the younger men. They'd done the groundwork. They'd spent their free time and their tireless energies to get the marriage movement and the Catholic Action initiatives going. Instead of being congratulated by the cardinal and thanked for their efforts over and above their teaching duties, they were firmly reprimanded for giving up their free time to guide the original Cana and Catholic Action groups. The cardinal chided them for neglecting their duties to the seminarians. Dedicated and competent teachers, they had never been negligent. They were actually being punished for their zeal. Their superior, a man who seldom left the cathedral rectory after he finished his daily duties at Quigley, could not tolerate their barreling off on their apostolic activities while he burrowed into card games on the sixth floor. He'd reported their apostolic activity to the cardinal as insubordination. "That was a great injustice," Father Egan says. "Voss deserved the job of director of the Cana Conference more than I." Both men, Voss and Marhoefer, suffered acutely from that setback. Patty Crowley, with her husband founder of the Christian Family Movement, concurs: "Father Voss had worked with the men. He was one of the chaplains for the men's groups, and he thought sure he'd get it. I think he never got over Egan getting it. That was a sore point."

Nonetheless, however hard the decision was on Father Voss, the ebullient Egan, with what Patty Crowley calls "his marvelous organizing ability," was a brilliant choice for the first full-time director of the Cana Conference. Monsignor Edward Burke was impressed with the marriage education work Father Egan had done at St. Justin Martyr, and he "didn't think Father Voss smiled enough," as the story was told. Monsignor Reynold Hillenbrand was in favor of Jack Egan's appointment because he dismissed marriage education as a lightweight burden. He expected Jack to give the bulk of his time to Catholic Action, Monsignor Hillenbrand's full-time passion now that he was a pastor at Sacred Heart in Hubbard Woods and no longer the rector at Mundelein. These men carried great weight in the archdiocese.

What was needed at the helm of the first lay-directed, archdiocesan-wide marriage program was a prodigious workaholic with the sure conviction that the people in parishes could make their own change without Father Pastor standing over the till. He had to be a zealous recruiter. He had to have sufficient grit to bear the grind of visiting two hundred and fifty rectories—the Chicago archdiocese included the Joliet diocese in 1946—and persuading the pastors, the crusty old pastors, the laid-back pastors, the gentle souls, the my-hands-on-and-your-hands-off pastors, the effectual and the ineffectual, the confident and the truculent, the kindly and the soulful, that it would be good for their young people—and for them—to have standardized, informed, discerning, quality marriage education. Some pastors were hard cases. Many of them wouldn't let Pat and Patty Crowley in the door when they came for names of couples-about-to-be-married for the first Pre-Cana Conference they organized.

Jack Egan had a vision for the casually structured organization he'd just been appointed to head. Its genius, as defined later by Father Walter Imbiorski in *The New Cana Manual* was creating a new apologetic of marriage, "translating the spirit, the joy, the truth of Christ's teaching into terms sometimes homely, sometimes dramatic, terms which are applicable to the real problems of real people." As Father Imbiorski put the case, a Cana day for married couples starts at one p.m. with "trying to understand crying babies, unpaid light bills, irate bosses, leaky faucets, fatigue, boredom, and concupiscence." During the three conferences interrupted only briefly for beef sandwiches at three, the priest conducting the Cana Conference would relate those realities of life to the "wisdom of the Church and the grace of Christ" with "rich, meaningful, persuasive solutions." The day ended at six p.m. after recitation of the rosary and the celebration of Benediction.

A Pre-Cana Conference set up for couples planning to be married began with a similar Sunday afternoon regimen of talks and lunch, climaxed by Benediction. During the week following that initiation, the couple would return three weekday nights: Monday to hear an experienced couple talk about their marriage, Wednesday to hear a doctor describe the physical aspects of marriage (always in the "light of faith"), and Friday to hear the priest conductor draw together all the aspects of marriage they were trying to assimilate in such short order.

A third important feature of marriage education in the archdiocese were the Lenten Marriage Forums, six lecture/discussion sessions in twelve to fifteen parish halls on the six Sundays of Lent. Four of those sessions were conducted by a priest, one by a married couple, and one by a doctor. By 1957, there would be 4500 young people attending these sessions titled, *Let's Talk about Love*.

Father Egan had taken on a demanding assignment. His pastor urged him to operate out of the St. Justin Martyr rectory. That would have been pleasant. Jack had roots there now, a large following of parishioners whose devotion to him would not fade with the years. Jack resisted the pull, knowing that the energies he had put into his work at St. Justin had to be totally redeployed into his current appointment, even at the risk of loneliness and temporary dislocation. It meant a great deal to him personally, as well as institutionally, that this archdiocesan venture should work. It was a chance to show what lay people could do, as well as what he could do with the help of lay people.

The roots of this program to enrich and deepen individual marriages, like much of the ferment in the pre-Vatican II Church, grew in France, with family retreats. Observing their impact during a 1937 visit, a New York Jesuit, Father J. P. Delaney, transported the idea from Paris to his home base. In 1945 he gave over forty retreats—Family Renewal Days—to five distinct groups of married couples. When Edward and Marie Kerwin of River Forest, Illinois, read about Delaney's renewal days in *America* magazine in 1944, they asked him to conduct three Family Renewal Days in the Chicago area late that summer. They invited couple/friends from Marie Kerwin's days at Sacred Heart Academy, including Pat and Patty Crowley.

Patty, who'd been married three or four years, says, "I remember being so thrilled with the renewal day. We hadn't had any marriage instruction. In fact," she notes wryly, "Jesuit Father Edward Dowling had given us our only marriage instruction at a bar at the Bismarck Hotel."

Concurrently, the men's Catholic Action group of which Patrick Crowley was a member, realized that their mix of salesmen, lawyers, and managerial types had only their married state in common. Pledged as they were to "change the world," to bring it more in line with Christianity, they decided to concentrate on observing the current state of wedded bliss, and acting to foster its spiritual aspects. They began to sponsor some of these Family Renewal Days, soon re-christened Cana Conferences.

Whether or not the catchy cognomen conceived by the same Father Dowling who'd instructed the Crowleys on barstools made the rose smell any sweeter, Cana Days spread like butter on hot toast. According to Monsignor Harry Koenig's history of the archdiocese, "the group used the mechanism of the infant Catholic Action Movement to give impetus to the idea (of Cana)." By the time Father Delaney returned six months later, the North and South Side groups had enlisted the talents of Fathers Voss, Marhoefer and Martin Carrabine, S.J., "who worked assiduously over the next two years to promote the work of days of renewal for couples." The West Side group developed an organization plan which became the pattern for Cana in Chicago. By the time Father Egan was appointed director of the first official Cana Conference in the country, there were twenty diocesan and religious clergy conducting Cana Days. A lay panel (the Robert Podestas, Joseph Joyces, Frank

Gleasons, Fred Becklenbergs) had applied to the chancellor for a permanent director.

In 1947 there was still a subtle—some would say not too subtle—Jansenistic tone to the Catholic attitude toward marriage. As the perceptive Canadian psychiatrist/author Karl Stern described the Catholic outlook at a Christian Family Movement convention, "Now a great number of Catholics have toward sexuality a strange, puritanical attitude; a Manichean attitude of fear as though the flesh in itself was something evil or dirty." Stern was aware that the Church had always condemned this notion."But it is very prevalent. The strange thing is that the child in contact with a mother who has this kind of inner attitude towards sexual morality, even long before a conscious awareness of sex, is imbued with (the same attitude).

"This means," he told CFMers at Notre Dame, "that a child approaches puberty with a strange sense of fear and anxiety." Stern believed this fear was unhealthy. "This is something very important to understand not only in family life but in the life of society. We see such a great number of Christians, Catholics as well as Protestants, whose entire morality is basically a negative one, one of the 'don't.'" He saw, he said, an astonishing host of Catholics who "actually never experience the primacy of the positive command, the command of love."

For Jack Egan and Cana pioneers who believed in the primacy of love, the revered Dominican priest Gerald Vann came closer to their ideal in his notion that the Church blesses physical passion in the marriage ceremony. Physical love is a good thing, Vann assured his readers. "The Church does not say: 'This is a rather shady affair but given certain conditions and circumstances it may be allowed'; the Church says, 'This is a good and lovely thing in itself, but the divine life which is given it in the Sacrament turns a merely humanly lovely thing into a divinely lovely thing.'"

What Vann conveyed to people was that their love for each other, "two body-spirits, is a thing that has to be made by them; and it takes a very long time, and great efforts, efforts to understand, efforts to curb greed and selfishness, efforts to achieve unity of mind and heart." Cana was needed in those post-war years because marriage itself was "taking a beating," according to Monsignor Reynold Hillenbrand. He quoted Pius XII who described the evils harrying the family: "levity in entering into marriage, divorce, the break-up of the family, the cooling of mutual affection between parents and children, birth control, the enfeeblement of the race."

In post-war 1947 the Church was in the marriage business. The young couples Father Egan was marrying at St. Justin Martyr week after week were representative of thousands in the archdiocese who'd waited in foxholes and the home front with the same eagerness Jack waited for his ordination. They'd seen marriage as the dream at the end of the nightmare war. Their expectations were unrealistically high; their resources, few. They were moving the country into a passion of togetherness. Those who had been apart wanted to be close, to get more out of the marriage relationship themselves than their parents had got out of theirs, to put more in. They needed a new theology of the laity's ministry based on Pope Pius XII's teaching that lay people shared priesthood with priests. What did the notion of the Mystical Body mean for married people? Some work was being done on this question in France, but little in the United States.

It wasn't as if the Cana Conference, under Jack Egan, could pick up a dossier of material and hand it over intact to the couples coming for enrichment of their marriages, understanding of their sacrament, rules for getting on. The dossier was being created as the participants went along, just as the rules for lay direction were. It was a heavy duty.

From Monsignor Hillenbrand Jack had learned that his role as priest was to be servant, servant of the servants of God. "The lay people were central. They were truly the Church, so that the hierarchical model of the Church—the Pope, the bishops, the pastors, the lay people—was not only outmoded. That mode was irrelevant to the work of the Church in the world." As the foot-washers of the world, priests served, in Jack Egan's words, "by opening the book and telling the story, and offering the Eucharist with the people."

How was Jack Egan going to get lay people to take the responsibility that he had been taught was theirs? For most of their American church experience, the people had been expected to stay in the pews, paying, praying and obeying. Now the lay people were to be leaders? Think for themselves? Any change in the lay people would affect the role of the clergy. Jack had to educate the pastors person-to-person, Father Egan to Father Pastor on a one-by-one basis. "I knew I had a selling job to do, selling myself. The pastors didn't know me. They were all a generation older than I. I was only out of the seminary three and one half years when I got this assignment." As Monsignor Gerald

Kealy assessed the Cana Conference for his associates at the time: "It mustn't be very important if they put a young priest like that into it."

It took dogged drudgery to surmount that prejudgment. Some of his early difficulties when Cardinal Stritch assigned Jack Egan to marriage education were territorial. Innovators who had initiated couple retreat days in their area wanted to hold onto them.

Pastors, when they allowed Cana Conferences, liked to keep control. As part of his routine, Jack made Sunday rounds, observing how Cana Conferences and Pre-Cana Conferences were going, whether the priest-conductors were following the guidelines and giving the participants the same input on the uniqueness of their vocations and the importance of spending time getting their marriages in line with the Church's vision of Christian marriage and family life.

One Sunday, early in his Cana career, Father Egan dropped in at Mallinckrodt High School in Wilmette where Father Edward Dowling was giving a Cana Conference for St. Mary's Church couples he'd been connected to since his teaching days at Loyola Academy. This group loved Dowling, "a man of great generosity who would take the train from St. Louis to Chicago, sit with a couple in difficulty, and get on the midnight train back to St. Louis for work the next morning," according to Jack Egan.

When Jack arrived, he suggested confidently to the moderator, "When Father comes to a break, I would like to say a few words." The chairperson was apologetic: "Monsignor Hillenbrand (Frederick, Reynold's brother) told us that only Father Dowling is to speak to the group." Although he was able to say coolly, "That's perfectly all right," Father Egan was taken aback. He pondered his next move. Should he simply leave? He'd covered a good part of the city already that day. Besides, he had always been afraid of Monsignor Reynold Hillenrand's brother, a formidable pastor. He opted to telephone the pastor of St. Mary's. In his friendliest, most open, hard-to-refuse, humble-curate-to-revered-pastor manner, he cooed, "This is Jack Egan. I'm over here at Mallinckrodt High School. I would like permission to speak to the group."

Monsignor Hillenbrand's brother was impervious to blandishment, or simple courtesy. "What are you doing there?" he demanded peremptorily. "I will thank you very much if you will kindly leave now." Then he hung up.

Was Jack checkmated or could he find another move? "If you are going to run away from this, you are going to run away from a lot of things," he lectured himself, and drove directly to the rectory at St. Mary's where he rang the bell. All these years later he can visualize his telling the housekeeper that he wished to see the pastor, his climbing the stairs to the pastor's quarters. "He's reading *Time*. And quite surprised to see me!" Jack sat down and asked Monsignor Hillenbrand's brother what was wrong with his saying a few words to the group. "These are my parishioners," the pastor of St. Mary's growled proprietarily. "They got Father Dowling and I don't see why any outsider. . . ."

Jack Egan knew he had to make it clear to the crusty pastor of St. Mary's that he, Jack Egan, was no outsider in the marriage education movement. "Monsignor," he said, softly but forcefully, "you have to realize that I have been given the obligation and also the authority by the cardinal to develop this work. What I am trying to do is to get to know the work, get to know what is going on, so that we may be able to improve it as the years go on." He also pointed out that he was trying to get to know all the pastors in the archdiocese. "I probably should have asked you for permission, but I just took it for granted because every Sunday I visit every Cana and Pre-Cana Conference in the diocese."

The autocratic priest was impressed. His expression softened and he allowed that he had been "a little impetuous." The rest of the interview was pleasant.

The effect of Jack's initiative was permanent. Some years later when Jack telephoned Monsignor Hillenbrand's brother about a Pre-Cana Conference at St. Mary's, the Monsignor was more than conciliatory. "Jack," he said, "I want to tell you something. Anything that you want in our parish, you can have. You are the only priest I know who goes around to the pastors to sell the work they are doing. So whatever you want, you tell me and it will be done."

Crusty pastors were not the young priest's only challenge. As he made his Sunday rounds he found priests not following the Cana format. "It was incumbent on me to fire (them)." He almost missed an entire Cana Conference when he arrived at 1:45 p.m. for a session that began at 1 p.m. "It was supposed to go on to six p.m. and end with Benediction in the church. I saw the priest about to leave."

Jack went up to him. "Ed, what's going on?"

The Cana conductor had a ready explanation. "Well, I told them everything I know." Jack had a ready solution. He fired him. "Lookit, Eddie, will you knock it off!" Difficult as it was for him, Jack was willing to dismiss a peer for the sake of the work. "He was a bright man, much brighter than I, but he never gave another Cana Conference."

Some of the conductors who predated Jack's ascendency were satisfied to continue with their old content, like teachers in comfortable ruts re-using notes. When Jack pointed out the agreed-upon agenda, he warned conductors to conform or quit. It wasn't Jack's style to simply drop a conductor off the schedule. "I'd rather face them head on. I thought it was cruel to treat people with silence, not to invite them back, if you didn't like what they were doing." He would tell people, "I may be wrong, but it just happens that I am in charge of the Cana Conference. If the cardinal wants to do something else, it's all right." He wouldn't argue the theology. He'd simply state his view. "In terms of giving Cana Conferences under our jurisdiction, it would be better if you didn't."

Although he tried always to be fair and give the conductor a hearing, Jack cherished his mandate from the cardinal and his responsibility. Anyone could do marriage education, but a Cana Conference was organized up to the standards of the director, the priest conductors in joint agreement, and the lay board. There would be no free agents while Jack Egan reserved the right of veto power over any of the conductors.

Possibly it was in standing up to the Church's powerful pastors like Monsignor Hillenbrand's brother and Monsignor Molloy that Father Egan primed his chutzpa to stand up against Chicago's powerful in Hyde Park/Kenwood later on. Monsignor Patrick Molloy, the priest exiled because of his misadventure as go-between the mobs, was as formidable a presence in his dominion at St. Leo's, as Mayor Richard Daley, a pal of Molloy's, was in his. As pastor of St. Leo the Great at Seventy-eighth and Emerald Avenue, he ruled in style—his style.

Monsignor Molloy was not a tall man, but he was strong, well-built. He'd been a boxer in his early days and may very well have been the founder of the Catholic Youth Organization, Father Egan suggests. He'd put on amateur boxing nights at St. Brendan's Church when he was an assistant there. "That was probably against the rules," Father Egan adds, "but Pat Molloy never bothered about any rules—either of God or man or Church. He was a law unto himself."

Jack recalls a movie-quality car chase one night when Monsignor Molloy commandeered first Jack for a companion, and then a police escort, to buttress his precipitate race from Seventy-eighth and Emerald down Shields Avenue to Comiskey Park. "We started down Emerald Avenue in Molloy's car and when we approached Sixty-seventh Street where it takes a short dog-leg and continues north, Father Molloy flagged down a policeman passing on a tricycle. The cop recognized Molloy as the priest who got him on the force. Molloy didn't ask him for an escort to the ball game, he ordered one.

"Down Emerald we went with siren screaming and horns honking. The streets were jammed. The police lights were switched on. We were behind the motorcycle, and people were moving over. They put their cars up on lawns, on sidewalks, and turned down alleys to get out of our way."

Jack was "scared to death," but Molloy was in his element. "He never shut up. He was talking all the time." Exiting in front of the ball park at Thirty-fifth and Shields, he arrogantly threw his keys to the policeman coming over to tell him to get his car out of the street, and called, "Sergeant, have the car facing south at the end of the ninth inning, and we'll be on our way."

Once he recognized the lord of St. Leo's, the sergeant shifted from lion to lamb. "Yes, Father Pat," he said, and turned away as Molloy whistled for a guy in the alley to produce tickets for the jammed White Sox/Red Sox game. The pennant race was close that year. "He didn't even tip him," Father Egan recalls. He recalls everything about that night. "It was a night I shall never forget." Egan adds, "Only in Chicago . . . only in those days."

Egan hasn't forgotten either a time when he was forced to confront this politically well-connected pastor who clubbed with Mayor Daley. The Cana Conference was funded largely by the modest fees organizer couples collected at Cana and Pre-Cana Conferences. Usually, they'd count the money Sunday night and have the check in the mail on Monday. Father Egan depended on this steady flow, especially the checks from large parishes like Pat Molloy's. When there was no Tuesday check from St. Leo after a large conference of one hundred and fifty couples, Father Egan called the chaircouple who reported that Father Molloy had taken the envelopes.

Telling the volunteer couple not to worry, Jack immediately got Monsignor Molloy on the phone for an explanation. "Well, listen, Egan," Monsignor Molloy said, "I want to tell you something. The priest gets paid. The couple gets paid. The doctor gets paid. And nobody pays the parish. I had a janitor here, I had lights on, I had the chairs put up, and had it cleaned afterwards, and the parish doesn't get anything."

"I'd like to come out and see you," Jack said evenly, although his Irish was up by this point, aggravated by his real need for his operating funds. Monsignor Molloy said amiably, "I can see you any time." For Jack, "any time" meant right now. Following the Hillenbrand incident pattern, he bolted out to Seventy-eigth and Emerald. "I heard you over the phone," he told the surprised monsignor. Then he outlined his case. He explained that Cana's only expenditure was the $25 received by the priest-conductors. "The couple never gets paid anything. The doctor is paid nothing. This is the only way I support my office.

"I want to tell you, Pat, you are the first and only pastor in my several years in the Cana Conference who has objected to this. And I'll tell you what you can do. You can keep all those envelopes and not send me a damn cent. We'll get along without you. But we'll never have another Pre-Cana Conference here, Pat."

Then he walked out, fairly certain that he had embarrassed Pat Molloy who wouldn't like the story of his penuriousness circulating in the archdiocese. Father Egan was right. The check was in the mail the next morning.

When there was disaffection among the lay people, Jack worked with it by personal contact, "by sitting in their homes, having dinner, talking to them about their work," he says. He is a past master at bringing people around as well as recruiting them. Kathy Pelletier Moriarity describes this skill as "putting the right sinker into each individual person." Nina Polcyn Moore, doyen of St. Benet Book Shop during the Chicago Church's Golden Age, suggests that everyone is hungry for the kind of attention that Jack Egan dispenses. He functions as a mirror for people, reflecting them back to themselves as glorious, as a character in Arthur Miller's *After the Fall* describes himself. "I feel like a mirror in which she somehow sees herself as glorious." Jack Egan knows that people need to interact with others who recognize and mirror their identity as it actually is, empathize with their feelings, respond to their needs with what psycho-analyst Heinz Kohut calls "nonhostile firmness and nonseductive affection."

Jack Egan was prepared to attend to the needs of the couples he recruited. Peggy O'Dowd', who met Jack the night he was appointed director of the Cana Conference, describes Jack gathering "all the bright young people he could charm into following him" and laying out on the O'Dowd's living room floor "a skeleton of what he thought could come about. We couldn't believe his large dreams for Cana could come true." Her assessment years later: Jack Egan fulfilled his two goals, 1) forming lay men and women to serve Christ through the Church, and 2) finding ways to enrich marriage and family life.

Early Cana board co-chair Berenice O'Brien reflects that she and her husband felt "rather flattered and pleased to be asked" when Father Egan suggested they would be a superb speaker couple. After Jack had described the format of Pre-Cana and the training the O'Briens would get from experienced speakers, they began working on their talks, "not too definitely, no idea really what we should do."

Their next Cana contact was the legendary Katie Murphy who ran the Cana office with solicitude for the persons she met and superlative organizational skill. She had a question: had she slipped up or had the O'Briens forgotten they were supposed to speak at some parish the previous day?

"It was a shock to us that we had been scheduled when we had had *no* other contact with Cana but that visit from Jack and perhaps a conversation with Peggy O'Dowd," Berenice admits. "It was a warning to us that 'we would not know the day or the hour' when the Cana call might come, a fact we learned to live with for the next ten or twelve years; a fact that made our life interesting and challenging, that permitted us to meet some of the most interesting people we have met in our lives, and through which we forged friendships which are strong with us still."

Pat Hollahan Judge recalls the Judges' recruitment for speaker couple as standard. First, the friendly phone call from Father Egan who remembered Pat from the days when she'd organized a high school Catholic Action cell at his suggestion: Father Egan just happened to be in their neighborhood and would like to drop up to their third floor apartment on north Glenwood. "What a salesman," Pat says admiringly.

"Selling God, he got us. I should have known. Once you were part of his network you were caught for life."

Over a cup of coffee and a cheese sandwich—"you just wouldn't have a piece of cheese around. I never had a chance to stop for supper"—Father Egan described speaker/couples' responsibilities and opportunities. "You'd have so much to give," he assured them. Pat recalls that she knew the idea was impossible, ridiculous. "We lived on the third floor, we had a child, we had no car." But Jack Egan left with a yes.

"Two weeks later we were working in Cana. I don't even remember him staying that long."

7

"I Am Myself"

"Whoever speaks at my funeral will not say I was a priest's priest. I was a lay person's priest," Jack Egan muses. It's not that he doesn't have close priest friends, "a variety of people in Chicago related to me because of my work." It's simply that from his earliest days in the priesthood Jack Egan has spent his free time with lay people. Early on, they were Young Christian Workers and Young Christian Students.

"This is what I liked doing, this is what I thought I should do, and as a result, I became far more close to the laity," he says. This was true in spite of the fact that Father Egan was working very closely with hundreds of priests across the country in his Cana organizing. Although the generosity of the clergy in Chicago "overwhelmed" Father Egan, "in a certain sense I was hesitant about asking the clergy (to participate in Cana), but I was never hesitant about asking the laity."

Early Cana co-chair Art Schaefer recalls the night Father Egan called to say he was in the neighborhood. "Could I drop in for a few minutes?" As Jack Egan laid out the role of speaker couple, Art and Virginia Schaefer were shocked to think of themselves as an example for others, although, Art writes, "we were about as compatible as man and woman can get." The Schaefers' association with Cana in 1948 "didn't rescue a marriage, may not even have made it better," Schaefer says, "but it enriched our experience" by training the Schaefers' attention on the spiritual reality underlaying their union. To give the feel of Egan's effect on him and his wife, Schaefer quotes mythologist Joseph Campbell, "We're so engaged in doing things to achieve purposes of outer value that we forget that the inner value, the rapture that is associated with being alive, is what it's all about." Jack Egan communicated that rapture to the Schaefers.

An able pair—Art was a vice president at DePaul University, Virginia the mother of nine—the Schaefers evaluated current board practices of pioneer chaircouple Eileen and John Farrell and Executive Director Jack Egan. They proposed refinements in the structure. In line with Father Egan's pitch on the primacy of the laity, they suggested lay couples take charge of the Cana program. Father Egan could function as chaplain with the power of veto if the board's actions contravened the goals of the archbishop. Once Jack agreed, the Schaefers and Frank O'Dowd (whom Jack had met at that first October 9, 1947, gathering) drafted by-laws providing for a nine couple board, each with three-year terms. A senior couple, elected chaircouple, would serve a fourth year. The system worked, but it wouldn't have, Schaefer wrote Father Egan, "without your extrovert nature, your people-managing ability, and your faith in the idea that there was plenty of talent among the laity to accomplish the Cana mission."

Father Egan's faith in the Schaefers was well placed. The couple, whom Art once wryly described as "professionally happily married," were a premier speaker couple as well as board chairman in their day, addressing thousands of couples at Pre-Canas, Lenten programs on marriage, and on road shows to demonstrate Cana style in other dioceses. They quoted St. Thomas Aquinas to their audiences, telling how the natural impulse toward fleshly union is the beginning of the virtue that leads to psychological and spiritual depths that make marriage, in Virginia Schaefer's words, "the best idea God ever had."

Not all clergy were as willing as Jack to ascribe competence to laypersons. Sociologist Father John L. Thomas, an authority on marriage relationships as author of *The American Catholic Family*, wrote a draft of a marriage manual for couples making Pre-Canas. Jack Egan suggested a review by a lay committee. What could be more natural than to consult couples doing a good job at being married? As Peggy O'Dowd recalls, "Father Egan had continually encouraged our thinking" as well as a freedom of expression his priestly contemporaries found unsettling and unnecessary for the laity. Committee members, all of them now in marriage education for the archdiocese, felt completely free to critique Father Thomas' work. Father Thomas, astonished if not dumfounded, felt free to critique their effrontery.

"Father Thomas was not accustomed to this mode of operation at all. He was outraged. He left our house in a huff," Peggy O'Dowd relates.

It's probable that Jack Egan intervened, smoothing over the rift—one of his superlative skills—for eventually Father Thomas used many of the committee's suggestions. Once acclimated to this singular lay behavior, Father Thomas became a staunch supporter of Cana.

Father Thomas himself dumfounded participants at a study day when he pronounced that women were men's intellectual equals. "There was quite a rumble," Peggy O'Dowd reports. "I had never been told that in my life. It even startled Mary Cronin (Peggy's co-hostess whose inequality had kept her out of the main dining room of the Chicago Athletic Association). Forever after, Father Thomas became a beloved friend."

These couples were learning more than they could have hoped as they took responsibility for creating a body of religious, psychological, and physical information about marriage. In Father Egan's first ten Cana years as chaplain, those insights were transmitted to 71,430 men and women who attended 600 Pre-Cana Conferences in 250 parishes. Those post-war days were a unique time. Drawing on the enormous energies of young married women not carrying double career loads as their daughters would, and young men not yet overwhelmed by managerial responsibilities, Jack mobilized the vitality and good will latent in people grateful that the world-wide conflict was over. Like Jack, they sought deep spiritual meaning in their lives. Some of them were the CISCA "graduates" whom Father Carrabine had primed for responsible service to the Church, some graduates of Catholic schools where they'd been reared on the same encyclicals that radicalized Hillenbrand's seminarians. As Jack himself says, "The kind of laity that had developed had not been available in the Church before."

Jack Egan skillfully harnessed that new energy, directed it, educated it. From Monsignor Hillenbrand he'd learned how to nurture good conscripts with good coaching. He gave them visiting scholars and theologians. He provided electrifying study weeks at Oxley, Ontario. He organized training courses and planned retreats. Now, when he called to say he was in the neighborhood, he'd arrive with a great new book on marriage, maybe one recently translated from a French theologian. Under the other arm he'd have a bottle of wine.

Two generations before Thomas Peters and Robert Waterman wrote *In Search of Excellence* in 1982, Jack Egan instinctively provided the concentrated personal attention that pushes an individual to his or her best performance. Peters/Waterman observed that good companies motivate people "by compelling, simple—even beautiful—values." Jack motivated his Cana people with all the compelling, simple, beautiful values he'd learned so well from Monsignor Hillenbrand.

He added zest. "If we're going to do it, let's have fun doing it," Father Egan would urge volunteer speaker couples and doctors.

Priest-conductors earned only a pittance, as Father Egan had assured Monsignor Molloy. Their bonuses were Cana parties in the basement of Old St. Patrick's or at near North Side hotels, dinners with visiting Church luminaries, late night talk sessions. These events galvanized the organization. Most everyone experienced the conjunction of laity empowerment, equality of women, searching theological inquiry, and service to the Church as a heady mix. Jack Egan told his Cana recruits that they were the Church in Chicago, that the Church in Chicago was wonderful, that they were wonderful. He made them believe they were doing work that was important and necessary, fruitful and long-lasting. Some of them smiled at his hyperbole—could every occasion be historic?—but generally they were willing to let his elixir do its work. That was good for them, but was it always good for Father Egan?

"I used to be getting my meals here and there," Jack mentions casually. He never clocked his solo hours in his car. Only later could he admit how alone he felt in his early Cana days. "There was nobody I could go to who knew anything about the development of an organization like this." Father Voss would have been his natural ally and teacher, but Father Egan felt "a coldness there, an understandable coldness."

Nor was Jack Egan's charm proof against the politics of marriage education. The priest director of the Family Life Bureau in Washington suspected Cana was preempting his life work. Within the archdiocese, the West Side Cana group, who worked with the Dominican priests in River Forest, distanced themselves from the North and South Side groups which had developed originally as actions of Catholic Action men's cells. They, in turn, were separate from Pre-Cana founded in 1944 when (Christian Family Movement co-founder) Patty Crowley thought that a Pre-Cana Conference "would be wonderful" for her sister who was getting married. She and Dorothy Drish of the Catholic Action Women's Group enlisted the help of the girls' Catholic Action Federation to organize the first program for engaged couples at Mallinckrodt High School in Wilmette. They were consistently rebuffed as they went from North Side parish to North Side parish to collect names of couples planning imminent weddings. "Most of the priests turned us down.

Some wouldn't let us in." As Patty says of the first Cana Days, "Those were the days in the Church when women and men were never heard of together." These women were not to be encouraged!

By patience and persistence, Dorothy Drish and Patty did manage to get a few names. They arranged the place and found a priest willing to do the marriage instruction. They organized all the incidentals they thought necessary to give these young persons the kind of experience that Patty had known at the Father Dowling Cana Conference she'd gone to. The young couples arrived at Mallinckrodt eager for information about Christian marriage. The priest did his best at this eventful birth of a new concept. But it didn't work out exactly as Patty had planned. "Everybody liked it but my sister and her husband," she recalls. "They thought it was awful."

It wasn't Jack's style to schedule R & R between assignments. The night of his appointment as Cana director he accompanied Father Voss to a big meeting of the West Side group. His first day on the job, he began to replay the St. Justin Martyr' census plunge. His priorities: to introduce the Cana concept to all archdiocesan pastors, to recruit and educate additional priests, to develop the lay organization (that meant unifying the North, South and West Sides), and to multiply doctors and married couple speakers. By this time, Pre-Cana was growing exponentially. Even so, Father Egan had one rule: "I only asked volunteers to serve two years. I wanted them to know it wasn't a lifelong commitment." They could continue to serve if they wished.

Jack didn't have options. He felt beleaguered. Goaded by his self-expectation, his need to succeed, the largeness of the task, the nagging politics in the movements locally and nationally, the physical strain of interviews—and meals—on the run, the apparent need of all the young couples in the archdiocese, he saw his task as larger than his present capacity to cope.

Soon after his Cana assignment, Jack had been invited by a friend, Father Fred Mann, to a conference concerning the priest and counseling at Catholic University in the nation's capital. His interest piqued by his experience with Carl Rogers, the new Cana director carved out the time to do himself what would prove to be a great kindness. For at that conference he met the therapist and ally he was soon to need desperately, "this genius, Father Charles Curran."

Curran, Carl Rogers' first Ph.D. in counseling at Ohio State and a scholar relating Rogerian theory to Thomistic philosophy for a book called *Catholic Life and Education*, was by 1955 a pastor in a little parish in Carmel, Ohio, and a teacher in the minor seminary in nearby Columbus. The country around Carmel was pretty, rolling corn belt land merging into the fertile hills and valleys of the Appalachian plateau to the east.

In Chicago, Jack Egan was hefting prodigious responsibilites. He felt unsupported by his natural father figures, cut off from any shared life with peers. However rigid the discipline in some rectories, parish priests knew where they fit in the clerical scheme. They came home to dinner—it was often compulsory—around a table of people who understood their concerns. They met with classmates every chance they got, golf club or wine glass in hand. At a time of life when it was natural to question celibacy and the nature of authority, Jack had no one with whom to share a nagging disquietude. He lived in a parish, but he wasn't one of the regulars. Besides, he was always running about on Cana business.

He couldn't turn to his mentor, Monsignor Hillenbrand. Jack had disappointed Hillenbrand, as he had once disappointed his father. "He lost a lot of interest and respect for me because I devoted myself to the Cana and Pre-Cana Conference when he thought I should be working full-time in Catholic Action, in YCS and YCW." Hillenbrand was not satisfied with Jack's dedication in spite of the fact that Jack was still spending his day off from Cana as national chaplain of the YCW women.

On point as the first Cana director, Jack felt his inadequacies grating as unrelentingly as a charleyhorse biting into a calf muscle. "I knew my limitations. Monsignor Hillenbrand once said it is a good person who knows his limitations. I knew I wasn't bright and didn't have a real understanding of all the intricacies of the philosophy and the psychology and the theology of marriage, the whole conjugal relationship." Besides the intellectual demands, Jack had managerial demands he hadn't been trained for.

He was trying to do too much too fast with too little support and preparation. If he stumbled, he'd risk himself—and Cana. He couldn't continue to rally Cana volunteers if his own zeal faded to zero. He knew he had "problems that (he) had to cope with." He felt trapped. Somewhere there had to be help available. He had experience now of helping people. He knew it was possible. "I had to make serious changes so I could grow spiritually and relate to people."

Emboldened by the boost in self-confidence that the people at St. Justin Martyr had given him, Jack did for himself what he was so willing to do for others. He called Father Charles Curran in Carmel, Ohio, and asked for help. He knew that "it's one thing to be liked and another thing to accept and integrate yourself." He could be of more service— he could go on, he thought—if he got to know himself better and like himself better. At Father Curran's encouraging invitation, Jack got in his car, for once not to listen to parishioners' woes, not to mitigate pastors' irritation, not to chaplain his YCW group, not to recruit or encourage new speaker couples. He drove to Carmel, Ohio, to do for Jack Egan what he desperately knew had to be done, to scrutinize and analyze his life with the help of a counselor. Again, he had picked the right person, a truly tutelary genius.

For ten days Jack Egan met for an hour counseling session morning and evening with Charles Curran in his pleasant lakeside rectory in the quiescent Ohio backwater town. "Charles Curran was the premier counselor that I ever encountered. He pulled everything out of me, my past life, my guilt, my relationship with my family, myself, the seminary, the priesthood. He helped me examine my whole life in that magnificent non-directive way."

Actually, it wasn't necessary for Curran to pull anything out of Jack Egan. Jack poured it out. That's why he'd come. Never one to waste time—he had too much to do in life—Jack dived down to those depths he didn't want to face alone. "I knew I was the only one who could solve my problems. He helped me open up so I could see the solutions."

As a Catholic priest, Curran could understand the pressures of celibacy and loneliness Jack was suffering. As Jack revealed the pressures crowding him, beginning with his relationship with his overcritical father, he began to see the picture of himself he was drawing with his own words. "Everything became clear in my life because for the first time, I was totally, completely, honest with another human being. I revealed the deepest feelings of my soul to this person with absolute confidence and without any pressure. He saw inside me because I opened myself to him." Tangentially, Curran deepened Jack's hold on non-directive counseling. "But, more importantly, he helped me see myself as I was, really was, with all my limitations." And he made it possible for

Jack to accept himself as he really was, for Curran accepted Jack as he really was.

Contemplating the gentle ripples lapping the lakeshore between sessions, Jack forgot Chicago and Cana and Catholic Action groups and archdiocesan politics. He concentrated on "my relationship with God, my relationship with people, my relationship with work, and my relationship with the priesthood. It was the first time I was able to separate myself really from my father." Jack speculates that he wouldn't have been able to deal later with Cardinal Cody—"I'd have buckled under"—without this experience. As he put the nature of authority into perspective, Jack changed his perception of himself. "For the first time I really accepted myself as a person of value. Here I was, thirty or thirty-one (finally realizing I was) a person of value who didn't have all the answers, but who didn't need to have all the answers." How many people, like Father Kevin Conway, had told Jack, "I don't think you have brains, but . . ." Now Jack could tell himself, "I don't have all the brains in the world, but I do have certain qualities, insights, experiences that other people don't have. I am myself."

When Father Curran saw Jack Egan to his car after those intense ten days, Jack was a different person. "I felt completely clean, I felt completely washed. For the first time I was able to cope with my relationship with my father and my relationship with authority." Jack had eliminated fear from his life, "that unreasonable fear that prevents you from acting, that immobilizes you. Father Curran helped me appreciate my talents, and encouraged me to push them to the limit, and also to care for myself. He is the finest counselor I have ever encountered."

The people at St. Justin Martyr taught Jack Egan that he could be liked. With Father Curran, he learned he could like himself. He no longer felt the need to be someone else, "someone more competent, smarter, better at athletics, better at speaking, better looking." He could be happy being Jack Egan.

His time with Curran made it possible for Jack to persevere in his goal of attending people's needs. All the time he skimmed over the city, netting a cheese sandwich here and an additional doctor speaker there, Jack Egan operated at several levels. At the surface he functioned as full-time, really an over-time, director of Cana. Below the surface, he always nurtured a subterranean agenda. Just as he'd organized marriage preparation as a curate at St. Justin Martyr, now that he was in marriage preparation full-time, he was becoming known as a priest responsive to social issues.

In the early 1950s, he got a call from a group of University of Chicago students working with a Woodlawn priest, Father Leo Mahon, to help the city's newest immigrants. Hundreds of Puerto Ricans, American citizens who'd moved into the near South Side area, were at the mercy of the city. The police didn't speak Spanish. Firemen couldn't speak Spanish. Nor did storekeepers or landlords. Schools had no books in Spanish. The Puerto Ricans were desperate that cold spring. The Woodlawn Latin American Committee set up to assist them was in debt. Could "good old Jack" come to a meeting? And could good old Jack raise some money?

Aware that Monsignor Edward Burke, his champion at the chancery office, had a natural interest for he was already working with Mexican-Americans at a little Mexican church at Twelfth and Halsted, Jack contacted Burke at his cathedral room. It was Holy Thursday morning, the beginning of the heavy Holy Week schedule for all priests of the archdiocese. The chancery office was closed.

Nonetheless, Burke agreed to meet Egan at his office. Jack painted a poignant picture of the Puerto Ricans' plight and the efforts of the Woodlawn Latin American Committee, "what they were doing, their need for money, (volunteers) working there free."

"All right," Monsignor Burke agreed. "Let's go see the cardinal and I'll ask him for some money." After a quick phone call, Burke announced, "We're going up there right away. We'll use my car." Not as confident as Monsignor Burke, Jack pulled back. "Wait a minute. I've never been to the cardinal's house. What are we going to say to him?"

The chancellor reassured him. "Jack, don't worry about it. Leave that up to me. I'll take care of it." So, in Jack's words, "we got into his car and we go up to the residence" where Samuel Cardinal Stritch had lived since Cardinal Mundelein's death in 1939. The red brick mansion at the southeast corner of North State Parkway and North Avenue, just opposite Lincoln Park, was imposing both for its dignified portico, its multiple chimneys for the once-useful fireplaces, and its history since the Most Reverend Patrick A. Feehan built it in 1880. When Catholics gathered in Chicago for the 1926 Eucharistic Congress, Cardinal Mundelein hosted there what was probably the largest gathering of prelates in the Western Hemisphere. Eleven years later, Mundelein had

President Roosevelt to lunch after the President dedicated the Outer Drive Bridge. Cardinal Pacelli was received here before he was Pope Pius XII. And now Jack Egan.

If the residence was imposing, Cardinal Stritch was "down home casual" in his second floor office (the only time Jack was ever on the second floor of the cardinal's residence). In contrast to the ermine-trimmed trappings he wore for formal occasions, Cardinal Stritch was in his shirtsleeves, his suspenders around his waist, surrounded by piles of books, typing a pastoral letter warning that no Chicago Catholic could attend the World Council of Churches meeting in Evanston. Catholics were still very insular in the 1950s. ("Unbelievable," Jack comments, thirty years later.)

Taking in Monsignor Burke's urgency and Father Egan's hesitancy, Cardinal Stritch hospitably invited them to a comfortable alcove overlooking the well-kept grounds. After a succinct introduction to the Puerto Rican situation, Monsignor Burke turned to Jack: "Why don't you tell the Cardinal all about it?"

For Jack it was one of those times when the Holy Spirit endows the timid with sudden eloquence. The cardinal, already aware of the depth of social disruption on Chicago's South Side, listened as Jack Egan brought the poverty of the city's newest Hispanics into that rich room. The cardinal turned to his chancellor, "Earmark $10,000 for this work and give Father Egan $5,000 today so that it can begin." Not one to stop at one success, when Jack later found himself with the national director of Catholic Charities, Monsignor John O'Grady, he asked his advice about the Woodlawn Latin American Committee. "You know, Father Egan," he said, "what you should be doing is getting in touch with Saul Alinsky."

"Well, I've met him," Jack said.

"Well, meet him again," the Monsignor persisted.

Jack was approaching another decisive turning point. Saul—"don't give me any of that Jesus shit"—Alinsky was to be Jack Egan's next great tutelary genius. And dear, dear friend.

8

"What Do You Think of the Rosenburg Case"

As Jack Egan likes to say, "There's a little bit of history here. To get to Alinsky in 1955, you have to go back to those people who drafted me into the Woodlawn Latin American Committee—Father Leo Mahon, Nick von Hoffman and his wife Ann Byrne von Hoffman, Ed Chambers, Sally Cassidy, Paula Verdet, Fran Kelley, Lester Hunt."

As interested in people as he was, Jack Egan couldn't have the shortest commerce with the Latin American committee without quizzing them on the source of their concern for their Puerto Rican neighbors. When he found out that Paula Verdet had been president of the Young Christian Students in France before she'd come to study sociology at the University of Chicago, Jack revealed his hankering to study family movements in France and Belgium. American theologians still emphasized the precepts of canon law and the justice issues between husband and wife. "If you examine some of the marriage material (in the United States) of those days, it is very canonically ordered, truly bland, nothing of the romance and beauty and psychology which were beginning to be developed by good psychologists across the world," Jack recalls. In France, he thought, he would get a deeper understanding of conjugal spirituality.

Even as Verdet encouraged Jack in his European quest, however, he drew back. He had never traveled abroad. Even when he traveled in the United States for Cana road shows, in some sense he never left home. "I would be picked up and brought to people of comparable ideas and attitudes." Verdet assured him that her YCS contacts would get him through rectory doors in the French countryside and cities once he was "in the neighborhood." He could learn so much. Finally succumbing to the bait of wheedling knowledge from experience, Jack took a crash course in French, shopped for a black beret, and flew across the Atlantic on June 5, 1953, for three months of fieldwork/rest. "It wasn't until I went to France that I saw a whole new culture and development."

The friendly American priest, with his broken French and disarming manner, was welcomed in *foyers sacerdotaux*, French "bread-and-breakfasts" for traveling priests. Immediately, he was confronted by his own provincialism. The night of his arrival in Paris, at the first dinner he shared with French priests, they leaned across the table and inquired intensely, "What do you think of the Rosenbergs?" In the rectories Jack had been visiting in Chicago, the talk was of recent appointments at the chancery, White Sox chances for the pennant, the press of young couples eager for marriage, the "togetherness" that would be hailed as "almost the national purpose" in *McCall's* magazine the following Easter. There was no speculation in the average Chicago rectory about the fate of the couple accused of participating in a spy ring that sent hundreds of documents detailing every aspect of the production of the atom bomb to Moscow. Should the Rosenbergs be executed as Soviet spies? Jack didn't know. He was at a loss to explain the McCarthy era to people in this very poor and very Communistic suburb of Paris. How could he explain noisy American demonstrators waving placards which read, "Two Fried Rosenbergs Coming Right Up?" With that first shared meal, Jack realized that traveling in France would stretch more than his grasp of conjugal spirituality.

Listening more than he spoke, Jack lapped up the words of distinguished pastors like Abbe Michonneau, a great intellectual of the left, "but not the far left," author of *Revolution in a City Parish*. As Jack ranged through all France's large cities, visiting the priest-workers at several different locales, staying with the "marvelous" Stanley de Lestapis, S.J., he sought the theological substructure of their widening understanding of marriage, and techniques for teaching it. But the question of the Rosenbergs and the Catholic Senator Joe McCarthy followed him.

As he visited "all the finest theologians," Jack recorded daily reports with his typewriter, and daily pictures in his head. He remembers sitting in a kitchen with French theologian Henri deLubac, S.J., who assured him "we are just beginning to think about the whole question of conjugal spirituality here in France. We have not developed a theology yet." What Jack knew was that deLubac and Michonneau and De Lestapis—France's most original theologians—were passing on their insights as fast as they formulated them. As teachers to the chaplains of the Young Christian Workers and Young Christian Students, these theologians were formulating the input for YCW/YCS Gospel inquiries. The young people following Canon Cardijn were getting the best theology available at the time, the theology that would lead into Vatican II in 1962.

Actually, these theologians Jack was meeting were moving so fast that some of them were skidding into roadblocks. Father deLubac was only one of the French theologians silenced in 1954 by the Vatican. Another was French Dominican theologian Father Marie-Dominique Chenu who saw similarity between the current strength of European Catholic Action and the great apostolic movements of Saints Dominic and Francis of Assisi. Although they weren't allowed to teach the faithful in 1954, Chenu and deLubac were invited to teach the bishops at Vatican II. (Chenu was adviser to the French-speaking African bishops.)

These men, reading "the signs of the times," in Chenu's telling phrase, believed in small, committed groups as a theological source. As Jack had hoped, they shared insights on marriage. Jack had timed his summer in France at the watershed moment when theologians were "moving from a canonical understanding and appreciation of marriage to a personalist appreciation of the dignity of both persons wedding themselves one to the other."

At the *foyers sacerdotaux* set up to provide traveling priests lodging, breakfast and a place to say Mass for five hundred francs a night, Jack found contacts unavailable to France's casual tourists. One night a "marvelous" concierge in Lyons excitedly informed him that morning would bring the great Father Voillaume. "Who is he?" Jack asked, unhappy to be uninformed, but unwilling to miss an experience.

"You never heard of the founder of the Little Brothers and Sisters of Jesus who live with the poorest of the poor all over the world as a sacrament of presence? With the pygmies in Africa, the poor on the docks in Marseille, in the slums of Rome! Father Voillaume rewrote for them the rule of Charles de Foucauld who was killed in the Sahara early this century by one of the Arab tribes."

Intrigued, Jack rose early to serve Mass for Voillaume who returned the courtesy. "In those days you didn't concelebrate." Then the concierge interpreted as Jack asked about Father Voillaume's work, revealing that in the United States he had never heard of the Little Brothers or the Little Sisters. "We are a wealthy country," he said, "but we do have poor people." Then he put his usual question, the one that gives him his long must-do list. "Is there anything I can do for you?" When Father Voillaume admitted that Cardinal Spellman had refused permission to bring his order to the U.S., Jack was quick to absolve New York's archbishop. "Let's be fair to him. Everybody who gets off the boat in the United States expects Cardinal Spellman to set them up and do something for them." Jack promised Father Voillaume an audience with Cardinal Stritch in Chicago, making the gesture that was second nature to him, as usual with no thought for what he might be bringing on himself. In this case, once the message was in the tube, its course would affect markedly Jack's own future.

Father Voillaume contacted his dear friend Jacques Maritain, a distinguished French theologian who'd done several teaching tours in the United States, about Egan's offer. Maritain, in turn, wrote his dear American friend, community organizer Saul Alinsky. Alinsky called Egan: "I got a letter from my friend Maritain who wants me to take care of this fellow—what's his name?—who's coming to visit you." He added, parenthetically, "I've heard of you, Egan."

"I've heard about you, Mr. Alinsky," Jack rejoined. "Why don't you come over for lunch and we can talk about how we can make this man's visit as pleasant as possible."

From that day in 1954 throughout their long friendship, Alinsky kidded Jack Egan about the kosher salami sandwich and cup of coffee Jack called "lunch." If Alinsky didn't get a Caesar salad and a bottle of Pinot noir carefully held back for occasions such as this, he did find sympathetic sensibilities and a receptive ear. As Jack remembers the occasion, they established their common revulsion at seeing the common man—like Jack's black man on the streetcar—pushed around. They talked about the Catholic Church, community organizations, their own lives. Alinsky told Jack "about his first wife who was drowned trying to save their adopted children, tears running down his cheeks. He was really in love with his first wife, devotedly in love."

When they got around to Father Voillaume's visit, Alinsky suggested, "Lookit, Egan, when this guy comes to town, why don't you give me a ring and we'll go down to the Palmer House Grill and have lunch. Then you can go ahead and arrange whatever talks you want."

Jack demurred. "Mr. Alinsky," he said, "I met this man. I know how he lives, where he lives, the people who belong to these organizations, how they live with the poor. I think he would feel very out of place at the Palmer House. Couldn't we go to some ordinary restaurant?" Alinsky was impressed, he reported later to Maritain, that he'd found an American priest sensitive to the sensibilities of the poor. Meanwhile, Egan was arranging a number of lectures to "get this poor fellow Voillaume a bit of money to pay for his transportation," and planning a meeting with Monsignor Vincent Cooke of Catholic Charities in Chicago (a very influential man, Jack Egan says, who knew 268 ways to help poor people in the state of Illinois).

Because of a scheduling conflict, Jack drew the duty of bringing Father Voillaume's petition to Cardinal Stritch. The cardinal sat quietly, head in hands, as Jack explained how the Little Sisters wanted to take up residence in a poor Chicago neighborhood, asking no quarter except the opportunity to be friends with their neighbors, a presence among them. They wear a blue denim habit and a little scarf on their heads, Father Egan told the cardinal, find jobs in nearby factories or stores, and welcome neighbors to their prayer services. When he could think of nothing to add, Jack said, "Your Eminence, I would like permission for the Little Sisters to come to Chicago."

He waited patiently, silently, while the cardinal carefully removed his glasses and carefully set them on his desk. He watched the cardinal drop his head in his hands once again. The seconds dragged like the feet of reluctant schoolboys. To Jack it seemed an interminable five minutes, although now he says, "probably just a minute or two." Finally, the cardinal reached out for his glasses, arranged them across the bridge of his nose and behind his ears. He looked up into Father Egan's eyes and nodded. "Yes, I give them permission." The Sisters were moved into 1725 W. Jackson Boulevard. Merchant Sol Polk donated a refrigerator the Sisters refused when it was delivered. Their neighbors had no refrigerators! And Jack Egan had a set of new friends—the Sisters as well as Saul Alinsky.

When Monsignor John O'Grady of the national Catholic Charities office came through Chicago again some months later, he arranged dinner at the Blackstone Hotel on Michigan Avenue for his friend Saul Alinsky, Nicholas von Hoffman of the Woodlawn Latin American Committee, and Jack Egan. In 1939, Alinsky had come into Chicago to organize the Back of the Yards neighborhood, port of entry for Eastern Europeans who lived the desperate lives Upton Sinclair depicted in his powerful novel *The Jungle*. Alinsky had a great clerical (and fiscal) friend in Bishop Bernard Sheil, who, like Alinsky and Jack Egan, had great faith in the power of the people to get things done when they mustered around issues important to their lives. With support from Sheil, Alinsky had organized the people in the stockyards area to express their own interests, their hopes, sentiments, and dreams so they could "own" their own organization. He worked to convince them that together they were not helpless before their chronic social problems of unemployment, disease, child welfare, delinquency, and poor housing, that they could take a good deal of their own fate into their own hands. He'd enlisted the help of the Catholic Church (ninety percent of the population was Catholic), neighborhood organizations, and labor unions to support the people's efforts. By working together, Alinsky preached, you can promote the welfare of all residents, regardless of their race, color, or creed, so you can all find health, happiness, and security through the democratic way of life.

Now the executive director of the Industrial Areas Foundation, Saul Alinsky had not organized in Chicago since 1939. It was clear to Jack Egan that Saul Alinsky needed help "to get back into community organization work and maybe the one great contribution I made to Saul Alinsky's life and the city of Chicago and community organization was to help Saul (he would laugh if he heard me say this, but it's true) begin another career. He was not doing any organization work when I met him," Jack recalls.

At the dinner at the Blackstone with Monsignor O'Grady (whom Jack considers one of the towering figures of the Church in this century) Alinsky guyed von Hoffman about his assistance to the Puerto Ricans in a way he had of taking a man's measure by observing his reactions. Working in community organizations was abrasive; working with Alinsky meant being under constant appraisal. Even as he critiqued von Hoffman's efforts for the Puerto Ricans as muddle-headed, Alinsky was appraising and approving of von Hoffman's quick comprehension. It seems that when Egan went to Cardinal Stritch for the $10,000 to pay the Woodlawn Latin American Committee's debts, the cardinal had expressed interest in expanding the Puerto Rican work. Later that month after the Blackstone dinner, Alinsky offered von Hoffman one hundred dollars a week (of the cardinal's money) to study the Puerto Ricans' jump over the black community into the Dearborn Street area on the near North Side above the Chicago River. Bishop Bernard Sheil of the CYO and Sheil School had earlier been a financial supporter of Alinsky's initiatives. Now Cardinal Stritch was moving into that role through the agency of Jack Egan. Stritch put up the money; Egan, the life.

As Sanford Horwitt analyzed the Egan/Alinsky relationship in *Let Them Call Me Rebel*, Alinsky had "stumbled upon a young man who had the potential to become what Alinsky had found to be so elusive: a crack organizer with whom he could work as a brother, or perhaps as a father, sharing and rejoicing in the adventure, the jousting, the fun, the power, and the nobility of a just cause." For Jack it was the beginning of a relationship "that perdures [he likes that word and concept] to this very day even though Saul died in 1972. We were very, very close."

To the casual onlooker, Jack Egan and Saul Alinsky were, in Irish poet William Butler Yeats' phrase, "a crazy salad." Jack was the oil to Alinsky's vinegar. Always abrasive, determined to be in control, engineering all relationships on his terms, Alinsky charmed people into obeisance or irritated them into rejection. To those who paid him homage, his lack of modesty was part of his charm. His acid wit was tolerable because it was used most often to bite the hands restraining the community will. Besides, he was a fount of great stories from his days communing with the Capone mob as a student criminologist and functioning as a sociologist at Joliet prison. A superlatively entertaining companion, he was the most loyal of friends.

At base, what sealed the bond between the politic Egan and the caustic Alinsky was their common distaste, even revulsion, at seeing people robbed of their dignity. When Jack Egan asked Saul Alinsky how he got into community organizing and Saul answered, "Oh, Jack, I hate to see people pushed around," their pact was confirmed. That mutual urgency whipped their disparate personalities into a functioning unit. Jack Egan brought his spiritual conviction of every person's worth to Alinsky's skill at creating a setting "in which victimized people could experience and express their self with power and dignity."

In the mid-1950s, the Cana Conference was going well. Jack Egan's faith in laypeople had proved to be accurate and well-timed. Cana volunteers were dogged workers, meticulous organizers, and enthusiastic partisans of the intense family culture creating in the fifties a generation of outsize—baby boom—families. They were experiencing, courtesy of Cana, their own jousting, fun, feeling of power and satisfaction in the nobility of their high-minded cause. They were sharing Chicago's Catholic "high," the sense that for Catholics in the fifties Chicago was the fountainhead for the Church's transformation from immigrant backwater supernumerary to player on the main stage. Monsignor Hillenbrand still functioned as head of the rapidly growing Catholic Action movements. Pat and Patty Crowley were acknowledged leaders of the locally initiated, now world-wide, Christian Family Movement. Cana was being exported via regular road shows. Where in the early fifties Jack had gone to France to find the spirit and substance of the Church's vitality, in the late fifties seekers came to Three East Chicago Avenue or Twenty-one West Superior or the Crowleys' welcoming living room in Wilmette.

Jack's Cana work had brought him very close to Monsignor Burke, an intensely loyal man, who'd picked Jack as a comer and shepherded his talents into a direct line into the chancery office. Cana board members noted that there was little that Jack asked of the chancery office that wasn't conceded, even encouraged. Once Jack made the connection (through Burke), the cardinal saw Alinsky as an agent to expand the archdiocese's efforts for the city's poor. He wanted two things. Besides the report on the condition of the Hispanics in Chicago that Nick von Hoffman worked on, ("you couldn't do that today without a million dollar study," according to Jack Egan) the cardinal wanted a study of the New York Life Insurance Company housing development between Thirty-first and Thirty-fifth Streets and King Drive and the lake. "The cardinal was deeply interested in what was happening to the poor black people moved out of that area and those displaced by the Dan Ryan Expressway," Father Egan recalls. The cardinal told Egan, "I would like to find out how those people survived and where they moved to." Jack Egan would work on that. Both studies were funded in 1957 when the archdiocese allotted $118,800 to Saul Alinsky's Industrial Areas Foundation for an extensive study of community changes resulting from population shifts.

Jack knew the need for organization through the labor movement and his St. Justin Martyr experience that taught him that for "the voice of a single individual to be heard down at City Hall was an oxymoron. It was inconceivable." He brought the same enthusiasm to studying the area that included Lake Meadows and Prairie Shores housing complexes that he brought to the suburbs of Paris and Rouen two summers before. As he and organizer Lester Hunt gathered information about the people on the near South Side displaced by the Dan Ryan Expressway, Jack learned on the job. According to Horwitt, Jack "had been almost completely released from his clerical duties." If a parish census at St. Justin Martyr's was a baby step into community involvement for Jack, assignment to the IAF to find out how the Dan Ryan Expressway affected people's lives was a giant step. During the summers of 1956 and 1957, Jack Egan and Lester Hunt visited practically every home and store and church and business between Thirty-fifth and Fifty-fifth streets and from the lake over to State Street. This was the heart of the old South Side ghetto—the Grand Boulevard section of Chicago.

They met the poor and the powerful. Jack made an appointment with "The Man," Congressman Bill Dawson, who "individually and singly moved the black population from voting Republican to Democratic under Mayor Ed Kelly." Jack found the office of the most powerful black politician in Chicago (before Mayor Harold Washington) in a ramshackle old building on Forty-seventh Street, "a sort of 1920s office, books around." Now that he'd talked to all the Baptist ministers along State Street, to real estate operators, to the clients and proprietors in barber shops, "everybody I could find," Jack was primed to talk over the housing situation with the congressman.

Dawson said to the young priest, "I don't know what you have on your mind, son, but I want to tell you something and I want you to bring this back to your cardinal. I am very grateful for what he and you have done for my people."

Jack replied, "Congressman, we thought they were our people, too." Dawson laughed and said, "Yeah, that's right." Jack says now that if you want the honest-to-God truth, "I don't think either one of us had done very much for the blacks. But that was his perception." The cardinal had made some good statements in 1954. Jack had given some good talks. "I really hadn't done much."

Jack Egan was getting personal training in community organizing from Saul Alinsky, the master. "Every night I had to write out a report. What we did. Who we saw. What was said. Then Saul would take these reports and at the end of the week he would examine them and say, well, you saw these people on Monday. They gave you this information. Did you do anything to follow up on that on Wednesday? It was real training in the analysis of organization." Jack learned to keep his eyes open. "Did you really believe what these people told you? Did you check this with anyone else?" Alinsky would ask.

It was a time of great satisfaction to Jack Egan. He had found a community of simpatico activists bent on bettering people's lives. First, the organizers did good work on the streets finding out what was what. Then they had good times together while they exchanged, challenged, teased, lampooned each other's information, perception, and ideas. While Jack had natural gifts of ingenuousness and empathy to bring to his daily interviews, he could see that he needed the training he was getting. To tough it out on Chicago streets—dangerous, devastated, and daunting—took a discipline and a nimble acuity that came only with dogged practice. He'd found a challenging job that called out the best in him, and people who demanded that he give it. They grew very close.

Concurrently, Jack Egan found another ally unafraid of the unknowns in the Church/society equation, this one inside the Church. Father Joseph Gremillion, a forceful young pastor of a ninety-eight percent white parish in Shreveport, Louisiana, come to the attention of priests like Jack because he worked at improving race relations in his church in the Bible Belt. He also shared Jack's drive to bring laypersons into the action of the Church. "Shreveport is like a town in Texas," Gremillion says. "Northern Louisiana is as Pentecostal as Alabama." As a priest working to promote justice for Negroes in the South, Father Joseph Gremillion was walking a lonely road in 1954. To come in out of that isolation, he regularly bolted up to Chicago to seek out like-minded people like Jack Egan who shared his vision that priests should see past their parish boundaries, even their cities, to a national point of view, perhaps even international. It was a galvanic moment for Gremillion and Egan when they found reflected in each other the same zest for widening the horizons of their parochial worlds.

If their meeting could be so reinforcing and productive, Gremillion and Egan told each other, all their friends in creative ministries would profit from meeting each other. They consulted the veteran and respected Father Louis Putz, C.S.C., of Notre Dame. Think what would happen if the people we know in social ministry, in race relations, ministry to farm workers, international issues, peace issues and human rights, got together, they said. Wouldn't they be turned on—as we are—by finding how many people are laboring in the same vineyards? "It was clear to us," Father Gremillion says, "that we needed to cross-fertilize so we'd have a sense of where the U.S. church was going as a whole. This was long before Vatican II." Networking was not yet the social rage it was to become, but Jack Egan and Joseph Gremillion were natural networkers.

With the confidence of a Mickey Rooney saying, "Let's have a show," they said, "Let's get everybody together." In 1955 they faced daunting obstacles. According to Gremillion, "At that time priests were not free, especially on a national basis." Few bishops wanted upstart priests exchanging tidings of possible uneasiness in their dioceses. "Who are they?" the bishops would ask. "What are they plotting about?" It was Bishop John Wright of Worcester, Massachusetts—mid-century, the only intellectual among the bishops, Gremillion says—who permitted thirty-two priests, hand-picked by the co-chairs, to gather at his diocesan retreat house and talk about the meaning of the lay person in the United States.

Per pattern, Jack Egan, Louis Putz and Joe Gremillion procured "the best talent in the country" as speakers. Egan asked Monsignor Hillenbrand to speak on "The Specialized Movements" and Monsignor George Higgins on "The Economic Scene and the Church Today." Father Joseph Fichter, S.J., related the layperson's role to sociologists' findings. The godfather of the Liturgical Movement, Father Godfrey Diekmann, O.S.B., related lay people to the liturgy, and Monsignor Frederick Hochwalt, the bishops' chair on education, related them to education.

In off-the-record sessions, participants dared to say the unsayable, dared to beset the unbesetable. In those pre-Vatican II days, the Church rested in the confident unassailability of its infallibility. The Church had all the answers. The church people Gremillion and Egan gathered weren't so sure. They were asking questions precisely because they knew that they, as priests, didn't have all the answers. The organizers had provided a safe place where they could admit that. Gremillion and Egan were in their element as the talk went on through the coffee breaks, through dinner, and on into the night. Once the participants had broached the subject there was so much to say (this was 1955) on the *layperson's* role, and the priest's role in helping *laypersons* achieve their proper status. "It was so exciting," Father Gremillion remembers. "Finding like-minded people, we would not only talk and understand each other. We could start national programs together."

Participants were at once limp with exhaustion and lively with enthusiasm. "Gee, Joe, Louie, and Jack, thanks a lot. Why didn't we do this ten years ago?" Father Gremillion, looking back in the confidence of his lifetime of scholarship, sees himself and Jack Egan and George Higgins as national Church leaders. "We were saying, 'Look, Church, this is what you should be talking about.'" In 1955, what they thought the Church should be talking about was the role of the laity. Two years later when Egan and Gremillion organized a second conference at Hinsdale, Illinois, the theme was communication in a pluralistic society.

Participants admitted that the Church was in open competition in the open market of ideas. How was the Church to communicate its message to the countless groups for which it had a message—"a bearing of witness to what it thinks is the Word of God?" As they made up the program, Gremillion and Egan realized how little experience the Church had had with pluralism. "In the past (the Church) has been either the sole officially accepted way of life, or the leading opponent of the established order." What they saw as changed was the Catholic population. Catholics were "being swept into the mainstream of American life." The Church would have to adapt, but how?

Two years later there was a third meeting, this one on ecumenism at Oxley, Ontario, in 1959. At the first meetings, Jack Egan and Father Gremillion, along with Father Louis Putz, CSC, of the University of Notre Dame, had quarried their prodigious contacts for the most sound and sophisticated church thinkers nationwide. At Oxley they brought Jaroslav Pelikan of Yale University, editor and translator of Luther's works and dean of American church historians, and the Very Reverend Alexander Schmemann, dean of St. Vladimir's Orthodox Seminary, Yonkers, New York, to their hand-picked Roman Catholic activist audience. Their coup advanced the admissibility of ecumenism in the United States, according to Father Egan, before the watershed decrees of Vatican II. Actually, their convocations undoubtedly provided some of the loam for the ideas that would sprout at the council. If projects need seed money, councils need seed studies.

By 1959, Father Gremillion was in Rome studying for a degree in sociology as Putz and Egan arranged the Oxley conference. The Vatican Council was in the offing. Because their national sharing had helped them see the need for an international council, Putz and Gremillion and Egan didn't share the general surprise when Pope John asked himself one morning (as he was pulling on his socks, according to Father Theodore Hesburgh of Notre Dame) what he would say to the cardinals at their meeting that morning and decided to tell them he was calling all the bishops in the world to Rome for a council. In some quarters, that was not good news. For participants at Worcester, Hinsdale, and Oxley, it was their little conferences writ large.

9

"You Have to Fight Injustice Wherever You Find It"

All this time Jack Egan was keeping up with his friends from the seminary. Once a month on Sunday night at seven, after they'd finished their parish duties and had a visit with their families, a small group of priests gathered at Annunciation rectory, centrally located on the North Side at Paulina and Wabansia where Father James J. Killgallon was an assistant. They were still "Rynie's young men." They'd started meeting regularly with Monsignor Hillenbrand soon after they got their parish assignments—once they'd come to appreciate how much they were going to need mutual support. In some sense, they were a clerical counterpart to the Alinsky group.

"It was a comfortable room in a great old rectory," Jack Egan recalls. "High ceilings, fitted out in good taste. Jake Killgallon was the artist in the group, a singer, piano player, devotee of the theater. A man of great integrity. A risk-taker. He couldn't abide any cant or phoniness." That they were risk-takers with short tolerance for phoniness might have been said of any of "this few, this happy few, this band of brothers." Like Henry V's soldiers before the battle of Agincourt, they were bound to each other, they believed, "from this day to the ending of the world." It wasn't going to work out that way.

It was their mutual mission that bound them, their determination to be a support group for each other as they teetered at the cutting edge of change in the Chicago Church. "We came together for play," Jack says, "for gossip, sure, but basically because we knew we needed each other. We were always concerned about how we were going to implement what we had learned in the seminary, how we would respond to new needs. We were feeling our way."

On those Sunday nights at about seven, Jake Killgallon opened the rectory door for Fathers Jack Egan, Gerry Weber, Dan Cantwell, Larry Kelly, Walter Imbiorski, Thomas McDonough, and Bill Quinn. They were the regulars, along with Monsignor Hillenbrand. At some periods the group included Fathers Leo Mahon and Andrew Greeley. After they'd settled down with a drink and joshed around some, they began to tell, like Catholic Action cell members, where they'd walked that week, what they'd found, what they'd thought, and what they'd done. Actually, they constituted the premier Catholic Action group in the city, although they didn't think of themselves in those terms, observing their city, judging how its needs were being met, and taking action to fill those needs.

In some rectories, of a Sunday night, the talk would circle around past victories and losses. But this group was interested in current circumstance and happenstance. What are new needs? How will we respond? What problems are we facing with the chancery? With our pastors? With our organizations? How can we relate to each other? Support each other? Support the lay people?

When they wanted feedback they got it. No one, except perhaps the gentle Dan Cantwell, held back. Certainly not the redoubtable Monsignor Hillenbrand who, however much he theorized about equality, continued to trail a protective garment of infallibility. Not the upfront, controlling, innovative Gerry Weber nor the thoughtful, hard-working, dependable Larry Kelly, both young priest regulars of the Annunciation group.

Hillenbrand still demanded strict allegiance—and got it. This spirited lot of young priests deferred to him even though they now had experiences of their own to toss into the Sunday night hopper. They had opinions, too, strong opinions. They had a mutual mentor, Hillenbrand and his young firebrands, in the great Canon Cardijn. As Hillenbrand preached the Mystical Body of Christ in season and out, the Belgian founder of the Young Catholic Worker movement preached the dignity of the young worker. "He had only one talk," says Jack Egan. A single powerful theme. Hearing Canon Cardijn in Brussels in 1935, a close priest friend of Father Egan's, Father John Fitzsimons, later chaplain of the English Young Christian Workers, thought to himself, "This must be what Hitler is like." Fitzsimons, like everyone in Europe in 1935, knew the Fuehrer's reputation for mesmerizing dispirited throngs hungry for affirmation. Fitzsimons could see that Cardijn shared Hitler's command of an audience. He also recognized how divergent were the goals of the two spellbinding personalities.

According to Father Fitzsimons, Cardijn never set out to create "Catholic Action." He simply wanted to help young workers solve their problems "because he believed in the apostolic potentiality of the simplest working man." The four men who conveyed Cardijn's conviction of the worker's innate dignity into the Western Hemisphere were Father Fitzsimons, Father Tomislav Kolakovic, Patrick Keegan, and Eugene Hopkins. In 1947, Jack Egan, Edwina Hearn Froelich and Mary Irene Caplice Zotti were part of a Chicago delegation initiated into Cardijn's insights at a ground-breaking Young Christian Worker Convention in Montreal.

Jack Egan assesses that Montreal meeting in 1947 attended by a large contingent of Chicago YCW people "as a watershed because we met all the people who were doing YCW in Europe. People like Canon Cardijn made it clear how action for justice was the work of the Church. It was the first time those young people we took with us knew what it was to be a Catholic. Their lives were transformed. Their lives were different from that time on."

All the young priests at Annunciation on Sunday nights were using Cardijn's principles in Catholic Action ministries: McDonough working with young persons at the University of Chicago; Dan Cantwell with the Catholic Interracial Council and the Catholic Council on Working Life; Kelly and Imbiorski with Egan at Cana; Quinn and Weber and Killgallon with CFM, YCS and YCW; Mahon with the Woodlawn Latin American Committee. Like Cardijn, they worked with groups that applied specialized Catholic Action techniques to societal problems. Jack Egan wasn't looking for a social apostolate when he was appalled at the housing problems of the young married people at St. Justin Martyr or when he solicited funds from Cardinal Stritch for the Puerto Ricans, any more than Cardijn was. He was looking for houses and money as solutions to needs. That's what Catholic Action had trained him to do. But Catholic Action didn't give him sufficiently effective tools for confronting entrenched injustices. That's where Saul Alinsky's community organizing tutelage came in.

In the 1950s, most Catholics were held back from an interest in social concerns by their traditional religious practices. They'd been trained to seek a person-to-God relationship over a person-to-person relationship. They knelt before the altar, beads trickling between their fingers, "Glory Be to Gods" on their lips. Like Jack Egan's parents they faithfully turned up at novenas—weekly pleas to, usually, Our Lady of Perpetual Help or Our Sorrowful Mother for the petitioners' intentions. Novenas were as popular as free dish nights at the movies. Religion, as popularly practiced, was vertical—me to God. To these new-breed priests, that kind of spirituality was not Christian at all. They'd learned in their seminary days with Hillenbrand that an individual can have a personal relationship with God, but never an individual relationship.

Each of the priests who sat back and put his feet up at Annunciation on Sunday nights had a particular agenda out of his experience. Father Killgallon and Father Weber would pioneer what Father Koenig's *A History of the Parishes of the Archdiocese of Chicago* described as "a new religious education program that eventually revolutionized the teaching of catechetics in the United States and was adopted in dioceses all over the world." Father Imbiorski would write *The New Cana Manual* incorporating the most powerful psychological, spiritual, theological, and biological insights available at the time.

Father Tom McDonough would get a law degree—"to join the club," according to Jack Egan—at the University of Chicago where he was chaplain to the Catholic students at the Calvert Club. Monsignor Cantwell was the sustaining presence behind the lay people working for interracial justice and the rights of the worker. Father Larry Kelly ("if you have a man on second, you'd put Larry at bat") worked with Jack Egan at the Cana Conference and then followed Father Quinn as Director of the Catholic Action Federation in the archdiocese. Their varied contributions drawing on their experiences made for a exuberant Sunday night stew.

During this time in the early fifties when the group met regularly, Jack Egan's experiences were leading him away from their consensus. At first the division was imperceptible because he was identified so closely with the Cana Conference. However, as the crack widened, the experience was painful in the extreme. The way Jack Egan expresses it, "I entered into city government in a way which surprised and angered Mayor Richard J. Daley." The way he entered—and stayed in—city government was also to surprise and anger many priests, including some in the Sunday night group.

Jack went public when the Metropolitan Housing and Planning Council (of which he was a member) asked him to testify before the Chicago City Council for a new housing code in the early 1950s. Jack knew that he was being used, in some sense. He didn't have any special expertise in housing. What he had was a Roman collar. A little ecclesiastical clout. "I was never, never fooled by the fact that I was being used and I didn't mind being used for the appropriate purpose at the appropriate time," Jack admits. There was no doubt in his mind from his experiences at St. Justin Martyr and his study of the Grand Boulevard area that the city needed new housing built as expeditiously as possible. He was willing to do what he could.

But he wouldn't make a fool of himself. Before he testified, he wanted his mental file cabinet loaded with the particulars of city living. What was it like for people out there in substandard housing that couldn't be replaced because of antiquated regulations? By now Jack Egan had made a lot of friends in the body politic; among them, policemen, firemen, realtors. He turned to them now for a cram course on housing in the city. First, to black police detectives working a squad car at night who squired Jack around three or four nights to areas "where it was rough and tough, where there were whorehouses and where drugs were sold in neighborhood basements."

The detectives made raids for gambling, prostitution and drug use with Jack in their back seat. They'd shush him when they sent out calls for other squad cars, "Just keep your mouth shut and look like a detective." An easy assignment for an Irishman in a city of Irish police. "I saw the real city," Jack says. "Those police knew I wanted an education and they gave me one."

Next Jack approached real estate men he knew. "If I was going to talk about the housing code I wanted to know conditions. Some of them trusted me, although I must admit I didn't much trust them because I thought the almighty dollar was the thing that was keeping them moving. However, I cajoled them into bringing me around to see some of the homes where there were code violations. I was appalled at what I saw. If there was a fire, a family couldn't get out if flames should block the one door."

His best teachers were the fire inspectors because they had unconditional *carte blanche* authority. "They were marking down violations so they had absolute access to every home. They'd root out the owner or manager and go through every apartment. I thought it was very disgraceful. They'd open bedroom doors on couples having intercourse. I was with them three, four, five days, all over the city."

Armed with that firsthand information gathered on the streets, Jack wore his Roman collar to City Hall where he testified for the 1956 housing code along with other citizens interested in improving the city's housing stock and making the city more livable. That legislation passed. For Jack, that opportunity was a dress rehearsal for his testimony in the Hyde Park-Kenwood urban renewal battle two years later. That experience would change his life. That time he didn't do enough homework, and his side—the side of the poor at whose expense the neighborhood of the University of Chicago was going to be renewed—would lose. It wasn't only that Jack Egan could have been better prepared. It was also the meager number of advocates for the poor who figured in the contest.

In taking on a public role, "putting one foot outside the Church," as his friend Father Gerry Weber would say, Jack Egan threatened the bonds that held the Sunday night group together. In the abstract, everyone in the Sunday night group agreed that the task of the priest was, in Jack Egan's words, to find the right laypeople to fight injustice, to "encourage them, mentor for them, train them, build bridges for them, so that they will do the job." Monsignor Dan Cantwell held rigidly to that prescription. But Jack Egan included a mental reservation in that formula, an added caveat: if there weren't any laypersons ready to do the job and the need was immediate, he was willing to step to the front and fill in until his lay associates were available.

The Rev. Richard McBrien, Chairman of the Theology Department of the University of Notre Dame, suggests that form follows function in theology as it does in architecture. He insists, however, that it's the function that is important. If the form gets in the way of the function, then "we have to have the freedom to abolish the form." That was Jack Egan's position. Good clerical form might mean seeing that laypersons did any necessary public testifying. Good civic functioning meant that informed people testified on public matters whether they were clerics or lay persons.

Jack took on a public role, in a sense, as soon as he began training with Saul Alinsky. After Jack reported to Cardinal Stritch on the results of the Grand Boulevard area study that he and Lester Hunt did under Saul Alinsky, Cardinal Stritch told Monsignor Burke, "I think that Monsignor Egan should be appointed to the Archdiocesan Conservation Committee."

"So I was appointed," Jack recalls, "without any consultation with any of the people on the committee. And I was put in almost as director. It was badly handled." Jack describes the pastors on the committee who questioned his appointment as "very fine men who were trying to determine how best they could prepare their people so that their neighborhoods could be integrated when blacks moved in." The movement of blacks into new areas was a foregone conclusion. Their numbers had increased dramatically during World War II when they had been invited North for jobs, the second great migration from the South described by James Grossman in *Land of Hope*. Blacks could no longer be sandwiched into the corridor between Lake Michigan and State Street south of Chicago's Loop known as the "Black Belt."

Coming under the influence of Saul Alinsky as he was, Jack believed the intransigent problems developing in the city demanded community solutions and intrepid intervention. What was needed was community organization. The committee members didn't think of that, of course, for they had no understanding of organization. "Nothing in our training enables priests to be administrators or organizers," Jack points out, "although those are the two skills that, in a certain sense, we are expected to know in a parish. We're also not trained to be counselors and yet one of the crucial things a priest has to be is a counselor."

Jack, eager to ply his new-honed skills, was "dumped in the center of these men and they resented it very, very much. They were all a generation older than I, Monsignor William Gorman at St. Columbanus, Father John Gallery, Monsignor Vincent Moran, Monsignor Jack Fitzgerald, Monsignor Tom Reed." These priests identified Jack Egan as Director of the Cana Conference and questioned the appropriateness of his appointment to their committee. Used to getting together at Marshall Field's for lunch irregularly, at Father Gallery's convenience when he was downtown, they had combined sociability with a mutual determination to shore up their churches against change. They were influential at City Hall. Now Monsignor Burke, with his plenipotentiary powers, had delivered them this interloper. Worse, this activist.

About this time, Jack Egan experienced another potentially damaging rejection over another stand divergent from accepted orthodoxy. From his point of view, the Young Christian Worker women whom he chaplained had made tremendous strides in achieving autonomy. Edwina Hearn Froelich and Mary Irene Caplice Zotti endured real hardship, actually going hungry at times, during their epochal European sojourn with YCS people in various post-war countries. They'd risked their business careers to take up Catholic Action work full-time. A good group of women had taken Canon Cardijn's faith in their dignity as workers to heart after the international meeting of Young Christian Workers in Montreal.

Up to that time only a movement formally mandated by the bishop could be designated Catholic Action. Much spiritual energy was sapped by arguments over which group had that mandate. As Jack Egan explains, "Following false premises, before Vatican II, it was believed the laity, at their very best, were helpers of the hierarchy in the apostolate instead of having an apostolate of their own coming from baptism and confirmation."

From Canon Cardijn's "practical, down-to-earth application of theology at Montreal," as Jack Egan describes it, participants took to their hearts the message that the role of the priest is "to open the Word of God, tell the story, break the bread, feed the people so that they may go out and bring the bread of Christ, broken and wounded, to the world." Priests had their role. Lay Christians had their own. Having internalized Cardijn's assurance that lay persons bore Christ out into the world, the group that came back energized by Montreal kept Three East Chicago Avenue jumping with programs to bring Canon Cardijn's theology to other young Catholics.

From Jack Egan's point of view, the men's group wasn't nearly as active and effective as the women's. When the men (supported by Monsignor Hillenbrand) agitated to unite the two groups, the women objected. They liked their autonomy. Father Egan supported them, respecting their effectiveness and doubting the men's competence. Monsignor Hillenbrand sided with the men. Already irked that Jack Egan didn't put the major portion of his energy into Catholic Action, Monsignor Hillenbrand decided that Jack Egan needn't put any energy into it at all. Having made the decision that unification was the next step, Monsignor Hillenbrand brooked no opposition. He was deaf to this young priest who'd worked tirelessly with the women's group and understood their concerns.

After more than a decade, the YCW women were a big part of Jack Egan's life. He was still in the seminary when he started recruiting young women students for Catholic Action groups. Working with YCW women was so much a part of his self-identification that he'd risked his health by giving up his free days over the years to their development.

He never regretted a moment of his commitment. He wanted to continue it. But now Monsignor Hillenbrand summoned Jack Egan to YCW's new offices at Jackson Boulevard and Paulina. Jack was at his most vulnerable. Before him stood the man who represented what Jack Egan believed best about the Church to which he had pledged his life. Monsignor Hillenbrand had held up for his boys, Rynie's boys, an ideal template, and Jack had stepped into it, meaning to become Monsignor Hillenbrand's kind of priest. He had not succeeded. As Jack had disappointed his father, now he had disappointed his father figure. Monsignor Hillenbrand was forcing Jack to chose between faithfulness to him and faithfulness to the vision that Monsignor Hillenbrand himself had commended to Jack as a seminarian.

Jack's stand for the women was interpreted as opposing Monsignor Hillenbrand's will for unification (although Jack was following the women's preference). Monsignor Hillenbrand's eyes behind the glasses with their heavy corrections were fixed and flinty. He told Jack Egan that he was fired as national chaplain of women Young Christian Workers. Theoretical proponent of the dignity of every woman and every man as he claimed to be—and wanted to be—Monsignor Hillenbrand saw no need to ask Jack Egan or the women how they would feel about this high-handed decision.

The women were deeply hurt. They felt their accomplishments diminished, rejected, by this man who was everyone's ideal. How many times they had heard him tell how Christ did His work through them and that he wouldn't get His work down without them! How hard they had tried to do Christ's work! And now they were to lose not only their autonomy, but also their devoted chaplain. Jack himself was in a state of shock. He reeled internally as he felt an important part of his identity wrenched from him. He would miss the women, he would miss the work. At a deeper level, he was wounded by this deep personal rejection by his long-admired mentor. "Here was a man I idolized asking me to stop doing work that was so much a part of my life and was so important."

He didn't question Monsignor Hillenbrand's ecclesiastical competence to make this decision. "He was my superior, with a mandate from the cardinal. For me to say no or to start a rump movement or boycott it or create opposition would be unseemly, improper, and unpriestly." Jack accepted the bald power play. That, too, was part of his training. "If that's what he wanted, I had other things to do. But I was hurt."

And so was the YCW movement.

As it turned out, the unification progressed and the Young Christian Workers regressed. The men, as Jack saw them, were "unbelievably peculiar chauvinists" who looked on themselves as the leaders of this new coalition. Not as theologically advanced as the women, the men looked on them as "the hewers of wood and the drawers of water," as Jack recalls. "They wanted them for secretaries." The women rebelled. There were a number of battles. The decline of the Young Christian Workers as a potentially effective Christianizing force was inevitable. The women were changed personally, as they generally testify today. But their potential to "change the water," to effect changes in their community, was aborted. In Europe, two decades later there would be former YCW workers in many governments. In South and Central America, YCW people would have influenced the rise of the "base communities," liberation theology, and the advances at Medellin. In the United States, the effects were not comparable.

Jack Egan had finished his apprenticeship with Monsignor Hillenbrand. Bolstered by the self-confidence gained by his therapeutic sessions with Father Charles Curran, he had the psychic and spiritual muscle to exercise some independence. He would never go beyond authority, any more than he did with Monsignor Hillenbrand. Like Canon Cardijn who ingratiated himself with the Vatican to promote his apostolate, Father Egan would stay carefully within the confines of authority. At the same time, he'd keep pushing at authority's limits to serve the laity to whom he'd promised his allegiance.

He'd plotted himself a lonely course.

10

"He Was the Only Guy to Stand Up to the University and City Hall"

By 1958 Chicago was one hundred and twenty-five years old, a grand old dowager with a proud face, dirt under her nails, and many poor children hidden under her skirts. Much of the inner city housing stock dated from the city's rebirth after the Great Fire of 1871.

Too many of the old lady's children lived in that historic area's substandard dwellings. Others who couldn't afford downpayments in the city's substantial neighborhoods were fleeing decaying areas for suburban ranch houses. Those who loved the city remained, those well-off enough to insulate themselves, those comfortable with the city's faded glories, those with hope for her future, and those too tired and poor to make a change.

The city's charms were still potent and real. And well worth working to save. This was particularly true of the Hyde Park-Kenwood area settled as a suburb when the Illinois Central Railroad opened its 54th Street/Lake Park station in 1856. By 1890 Hyde Park was the largest suburb in the world with 85,000 inhabitants, a natural candidate for annexation to the metropolis and for the resplendent 1893 Columbian Exposition. Early on, Chicago's railroad and meat-packing barons built summer homes there, later their primary residences.

The fabled Frederick Law Olmsted, designer of New York's Central Park and the first person to call himself a landscape architect, created the park system that girded the neighborhood. Using the Midway Plaisance to link Jackson Park and Washington Park, he attained his aspiration of bringing to the heart of Hyde Park the atmosphere of the smiling and beautiful countryside.

During the early part of the twentieth century, as the University of Chicago grew on the Midway which Frederick Olmsted designed and which John D. Rockefeller paid for, Hyde Park-Kenwood offered a rich life to the cultured. Ringed with parks, close to the Loop, blessed with excellent transportation, clustered around the University of Chicago, chock-a-block with amenities geared to the university population, the area was home to a mix of liberal thinkers, intellectuals, Bohemians and artists, and middle class people who liked the ambience and conveniences. It was at once Chicago's Greenwich Village and Harvard Square.

North of 47th Street, the natural boundary, however, was the South Side area described in a 1945 publication as "the largest contiguous slum area in the United States." There was little but "poverty, disorder, dirt and human misery." Louis Kurtz (quoted in *Growth of a Metropolis* by Harold M. Mayer and Richard C. Wade) said, "I have seen pitiful, pathetic, deplorable, rotten and damnable shacks, hovels, leantos and hell-holes in my travels, but when you see these Negro families huddled together like cattle in dilapidated wood sheds, garages, make-shift huts made of old lumber, old tin signs, cardboard and whatever could be picked up and fastened together as a shelter, one cannot help but realize that, rotten and deplorable as all slum areas area are, the '*Black Belt*' of Chicago beats them all when it comes to *Misery at its worst*."

Mid-century, as Hyde Park-Kenwood began to take on a stronger resemblance to its old dowager mother, poor children began to crawl in under the edge of its skirts, threatening its stability, its very existence. Those who loved the area began to ask each other how they could preserve their part of the city and its amenities. Led by the area's powerful institutions, they agreed to confront the growing crime rate and the illegal conversion of old houses and apartments. To work together to stabilize the area, there were several organizations in that highly organized neighborhood including the Hyde Park-Kenwood Community Conference founded in 1949; the Hyde Park Planning Association, and the South East Chicago Commission organized in 1952 with a skeleton staff, an office and a telephone number. The University of Chicago put up the $15,000 to set up the SECC's office in the Hyde Park YWCA. Julian Levi, brother to the dean of the university's law school, was SECC's first executive director, exemplifying the university's leadership role from the beginning as agent of the coming renewal program.

Between 1950 (when the Supreme Court outlawed restrictive covenants and blacks started moving in) and 1956, the number of blacks in the area increased five hundred percent. High-achieving blacks who bought in the lakefront high-rises and quiet side streets pushed out the less successful whites who moved away. At the same time, however, the housing on Hyde Park-Kenwood's encircling commercial borders was deteriorating in a way that area residents felt threatened by.

Urban renewal, untried and unprecedented in 1958, looked like a useful mechanism to control the borders. The federal government would provide money to help local communities buy up substandard properties like the old stores along Cottage Grove Avenue. Because the governmental machinery was primitive at that time, local planners could seize the initiative in claiming those funds coming into existence through the federal government, according to Peter Rossi and Robert Dentler in *The Politics of Urban Renewal*. Chicago, the first city to experiment with federally funded urban renewal, had a relatively free hand.

The Hyde Park-Kenwood planners were directly under the bidding of the South East Chicago Commission which meant they were controlled by the University of Chicago which funded the commission. According to Rossi and Dentler, Hyde Park-Kenwood was the only neighborhood in Chicago with an ambience of liberal intellectualism. "Few neighborhoods could be found in the urban North in which significant portions of the population were willing to achieve interracial or biracial neighborhood living. Of all upper-middle-class neighborhoods in the country, Hyde Park-Kenwood (was) perhaps the best equipped to tolerate and in some instances to encourage interracialism."

The problem rose not with the middle class blacks, but with the poor residents, black and white. Where were they to go when their substandard dwellings were pulled down? When the university published its Urban Renewal Plan in the spring of 1958 (which they had contracted with the city in 1955 to produce), a group of Jack Egan's friends in Hyde Park-Kenwood "and some city planners were so upset with the domineering and vicious tactics of the group that was engineering this project for the University of Chicago" (Jack Egan's assessment) that they came to him. They pointed out how many poor would be dehoused. According to Rossi and Dentler, by the time that group got a look at the university's urban renewal plan it had already passed its first test. In 1957 it was approved by the federal government, the funding source under the Federal Housing Act of 1954. Opponents' only chance to speak up publicly for the displaced would be at the Chicago City Council hearings.

Jack Egan took the story to Monsignors Burke and Casey who gave him their immediate and unwavering support. They took Jack's concern to Cardinal Stritch. "I had the total backing of the chancellor throughout the whole fight," Egan says today.

In his training days with Saul Alinsky when he had canvassed the area south of Chicago's Loop, Father Egan had seen the "pitiful, pathetic, and deplorable" dwellings cited in the 1945 report on housing in the Black Belt. He had a clear notion of what housing for blacks in Chicago was like. Were the University of Chicago's urban planners going to concern themselves sufficiently with the residents who would be uprooted as the people in the Grand Boulevard area had been for the Dan Ryan Expressway?

When he'd brought the report on his first Saul Alinsky project to the cardinal, the cardinal had reacted by appointing Jack Egan to the Archdiocesan Conservation Council. That position—and his symbolic Roman collar—gave Jack a warrant to raise the tough questions about relocation after the Hyde Park-Kenwood Urban Renewal Plan was published. When Jack Egan had testified earlier for the 1956 Housing Code, he had drawn a picture of families living in death traps—and dying in them.

Two years later in 1958, back testifying before the City Council, Jack Egan was still decrying appalling conditions. The housing code had worked marginally. Available homes were safer, some were less overcrowded. But the city's black population was growing, reducing housing opportunities for people in the middle as well as the lower income groups. Jack and his group looked past the plan worked out to benefit the University of Chicago to see how their plan would affect the whole city. They figured it might well function as a seed for the "consequent creation of new or worse slums" in other areas of the city.

As the spokesperson for the Archdiocesan Conservation Council, Father Egan used the *New World*, the archdiocesan weekly, to bring his views to the public—and to the Hyde Park-Kenwood urban renewal planners. As early as May, 1958, he called for adequate, nonsegregated housing in articles written by organizer Nicholas von Hoffman and signed by Jack. They pointed out that sorely needed urban renewal would encounter "increasingly fierce opposition" unless a vast number of new homes were built.

Father Egan called the segregation of the bulk of the Negro population into nightmarish shanty towns "the major moral problem of our generation." Bad as many of those "pitiable, pathetic, and deplorable dwellings" in Hyde Park-Kenwood were, however, Father Egan did not want to see them pulled down until other housing was available for those who would be displaced. As far as he could see, everyone involved was passing the buck. "There is no open housing market for Negroes. We all know very well that one-fifth of the population of Chicago and a tenth of the population of the whole United States is the victim of a gigantic silent conspiracy."

Jack Egan was serving notice that the archdiocese he represented refused to be part of that silent conspiracy. He described for *New World* readers how white flight was catalyzed by the success of one Negro family in buying a house in a white neighborhood. Jack Egan was against panic buying and panic flight. But he denied any opposition to urban renewal as a tool. "Is the answer to the dilemma to stop urban renewal? Certainly not. The houses we need must be built and our urban renewal program must keep pace." As Jack Egan saw the situation, the university had the right to protect itself. What was unhealthy for the community was the university's effort to encapsulate itself.

Jack Egan also objected to the university's appropriating all the city's chits for urban renewal to improve the University of Chicago neighborhood at the expense of others. The university had hired Julian Levi, whose brother would later be president of the University of Chicago, and Jack Meltzer as activists to preserve the university from any blight surrounding it. "They were going to have the first urban renewal program in the United States, and, of course, not only the first but also one of the largest. They got $20 million in federal funds, but they also ate up the $10 million in local bond money meant to be used for all the neighborhoods in the city of Chicago," Jack recalls.

To Jack the government was funding a moat to protect the great university. Where was their concern for the people presently residing in the pathway of the moat? "The overriding disaster of the plan," Father Egan says, "was that twenty thousand people were removed from that area—black and white—without any appropriate relocation housing for them." To him, that was intolerable.

To the university planners, Jack Egan represented pastors afraid that those displaced in Hyde Park-Kenwood would inundate parish neighborhoods presently white. Weren't Catholic parishes protecting their turf just as the university was? To Father Egan who had walked Thirty-first Street and Thirty-second Street and State Street between them, the issue was decent, affordable housing for everyone. That's what he'd testified for in 1956. That's what he was testifying for now.

Obviously, the university wielded more power. They had money to spend. What seemed to Egan as ominous as the urban renewal plan was the university's practice of buying up every single piece of property in the Hyde Park-Kenwood area. "Nobody could sell or buy property without going through their office. They were using all these federal funds and all this local bond money and their plans published finally in 1957 indicated no money for housing for the poor." This was not the way the federal funds were supposed to be spent.

It was fortunate that Cardinal Stritch and his chancellor and vicar general were in Jack Egan's corner. The crowd on the other side of the ring was soon heard from. Jack knew the articles were hitting pay dirt, as he says, when James Downs (a member of the University Board of Trustees, also a trusted advisor of Mayor Daley) called him for lunch. About the same time, Herman Dunlop Smith (also a trustee) called Saul Alinsky who'd recently returned from a European visit with Jacques Maritain and a meeting with Cardinal Montini, the future Pope Paul VI. Smith brought Alinsky to the University Club in the Loop where he pilloried the Church's stand on urban renewal in Hyde Park-Kenwood, and Egan's part in it. Meanwhile, Jerome Kerwin, the ranking Catholic intellectual on the university faculty, was contacting Pat Crowley, head of the Christian Family Movement, to get the help of Monsignor Hillenbrand, national CFM chaplain, in stopping the Church's attack on the university plan.

One of the persons who called Monsignor Burke was the popular, gregarious Monsignor Daniel Cunningham. He had heard from Mayor Richard J. Daley who wanted to know what this young priest was doing interfering with the urban renewal plans of the University of Chicago relative to the city. Monsignor Burke was curt with Monsignor Cunningham: "Diggy," he said, "I think it would be better if you minded your own business because he (Jack Egan) is operating with our approval. He is keeping us informed on everything he does. We are backing him. The cardinal is backing him." Jack Egan heard him say that.

People who might have been expected to support Egan's testimony saw the fight as futile. Saul Alinsky did not believe in entering a contest you couldn't win. The odds were enormous in Hyde Park-Kenwood. Saul Alinsky's criticism particularly stung Father Egan. "He really raised hell because he said we were going about it in the wrong way."

Unrepentant thirty years later, Jack Egan insists, "we weren't going about it in the wrong way." He suspects Saul was influenced by his friends in the Hyde Park-Kenwood area. "The basic thing was that they did not want their area around the University of Chicago to become a slum area. They didn't want their professors and students not to have adequate housing in the area. Well, that's all well and good, and I supported that. But that is not the way they approached the whole thing. They truly wanted—it seemed to me—to build a moat around it."

In the name of the archdiocese, Jack Egan was asking "for some public housing in there since they were using $30 million in taxpayers' money. But it is very interesting," he says. "Now it is October and the hearings for the Hyde Park-Kenwood program come up before the City Council—and we lose."

Jack's objections foundered before the power of the university and its trustees. "Just never underestimate it," he says of that power. "In those days it was frightening. The power of the *Tribune*, too." The only power Father Egan could commandeer was a united front among clerics, Church leaders, and lay people. Or solid support from the cardinal. Jack Egan had had the cardinal's support. However, Cardinal Stritch died in Rome before the vote in the City Council, tragically for the archdiocese which had blossomed under his permissive, supportive authority. Grassroots support for Jack's stand was not forthcoming. Too many Catholics were afraid of the growing black population.

Peter Rossi and Robert Dentler don't minimize the Church's objections in their analysis of *The Politics of Urban Renewal*. They characterize the archdiocese's opposition to the plan as formidable. "Final City Council approval of the plan was delayed for five months while the meaning and determination of the cardinal's committee was measured and tested." Yet the City Council's approval was assured once Cardinal Stritch had died. Without his buttress, Jack had only minimal support within the Church or without.

Actually, looking back, it is apparent that the recommendations of the cardinal's committee were hardly Draconian. They asked:

1) That land be cleared only as it was needed.

2) That every effort be made to insure that some of the new housing be within financial reach of families with small or intermediate income.

3) Provisions on rehabilitation be clear and precise.

4) The city's housing supply be jealously guarded by a close scrutiny of the demolition proposals.

With these considerations in place, the committee was ready to support the Hyde Park-Kenwood plan unreservedly. That statement was issued in July, 1958, months before the City Council vote.

When Father Egan came back to testify before the Housing and Planning committee of the City Council in September, his plea was general and pastoral. Every element of society has a vested interest, he assured the aldermen, "and the vested interest of the Archdiocese of Chicago is human beings."

Testifying on their behalf, he pointed out that the poorly housed he'd testified for in 1956 were still poorly housed. "Everything remains the same. The faces in this room are the same, Chicago's hundreds of thousands of ill-housed, under-housed, and de-housed people are also practically the same."

What he couldn't bring himself to do was condemn the plan outright. He stayed up all the night before the hearing with Hyde Park activist Lou Silverman wrestling with an expression of the archdiocesan position. In the end he conceded overall support of the plan in spite of his caveats. At dawn, he sent Silverman off in a cab to drop the statement at all the newspapers. Meanwhile, Jack Egan took a copy to the chancellor. "He blew his cork," Jack remembers. "I've seen Monsignor Burke mad, but I'd never seen him as mad as he was that day." After all they'd been through, Monsignor Burke's Irish temper was not going to suffer a mealy-mouth statement. He forced Egan to force the sleepless Silverman to retrace his rounds, picking up the statements he had so recently delivered so the archdiocesan position could be strengthened.

Looking back, Jack Egan sees he was naive in his expectations that the mayor of Chicago would fight for the people, that he would guarantee a relocation program and some public housing in the area. "There was none. I should have said the archdiocese opposed the plan."

Chicago attorney Tom Foran had used the power of eminent domain to clear land for the city's Kennedy and Dan Ryan expressways, also for the completion of the Congress Street Expressway. Now he was offered a contract with the city to clear the "dope hutches, Blackstone Ranger places and that sort of thing" (Foran's description) out of Hyde Park-Kenwood using the power of eminent domain. He, too, thought Father Egan was naive. Foran would run into Egan at public hearings in Hyde Park-Kenwood. "I used to fight with Jack. When he'd say we were driving blacks out, I'd tell him, 'You don't know your (ass) from your elbow. What we're trying to do is save the place. What's there? Terrible stuff like Bombay or Calcutta, filthy rotten terrible buildings without interior plumbing, filthy drug addicts, rats—if you think that's helping the Blacks . . .' Whatever was done was better than what was there."

To Foran it seemed that "Jack was absolutely sincere in what he was saying, and I was absolutely sincere in what I was saying." At base, Tom Foran objected to the Alinsky technique of community organization which Jack advocated. To Foran, Alinsky's "concept of getting people with problems brought on by their own limitations to try to correct them by attacking people who are more successful than they were was absolutely awful. I didn't need Saul Alinsky to tell me how to care about people, and I didn't think Jack Egan needed him either. And I used to tell him that."

In spite of their differing views on Hyde Park, Egan and Foran forged a close friendship. "He was a regular visitor to our house. Marvelous to our children." Foran, later U.S. attorney for Northern Illinois, was to be deeply troubled by the Second Vatican Council. Egan, on the other hand, felt vindicated. Foran describes their diversity of views as "a totally open and honest dichotomy between us. I think there was a tendency in the Church to act as a social agency, and they really are not. The people who have obligations to treat their fellow human beings well secularly are secular people. I have that obligation more than Jack Egan and, I think, have more talent for doing it."

Foran would tell Father Egan, "The best thing you can do for me, Jack, is shrive me for my sins and stick God in my mouth. I don't need your advice on social issues." He imitates Jack Egan's laughing retort, "I know you need your sins shriven." Foran remembers trying to persuade Mayor Richard J. Daley that Richard Daley and John Egan, both great guys, had a lot in common. Daley would demur, having been "fed things," information, Foran surmises. "Mr. Mayor," Foran would plead, "he's a terrific priest. For Chrissake . . .."

"Don't swear," the daily Mass-going Mayor would interrupt.

Later on, Tom Foran came up against Father Egan once again. Foran had cleared land on the city's near West Side, again by the power of eminent domain. From the point of view of the community organization directed by West Side activist Florence Scala, Foran "took" eleven hundred pieces of property. "And they still say I took it like Attila the Hun," Foran confides. While he considers Florence Scala "a great gal," and gets a big hug when he takes his family to her Taylor Street restaurant, Foran never doubts that he did the right thing in clearing the area.

Foran shrugs off the neighborhood perception that he was the personification of evil. With no rancor, he describes climbing over Florence's adherents lying prone on the courthouse corridors and the ketchuped cloth figure with a dagger in the heart left on the front lawn of his Sauganash home. He tells how he used infant mortality, tuberculosis, and syphilis figures to prove the need for land clearance when the case reached the Supreme Court. At that time to employ eminent domain one had to prove the property deleterious to the health, morals, and welfare of the community. When one of the judges showed interest, asking whether the figures for syphilis were really two hundred and eighty-three percent over other areas of the city, Foran answered confidently, "That's right, judge. That's what the statistics show."

One of Florence Scala's lieutenants, a large, dominating figure, leaped up in the court, overcome with anger at the presentation. Furious at this turn in the evidence, she pointed fiercely at Tom Foran and yelled for all to hear, "That man is anti-Semitic against Italians."

According to Father Egan, when the University of Illinois at Chicago saw the cleared land, they wanted it and so did the city of Chicago. Jack's position was that the city as a body politic had a right to change its mind and exercise eminent domain. "The community organizations were mad at me because I did not give them wholehearted support."

In the end, Tom Foran prevailed in Hyde Park-Kenwood and on the West Side. "I take considerable pride. I think we saved Hyde Park. It's a great location now, and I think we did it." He believes that if Jack looked at Hyde Park now, he'd have to agree that the area would be a shambles without the urban renewal. As for the University of Illinois at Chicago campus, "I think he knew we were right," Foran says, "but he felt an obligation to support community organizations." Once again, Foran's views are at variance with Jack Egan's.

Tom Foran saw Father Egan as an innocent. When Jack got together with Saul Alinsky for the obligatory post-mortem after the Hyde Park-Kenwood action, Alinsky assessed Jack's evenhandedness as innocence, too. He accused Jack of seeing too many greys. "It's very hard for you to see black and white," he told Jack. "In a fight like this you have to go for the jugular, to let people believe that you are trying to kill the plan."

Jack demurred. "That would be dishonest. I'm not trying to kill the plan, but I do want them to make some adjustments."

Saul shot back, "I said you have to give the *impression* that you're trying to kill the plan. Because you are working in grey areas, you are going to destroy all your work."

Three decades later, Jack Egan reckons Alinsky "was absolutely right." He feels compelled to add, "It was a vicious attempt on the part of the University of Chicago (which I respect very much). I want them to exist, but they could have done it far more unselfishly than they did."

Taking a stand on this issue was as important a course modulation within the Church as it was without. Chicago's politicians from the Mayor down were surprised and displeased by this seeming disaffection of an otherwise charming, ingratiating, intelligent priest of Irish extraction. The city thought it knew what to expect of such men. In this case it didn't. What were they to make of one of their own who didn't stay within his caste, who said, as Father Egan did, "From 1956 I became prominent in terms of social action in relationship to political action in the city and that was never to stop—even up to today."

Jack's public stance divided somewhat the unique liberal communities that were building within the Church at that time. One of these communities had formed in a tired old walk-up at Twenty-one West Superior where various groups reared on Catholic Action principles headquartered. There was nothing tired about the people who gathered there. They were, for the most part, young, vigorous, informed, idealistic, energetic, and unremittingly dedicated to action for justice in whatever area they specialized. To Jack Egan, Twenty-one West Superior, as the center for most of the comprehensive work of the archdiocese, "contained the dreams of some fantastic people who moved through the

Archdiocese of Chicago during the fifties and well into the sixties. It functioned as the mission control center for most of the good things that happened here."

Egan's Cana people on the first floor (before they moved to Seven-twenty North Rush) clubbed daily, mentally and spiritually, with the Catholic Labor Alliance people, the Christian Family Movement people, the Catholic Interracial Council, and the Catholic Guild for the Blind people on the upper floors. The unified spirit of this charged community was tested by Jack Egan's public testimony against the University of Chicago's urban renewal plan. Ed Marciniak, editor of *Work*, the monthly publication of the liberal Catholic Council on Working Life, wrote an editorial suggesting that responsibility for the relocation of Hyde Park's poor rested with the entire city population. He didn't disagree with Jack Egan's contention that families should be moved only for just cause, and then to decent homes. What he challenged was Jack Egan's intervention at the eleventh hour into a community-planned negotiation agreed upon by "major institutions of the community, local priests, ministers and rabbis, urban renewal officials and the leader of the community organization, a Catholic layman with a keen social conscience and a deep commitment as a Christian."

Was the authority of the secular Christian being undermined? After all, Jim Cunningham, chairman of the Hyde Park Conservation Council which voted to support the urban renewal plan, had been a longtime Catholic Action adherent, a member of Father Louis Putz' first YCS group at the University of Notre Dame. Here began a running disagreement that would continue for years on the role of the priest in political action.

That disagreement sundered the Sunday night community that gathered at Annunciation. For Jack Egan this was a painful blow. While it was true that his self-confidence had been sharply boosted by the therapeutic sessions with Charles Curran, he harbored a residual need for support and approval he could never entirely shake. Monsignor Hillenbrand's approval meant everything to him. The Sunday night group were his closest allies in the Church. Usually, they provided comfort for one another and convivial exchange.

Their last meeting was not that comfortable. The air rippled with uneasiness and inquietude at Seven-twenty North Rush Street, a once-handsome old mansion which housed the staff of several Catholic agencies. University of Chicago professor Jerome Kerwin, the pride of

Chicago Catholics, had called Patrick Crowley, Christian Family Movement co-founder, about Jack's testimony. Crowley contacted Monsignor Hillenbrand about his former student making trouble for the University of Chicago. Monsignor Hillenbrand, in turn, called Father Bill Quinn and asked him to get a group together. "To kick the hell out of Jack Egan," Jack described the agenda later. About twenty priests and lay people took the fine old staircase up to the high-ceilinged meeting rooms that alternately pleased with their stateliness and frustrated by their inconvenience. Monsignor Hillenbrand immediately took the floor for what Father Andrew Greeley would call the "Egan Heresy Trial."

Slight though he was, Monsignor Hillenbrand had a fiercely commanding aura. Now, as he charged his protege with a critical blunder, anger made his ordinarily powerful delivery devastating. He snapped rhetorical questions at Jack without giving him any chance to reply. Who was Jack Egan to take a stand on urban renewal in defiance of the University of Chicago? Why hadn't he left the matter to the wisdom of local lay Catholics like Jim Cunningham and Jerome Kerwin? Weren't they the experts on the scene?

Monsignor Hillenbrand had been revered by so many people, including for years Jack Egan, that he never thought to question his own omniscience. Nor did he expect anyone else to question it. It never occurred to him that he could be unfair. He saw his condemnation as a mechanism for pulling Jack back into line. Jack, who didn't intend to fall back in line, tried to defend his stand. Monsignor Hillenbrand would hear none of it, insistently excoriating Jack Egan for getting mixed up in the University of Chicago imbroglio.

"You had no business there because you are a priest," Hillenbrand flared. "This is not your role, the role of the priest, to question the university. You are just plain wrong, you who had the privilege of the best possible training on the role of the laity."

Next he disparaged Jack's competence. "And not only that, what do you know about urban renewal? You're a disgrace to the Roman Catholic Church and the priesthood. You should be in favor of that plan just because the University of Chicago is there."

Father Egan had supporters in the room, Fathers Bill Quinn, Jake Killgallon, Andrew Greeley and Walter Imbiorski, layman Peter Foote. "Maybe half the twenty or so there were with me. But it was Rynie's show even though a lot of people stuck up for me." What wounded Jack most deeply was the source of the accusations.

"Criticism hurts more when it comes from a mentor. Monsignor Hillenbrand's approval meant everything to me. It was so hurtful to attack me before my peers without letting me give my case. I was overwhelmed." Jack felt cut loose. He left Seven-twenty North Rush Street that night a man of sorrows. The bonds so carefully nurtured at the seminary to sustain priests cut off from family life were ruptured. Monsignor Hillenbrand was split off from "Rynie's boys," his boys. Their relationship changed, too.

Jack lay in bed that night rerunning the evening in his mind. He couldn't sleep for hearing Monsignor Hillenbrand's accusations. He tried to put the evening in perspective. He knew that you have to learn how to fail in life, that you have to accept being kicked around a little bit. Yet this was of another order, he told himself, as he tried to fit this evening into the pattern of other evenings with his old teacher. He was still wide-eyed when the first phone call signaled the beginning of a new day. The caller was Monsignor Hillenbrand who had had coffee and second thoughts. The hard edge of his voice was softened. His overture was friendly. "I was a little rough with you last night, Johnny," he admitted carefully. "I want to apologize for what I said."

Jack had had the night to assimilate his new status. "Rynie," he answered quietly, "you can't apologize to me. There were twenty-five people in that room. Do you want to call them all together and tell them you were wrong? Or to modify your opinion? Or your words? It is just too late to say I apologize."

Monsignor Hillenbrand was not willing to retract his criticism. His voice dropped as he finished lamely. "I just wanted to let you know I was sorry."

Remembering, Jack Egan says sadly, "He was just speaking to me. Of course, I idolized him. Those were the strongest words I ever spoke to him. You just don't want to push a friend to whom you owe so much." That was the breaking point. The Sunday night group had gathered for mutual support with the rector who had taught them how to be priests. They'd advanced to a place where he could no longer support them. The trial was the end of the group. Jack Egan saw Monsignor Reynold Hillenbrand only once again before he contacted his exemplar two weeks before his death.

The groups were diverging, in a sense, because Jack Egan and the others were diverging as persons. They were "following their bliss," in the Joseph Campbell parlance, their experiences having propelled them out ahead of their mentors. Jack Egan was entering a time of life when he would be known as an outsider inside the Church and an insider in the wider ecumenical society outside the Church. The elements that took him to their heart in society felt embraced by the Catholic Church itself when Jack took them to his bosom. As for his fellow priests, there were those who would have gladly thrown him out of their rectories. Some of them did. He claims to have been thrown out of some of the best rectories in the city.

Looking back at the urban renewal flap, however, Jack Egan doesn't recant, insisting that he was representing the interests of the whole city while the university represented only its self-interest as an institution. He was willing to hang there in the wind on behalf of the whole city, even if he must remember the episode to this day as a "terrifying experience."

To Tom Gaudette, a premier community organizer trained by Saul Alinsky, Father John Egan was a voice crying in the wilderness in the Hyde Park-Kenwood urban renewal fight. "He was the only guy willing to stand up to the university and to City Hall." In Gaudette's view, the purpose of the "program known as urban renewal was to move blacks out of Hyde Park and the federal government was going to pay for it. What we tried to do was organize support (for changes in the urban renewal plan) and we found damn little of it. The thing I remember most was not the politicians. Their reasons were understandable. But where in hell were the clergy in something like this?

"They were accusing Jack of wanting to be cardinal. Or saying the only reason he did it was because Cardinal Stritch wasn't here. Jack Egan?" Gaudette asks in disbelief, his blue eyes piercing his audience, his words coming out in short, sharp, spurts. "Some priests said he was creating scandal with our Jewish brothers. Some complained he was preventing the lay people from getting involved. Who? What lay people? In 1957? Hell, there they were, fat and sassy, talking about the prophetic role of priests. But they never brought out that blacks were being kicked out."

Nor did they think about Jack Egan, how vulnerable he felt testifying against the heavyweights the university had assembled to impress the City Council with the validity of their position. "I have never felt more alone," Jack Egan told author Sanford Horwitt. The cardinal was all the clout Jack Egan could possibly have carried into that chamber. His small group couldn't sustain him. With the cardinal gone, there was a vacuum where there should have been a retaining wall.

Yet when his fellow priests scolded him, Jack Egan, cool and respectful, answered their protests evenly, measuring his words, admitting his frailty, saying, "I do struggle with this. I do. I must admit that I've had sleepless nights. But I've got to do something." There was his only rationale. He'd seen that black man tossed from a streetcar. He'd talked to all those impoverished along Thirty-fifth Street. He'd gone with the fire inspectors into firetraps. He knew about cockroaches and rats. That was all he could say to defend his action, "But I've got to do something." What he meant was that he couldn't see the poor kicked out of Hyde Park-Kenwood without getting out on the road, a slight, beseeching, hopeful suppliant, in front of the bulldozer that would roll over him as easily as it would roll over the homes and people he was trying to save.

For once, Jack's natural ebullience failed him. Berenice O'Brien, who served with her husband as Cana Board chaircouple in the early 1950s, remembers picking up Father Egan and Father Walter Imbiorski on Michigan Avenue in Chicago on an October Saturday after the hearing. They had plans for a Notre Dame game at South Bend. "I never knew the particulars of the urban renewal fight. Jack was careful to keep each area of his life compartmentalized. And we were in the Cana slot.

"Yet, when Father Egan got in the car, it was obvious that he was terribly bruised. Walter Imbiorski treated him so very tenderly—as only Walter could do—that we knew that any further contact would be too painful. 'Kid gloves' wouldn't have expressed the care Walter bestowed as he ushered Jack into the back seat. He acted as a screen between Jack and anything that might further pain him." Jack seemed to shrink into the upholstery.

On their return, the four Notre Dame fans met two Dominican priest friends for dinner. Pope Pius XII had died on Jack Egan's forty-fifth birthday. The election of the next pope being the news of the day, the six dinner companions put the names of the leading candidates in a bowl and Bob O'Brien drew Angelo Roncalli's name. That week the cardinals in Rome picked the same man. He took the name of John XXIII. That could have been taken as a healing sign for Jack Egan, for the Second Vatican Council called by Pope John XXIII would ratify many of Jack's initiatives.

"When we dropped Jack off after the game, the dinner, and the drawing," Berenice O'Brien remembers, "he was obviously feeling much better. The day Walter had planned had done its work."

11

*"God You Know,
They Finessed Us"*

The University of Chicago Urban Renewal debacle was "terrifying" for Jack Egan because he had stepped outside the clerical culture. He'd left a safe, familiar and edifying place for a forum that was fairly much untried, unedifying, and unsafe—for a priest. In some quarters that testimony on behalf of the city's poor lent Jack Egan a mythic aura. Father Patrick O'Malley, first president of the National Federation of Priests' Councils, recalls hearing of Jack's testimony as a seminarian. "Of course Jack Egan's name was a household word even then among us priests-to-be."

Father John Hill, acting pastor at Presentation Parish, knew of Jack Egan's social concern before Jack arrived to take over as the new pastor. "I admired him when he came because of Hyde Park-Kenwood. I thought Jack Egan was on the side of the angels, and the only one who was—aside from Monsignor Kelly who printed all the articles in the *New World*. The entire Catholic liberal establishment did not support Jack."

To Jack Hill, Father Egan fought Hyde Park-Kenwood on his own. "He didn't win the day. He won some concessions. He conducted himself honorably although he didn't have an ally." As a result, what Jack Egan "won more than anything was the respect of the young priests of the archdiocese." Jack Hill thinks Jack Egan changed as a result of the urban renewal battle, as attitudes toward him changed. He gained some "charisma that wasn't there before, a new dimension. People could gravitate toward him automatically."

The camaraderie at Presentation was still seven years into Jack Egan's future the Monday morning after the Notre Dame game with the O'Briens and Father Imbiorski. That Monday, he had to come to terms with the basically lonely life he'd chosen. Even though a conviction he was doing the right thing helped him survive the rebuff delivered by the City Council, he'd felt so vulnerable. So exposed. There'd been so much power arrayed against him.

How could he apply to this situation the Saul Alinsky principle of reflection? he asked himself. Could he defend his position as a priest in a public forum? Were Monsignor Cantwell and Tom Foran right? Jack agreed with their general stand that opposing society's ills was a lay job. In fact, he was fiercely supportive of that principle. However Jack always left himself an out, "There are certain circumstances. . . ."

Working out his rationale, Father Egan decided that clergy should step into the political arena only in emergencies, "for if the laity have the right kind of training and formation, they are going to take the initiative and then the priest will take his proper role." As Jack Egan pondered all this, he had a call from Mayor Richard J. Daley inviting him to his office at City Hall. The two Irishmen, one a subtle, ex- perienced dispenser of Chicago clout (he controlled 40,000 jobs, repre- senting 400,000 votes), the other a cleric freshly reminded of the reality of Chicago power politics, faced each other. Mayor Daley was kind, if somewhat patronizing.

It was a revealing confrontation between two men deeply linked by roots and rites, deeply divided on social issues. Both men were sons of pious parents born on the old sod. As a child, Richard J. Daley went to daily Mass accompanied by his parents. He kept up the practice throughout his life. Both had paper routes as kids and started at DePaul University toward degrees in the law. Daley finished. It took him four nights a week for eleven years of night school. Neither man was a scholar, but both were shrewdly smart about how one pressed ahead in the city, and each was skilled in picking the brains of sources with pertinent information. Of the two routes to power open to city Irish, Daley chose politics, Egan the Church. Even there they were not that different. Egan was freely referred to as a religious politician.

Psychologically, the two men who faced each other over Mayor Daley's desk that morning in October, 1958, were not unlike. Although the people in Bridgeport generally had the bad habit of badmouthing everyone, according to Len O'Connor, author of *Clout: Mayor Daley and His City*, close-mouthed Daley did not indulge in this neighbor- hood practice. Rather, he "was eager to please everyone and seemed keen to learn whatever anyone else might teach him." These were also determining qualities in Jack Egan. Both men were studious and applied themselves to any task they were assigned. Bridgeport, according to O'Connor, saw Daley as trustworthy and not too smart, not a heavy drinker or a big talker, and eager to be fair to one and all.

Mayor Daley was only three years into his regime as "duh mare." He'd first been elected April 5, 1955. He was still consolidating the power that the election theoretically gave him. This meant juggling all the possible power centers. With the resolution of the urban renewal vote in the council, the mayor had taken care of the university for the time. He could afford to be gracious. "You fought a good fight, Monsignor," Mayor Richard J. Daley assured Monsignor Egan from behind his impressive desk that October morning. "I know your side was defeated, but I promise you your voice was heard. We will put in a decent relocation program for the people. I promise you that there will be at least 200 units of housing for the poor in Hyde Park." There was no doubt in Father Egan's mind that Mayor Daley was most sincere. "But neither one of those things happened. The University of Chicago and the Board of Trustees of the University of Chicago were just too powerful."

Already, as Mayor Daley was taking his measure, Monsignor Egan was mulling mentally new strategies for confronting the city's power bases on social issues. When the first articles on the University of Chicago's urban renewal plans had appeared in the *New World*, Julian Levi had arranged a luncheon meeting of the local Protestant and Jewish clergy to suggest that they should "counteract the Catholic attack," according to Rossi and Dentler. "Partly growing out of this meeting and partly on his own initiative, Kenwood Rabbi Jacob Weinstein wrote an open letter, which the *Sun-Times* published, sharply criticizing the *New World*'s attack on the plan."

To Jack Egan, clergy of every faith should have been his natural allies in his testimony for housing for the city's poor. He resolved that he would never again go into public combat without the support of his fellow clergypersons. That wasn't his only misstep, he realized. He hadn't contacted the Catholic pastor of St. Thomas the Apostle Church who let it be known that he was disconcerted. "That pastor was absolutely right," Jack concedes. Jack had allowed himself to be separated from his natural constituency. He would not repeat that gaffe.

He'd learned enough about community organizing by this time to respect the power of coalition. If the voiceless in the city needed spokespersons until they could voice their own case at City Hall, he now knew how to produce them, how to concentrate on what people had in common, not what separated them. He would organize Chicago's religious leaders to articulate the concerns of the inarticulate. Jack Egan called both Rabbi Irving Rosenbaum, director of the Board of Rabbis, and Edgar H. S. Chandler, executive director of the Church Federation of Greater Chicago, directly after the City Council decision. He admits he sought out the other religious leaders because "I was hurting. God, you know, they (the urban renewal planners) finessed us."

Jack chose a meeting place in the lion's den, a restaurant across from St. Peter's Church on Madison Street where Mayor Daley attended Mass every morning. Jack Egan's blue eyes shine tinsel merry as he recalls the scene. "Rosenbaum and Chandler and I were eating our breakfast. This was the first meeting of the Interreligious Council on Urban Affairs. As we are going about our business, Mayor Daley goes by. He recognizes a few of us, 'Good morning, Rabbi, good morning, Monsignor,' and goes to the back table in the back room to have breakfast."

What did the interreligious coalition work on? "Everything," Jack Egan says. "Everything that was important for the city. Transportation, streets and highways. Race. Housing. Urban development." Much of their agenda grew out of the ferment of the times. Civil rights led the headlines as blacks in North and South risked their bodies to free their souls. Chicago had known racial segregation since the race riots of 1919 when Mayor Daley was seventeen and Jack Egan three. At that time there were 109,525 nonwhites in Chicago. Forty years later, when there were 519,437 nonwhites in the city, pressed into roughly the same territory, the pressure to explode was growing as fast as the population. The Interreligious Council on Urban Affairs plugged into the life of the city by supporting blacks struggling to gain their civil rights. They also worked to create neighborhood organizations in Chicago based on the Saul Alinsky principle that people rally around their own causes, their own needs, their own priorities.

Early in their association, Father Egan, Rabbi Rosenbaum and Edgar Chandler joined a large group integrating Rainbow Beach on Chicago's South Side, a beach tacitly understood to be off-limits to blacks. Jack Egan, who felt well protected by Chicago police, suffered more from the reaction from his fellow priests. "They had all sorts of comments.

'Why don't you mind your own business?' 'Did you wade in with them?' 'Did you get wet?' and all that damn baloney."

The Interreligious Council on Urban Affairs was financed by Chicago's three principal religious bodies. For each $2,000 contributed, a religious group had one representative on the board. Because the Catholic Church gave $24,000, they had a large contingent. The Protestant churches had an equal number, and the Jews had three representatives. With that funding the council could hire "three of the finest people" in the city, according to Father Egan: Kris Ronnow from Edgar Chandler's staff at the Church Federation, and Douglas Still and Stanley Hallett to assist Ronnow part time.

When the Most Reverend Albert Gregory Meyer, archbishop of Milwaukee, came to replace Cardinal Stritch as archbishop of Chicago, directly after the urban renewal hearings, he met with the Archdiocesan Conservation Council. It was Jack Egan's first meeting with the new archbishop, and "one of the most embarrassing days of my life." Two members of the Archdiocesan Conservation Council, "really, really took me to task in front of Archbishop Meyer. (Their attack) was vicious. It was brutal. It was personal." The two pastors complained that Jack Egan had embarrassed the Church in the archdiocese of Chicago by entering into a fight about the University of Chicago "when we had contact with Mr. James Downs, a member of the Board of Trustees, and we knew exactly what was happening." They protested that Egan had created a terrible controversy and made enemies for the Catholic Church in Hyde Park-Kenwood, even though "he didn't know what he was talking about." They suggested to the newly appointed archbishop that Egan "should have his wings clipped and be prevented from continuing" this sort of activity. Archbishop Meyer sat silent throughout the attack, thrust as he was into an internecine controversy he hardly understood. Later, when Archbishop Meyer had an opportunity, he asked Father Egan whether he had to get embroiled in any of the urban renewal controversy. "Absolutely not," Jack assured his new archbishop.

About this time, Saul Alinsky asked Jack Egan if he could go full-time into community organization work. The idea appealed to Jack. During his summers training with Alinsky and during the months he devoted his entire energy to the urban renewal battle, Fathers Walter Imbiorski and Larry Kelly had taken charge at the Cana Conference even though Jack was still technically the director. Now it was time to legitimate their ascendency. When Egan and Father Bill Quinn had taken on their jobs at Cana and Catholic Action in 1947, they'd made an informal pact to serve about ten years and then let younger men take over. "In those days all the jobs were filled with people who'd been in them years and years. We agreed we'd like to change that. Not only that, they were all Irishmen," Jack remembers.

When Jack Egan approached Archbishop Meyer about creating an Office of Urban Affairs to focus the Church's power on the problems of the city, the archbishop naturally asked, "What about Cana?" He knew Egan's national reputation as the innovative Chicago Cana director. Statistics in the Chicago area were startlingly high. By 1956 most of the 410 parishes in the archdiocese sponsored Cana Conferences. More than 39,000 married couples had attended 803 Conferences since 1944.

"I've been in it ten years and we've developed it all over the country," Jack said. Figures for 1956 showed that in twelve years Cana had spread to ninety-two dioceses in the United States, to Canada, France, Germany, Ireland, Australia, Japan, Malta, South America, and the Philippine Islands. Road show teams from Chicago had gone into many of the ninety-two U.S. dioceses to demonstrate a typical Cana and Pre-Cana Conference.

Almost 36,000 engaged couples had attended a four-session Pre-Cana Conference since 1946. An extra evening session provided information for parents of engaged couples. Cana also sponsored a weekly high school marriage course in twenty-eight Catholic high schools, a Lenten marriage series on dating and courtship, and a speaking service for colleges, Newman Clubs, seminaries, and other interested organizations. All this was accomplished by a small administrative staff augmented by a dynamic, self-starting, Egan-ized volunteer staff of sixty-eight priests, sixty-four doctors, thirty married couple speakers, and 112 couples to do the organizational work. In the 125 parishes where there were Christian Family Movement sections, those groups assisted the Cana staff.

Reassured by Father Egan that this important national marriage movement would continue to flourish in his absence, the archbishop questioned Jack about his replacement. "I think that Father Walter Imbiorski should take my place," Jack said. "Does he have seniority?" the archbishop asked. Father Egan explained that while Father Larry Kelly had been with the program longer, Father Imbiorski had such an entirely different style that he would bring fresh insights and agenda to marriage education. "Larry Kelly's style is just like mine. Besides," Jack added, "we don't have any Polish priests in charge of any agencies in the Archdiocese of Chicago."

Father Egan had made a tough choice because the two priests covering for him (with Cardinal Stritch's permission) both shared fully his dedication to the apostolate of the laity, his views on conjugal spirituality, and his energetic pursuit of any lead or person that could enhance any aspect of Cana. Each of them would have continued the kind of informal education Berenice O'Brien remembers receiving as a Cana board member. Other board members remember hearing Father Daniel Berrigan, Margaret Mead, Father Walter Ong, Father Gus Weigel (peritus at the Vatican Council), Sydney Callahan, Nancy Rambusch, Father Bernard Haring, and Michael Novak—any luminary who came through Chicago—talking to small Cana groups. And so it was arranged. Father Imbiorski came in as director of the Cana Conference, and Jack Egan headed up the innovative Office of Urban Affairs, the arm of the Church set up to put the arm on the city for the good of the powerless. Jack set up a mixed clergy/lay board including attorney Tom Foran, the future Bishop Aloysius J. Wycislo, and Sister Ann Ida Gannon, president of Mundelein College, "to state the position of the Church relative to housing, planning, urban renewal, and all the social issues. Saul and I began working very closely. We were very close to Archbishop Meyer."

Jack was scarcely into the work when he had a call from Bishop William E. McManus, superintendent of Chicago's parochial schools, on the first day of December. "There's a fire out at Our Lady of Angels," he told Jack, "and I think you should get out there." Monsignor Joseph F. Cussen had given Jack Egan a room on the third floor of Our Lady of Angels rectory. The location on the near West Side at Iowa and Hamlin Streets was convenient to Jack's downtown office.

"I put on my hat and coat and jumped in my car and followed one of the fire trucks racing out Chicago Avenue. I couldn't park within two blocks," Jack recalls. Archbishop Meyer—only two weeks since his installation—and the pastor, Monsignor Cussen, milled with the thousands of people jamming Avers Avenue. Parents were struggling with the police to get past them to the school doors. A nun inside the building was screaming, "We are trapped. We are trapped." Children were jumping from the second floor windows. Some had leaped toward firemen's ladders and missed, falling to ground already littered with children and soaked with blood. Other children were clinging to the ledges. Scores of onlookers fainted at what Fire Commissioner Robert Quinn called "the worst thing I have ever seen or ever will see." Battalion chiefs wept. "We tried. God, how we tried, but we couldn't move fast enough. No one could live in that fire."

Firemen were battling through the flames to bring out the victims. Parents searched frantically for their youngsters as firemen emptied the smoldering building built at 909 N. Avers Avenue in 1904, substantially expanded in 1911, and remodeled in 1951. The *Tribune* reporter described priests kneeling to give last rites "to canvas covered forms which were once children." He described a desperate young father yelling at his wife, "Why didn't you tell her to stay home today?"

Tales of heroism were many. An eleven-year-old mourned his teacher Sister St. Canice, who struggled to get her students out the second story window. "She helped me onto a ladder there," Thomas Handschiegel told a *Tribune* reporter. "The last I saw of her was when she went back into the room and disappeared into the smoke. I think she could have gotten out, but she stayed to help the kids." A nun who wouldn't identify herself to the reporter made six trips into the building to lead out groups of sixth and seventh graders. She rolled some of her students down the stairs to get them out quickly.

The priests from the rectory had run to save the children at the first alarm. Father Joseph Ognibene, who'd been in the parish ten years and knew many of the children well, was part of a chain of rescuers. A father who'd heard girls shouting, "Save me, save me," straddled an open window from which he lowered the girls, one by one, through the window five feet down to a ledge above the school entrance. There Father Ognibene and another parent grabbed them and pulled them to safety. A neighbor who heard a priest yell, "There's children in there. It's on fire," made six trips in to lead children out until the smoke and flames made it impossible to enter. Later, a reporter saw Father Ognibene, near collapse, at the morgue trying to recognize the bodies of the children he knew so well.

"It wasn't a great fire," Jack Egan remembers, "but the smoke was unbelievable. The fire equipment was poor. The ladders didn't reach to the second floor. The children suffocated." Father Egan accompanied a fireman into a schoolroom where forty-four children sat in parochial school decorum, at their seats, heads in hands—dead. And at the front of the room, her head in her hands, sat their teacher, like the children—erect, disciplined and dead. As Jack Egan reconstructed their last minutes, "A lot of nuns asked children to sit there and pray. I'll never forget it. Everything perfectly orderly."

The fire had erupted at 2:40 p.m., only twenty minutes before the children would have been dismissed for the day. The alarm went in at 2:42. Fire trucks were on Avers within three minutes. But smoke engulfed the second floor so quickly—the firemen called the accumulation of smoke, heat and flames that coursed through the hall when doors and windows were opened "a hot box"—that three Sisters of Charity of the Blessed Virgin Mary and ninety-two children died. Seventy-six children were injured. The school was almost completely destroyed. "I have to admit it," Father Egan says, describing the firemen carrying child after child out, "I was relieved when they carried the body of a nun out. They carried three out. It would have been a greater tragedy if no nuns had died along with their students."

The whole city mourned, every citizen able to put him/herself into the position of the parents who had sent bright, lively, uniformed children to learn about the exports of Egypt that morning and now would never oversee another page of their scribbled homework. Chicagoans read about Mayor Daley's arrival at the scene, about Archbishop Meyer's visits to the injured at St. Anne's Hospital, and about the drab, yellow brick building at 1828 Polk where "three hundred mothers and fathers huddled in stricken groups or, crazed with grief, roamed the corridors trying to buttonhole hurrying attendants" at the county morgue.

Priests and Sisters from all parts of the city quickly gathered at the scene. "Thank God I was able to keep my composure," Father Egan says today, "and thank God for the priests and Sisters of the archdiocese of Chicago. As the firemen put each child into each ambulance, I put a priest or a Sister with the child. 'You stay with that child and you stay with that family,' I said."

Jack was firm with each of the religious, understanding the stress under which each of them was operating. "This is your family," he would stress with each one. "Now pay attention to me. You visit the hospital. You go to the wake. You sit with the family. You go to the funeral with them. You come back with them and then you visit them and visit them and visit them. You are their personal chaplain." He followed the same routine with the families of injured children. "I think that helped the grieving parents."

Both Fathers Egan and Joseph Fitzgerald quit their jobs and stayed at Our Lady of the Angels for the next month. "We worked morning, noon, and night," Egan recalls. Archbishop Meyer celebrated a Solemn Pontifical Mass for twenty-seven of the fire victims on December 5 at the Northwest Armory at North Avenue and Kedzie. Funeral Masses continued throughout the day in other churches of the archdiocese for the remaining victims of the fire.

Archbishop Meyer did his best to solace the grieving parents and relatives. He was comforted in turn by a little man from New York. As priests vested for the funeral Mass at the armory, Father Egan saw Francis Cardinal Spellman come up to the archbishop, holding out his hands. The archbishop looked down with gratitude at the fellow religious who'd come to his side in this time of greatest need. The two most powerful prelates in the American Church embraced.

12

"United We Stand, Divided We Fall"

Saul Alinsky and Jack Egan sat facing each other across a table at the Erie Cafe, a favorite hangout of Saul's, tossing out ideas like shuttlecocks, the contest electric enough for waitresses to take notice. "Egan and Alinsky beat each other up," community organizer Tom Gaudette recalls. "The waiters and waitresses used to stand there and watch these two great minds going at each other."

Gaudette saw Egan and Alinsky as insightful foils for each other. "Egan could see the motivation, the reason, the why we should do something." Saul Alinsky could see the how. "So he and Saul were a great team. When they got together it was marvelous." Gaudette struggles to capture the intense respect the two men had for each other. "Saul just loved Egan, loved him as a priest. 'Now there's a priest,' Saul would say, and then add, 'If you ever tell Egan I said that, I'll fire you.' Because Saul knew what a priest was! 'But there's so few of them around,' he'd say. That's why he admired Egan."

For Gaudette, to see Egan say Mass was an event, "so exciting when he gets up there and preaches. He makes the Mass a whole different thing, an experience, alive and real. You go to Mass all the time, it's so boring. Egan would talk (at Mass) about our common goals. It was marvelous. But that was the atmosphere." The beauty of Egan's life, for Gaudette, was his ability to "do both worlds." He cites Egan training seminarians. "I remember meetings we had at the cathedral every Friday night for months for priests, seminarians, or whoever. It was a very exciting atmosphere where some great people would just take your head and turn it around. That's where you met all the great people in Chicago. Egan created that."

Both Egan and Alinsky had a talent for drawing people out. Jack Egan had spent his life uncovering the action by intense and interested queries. Alinsky had a similar gut-deep interest in how people's lives

121

worked, how they related, how they could be hurt, how they could be helped. Now, the masters of the art practiced on each other at the Erie Cafe. As joyously as they resonated with the badinage, however, these were serious men. Having done their homework—Alinsky always insisted on that—they had a good fix on their mutual concern: how serious was the city's peril, how could they help.

Alinsky and Egan fit each other like a river fits its banks. If they fascinated each other, it was productively, in the way a Benedictine nun described years later. Sister Mary Benet McKinney heard on retreat that "we get faith from people who fascinate us," She wrote Jack, whom she found fascinating, about how he gave her faith. "I know that most of all, it is your grounded, consistent commitment to the people of God. Your belief in the Incarnate Word, present in all people, is touchable. It is surely that faith of yours, so obviously alive in your ministry, your relationships, your care, that has given me, over the many years that I have known you, a stronger and more viable faith."

Surprisingly, Saul Alinsky, a non-practicing Jew whose parents were Orthodox Russian immigrants, felt that same way about Father Egan. Alinsky's desire to help the little guy was reinforced by Father Egan's priestly vocation calling him to the same purpose.

They shared also a reliance on the leap of imagination. In Alinsky's veins ran the same Russian blood as the religious thinker Nikolai Berdyaev who taught in the early part of the century that God sent us Christ to make us more creative. For Berdyaev, truth was found through penetration of the environment by a creative act, "a light which breaks through from the transcendent world of the spirit." He saw man's greatness in his divine capacity to create.

Alinsky, in that same spirit described by Berdyaev, insisted his organizers be creative. Creative, inspirational, and funny. And this is what their allies in community development saw in Alinsky and Egan: creative imaginations able to conceive of a better future for the people in the city's neighborhoods. They saw ways to change neighborhoods of which others despaired. At a surface level, it was clear how Alinsky and Egan benefitted each other. Egan was Alinsky's funnel to the archdiocesan money bags. Alinsky was the archdiocese's handle on how to organize neighborhood communities facing societal change.

At a more profound level, Saul Alinsky and Jack Egan fed each others' deep needs to be known and accepted as persons. They could be honest with one another. As Tom Gaudette says of Alinsky, "I've never known anyone so honest as Saul. As a result you were honest with him. There were no secrets in his life. You never had any secrets from him." Alinsky and Egan shared as well their need "to keep the poor from being kicked around." In that they had powerful allies in Cardinal Stritch; after him, Archbishop Meyer; the chancellor, Monsignor Edward Burke, and the vicar general, Monsignor George Casey. These men saw very clearly that Chicago was at risk from the simmering confrontation between blacks and whites. In 1946 Cardinal Stritch made a strong commitment to the Chicago Commission on Human Relations "that the Catholic Churches of this city are open to Catholics from all minority groups and that this held for the parochial schools attached to the parishes." He directed the priests of the suburb of Cicero to deliver sermons on the equality of all men and property rights. He counseled parishioners in changing parishes to stay and welcome their new neighbors.

Archdiocesan leaders hoped that Saul Alinsky and his organizers could somehow modulate the population shifts taking place at a disruptive rate. They knew they couldn't stop the changes. What they hoped for was the integration of black Chicagoans into formerly all-white parishes without violence. They wanted to see the outflow of Chicagoans to the suburbs stemmed—for the good of the city and the good of the parishes.

They understood how limited were their powers. In the 1950s, a Chicago block a week was going from white to black. Churches were no longer anchors to security for parishioners. Perhaps they could be sources of generous response to the changes. The only route even the visionary Alinsky could see to integration was a quota system. "A lot of people didn't like Saul because they thought he was an integrationist," Tom Gaudette says. Alinsky was hard, dogmatic, but he wasn't hardnosed. He appreciated how aggravating it was for ethnics to live with blacks. Gaudette couldn't imagine Saul saying, "You must do this." Saul "related to people gently. He had great respect for suffering people, great respect for people who disagreed with him, but if you were a wise guy . . . wise guys got it right back. Such a nervy guy, so gutsy: he illuminated life."

Alinsky saw his quota scheme working several ways. He thought whites might accept the quota if they were guaranteed that black population would not exceed five percent in a neighborhood. Another possibility was contiguous white and black neighborhood organizations set up to work together. Their mutual leadership could negotiate agreements on such issues as housing sales and rentals. Sanford Horwitt explains, "Each organization would have accumulated enough power, (Alinsky) theorized, to be able to control real estate and mortgage lending practices, which had so much to do with the stability—or lack of it—in traditional communities."

The enemies were the panic peddlers, "block-busters." Jack Egan describes them coming into a community like Presentation Parish after the first blacks bought there. "Panic peddlers would buy up a house worth $20,000 for $15,000. A week later they'd sell it for $26,000 to someone who couldn't get a mortgage. And had to buy it on contract." Contract buyers often paid exorbitant interest; they didn't own their houses until the last payment. Many contract buyers lost their homes to see them resold to other hapless victims. It was an ugly system. The seller was taken. The buyer was taken. The community was taken.

If community organizations could work together to stem blockbusting and contract buying, everybody would benefit. Parishes all over the South Side were hurting. Where to begin? There was some interest in organizing the Grand Boulevard area where Jack Egan had trained with Saul Alinsky. That would have used Alinsky's template for two contiguous communities, Grand Boulevard and Back of the Yards, one white, one black, working together to solve local problems. Saul Alinsky had organized the white Back of the Yards Neighborhood Council—he was famous for doing it—in the thirties with the help of Joseph Meegan, Alinsky's first organizer; Bishop Bernard Sheil, and the young curates in the BYNC parishes.

Having first-hand experience of South Side neighborhoods from his training experience, Jack Egan dreamed of developing three neighborhood organizations: one in a changing neighborhood, one in a black neighborhood, and one in an ethnic neighborhood. His choice of where to move first was influenced by Monsignor John McMahon at St. Sabina's, "a man who should go down in history as a great priest," according to Father Egan. "He was totally opposed to white neighborhood councils whose only purpose was to keep blacks out of the neighborhood. He wanted to develop a parish where all colors would live in peace."

Monsignor McMahon had already experienced the trauma of seeing his parish of St. Charles Borromeo change from a totally white parish to a totally black parish, although, by working at it, the parish kept the parochial school integrated for two decades. This time he wanted to keep his church and school permanently integrated. "It had been a painful experience for this genteel and gracious man to be engulfed and overwhelmed by an outpouring of racial hatred," Sanford Horwitt writes in *Let Them Call Me Rebel*. Looking for a strategy to prevent a similarly horrendous racial confrontation, Monsignor McMahon talked to Father Egan about neighborhood organization. He talked to Monsignor Vincent Cooke at Catholic Charities about money. He talked to his neighboring pastors about the dilemma of saving their parishes.

Alinsky agreed to develop his first community organization in Chicago in twenty years on the Southwest Side, home of Monsignor McMahon and the autocratic Monsignor Patrick Molloy, whom Jack Egan describes as a "rough and tumble boxer, friend of mobsters, foe of integration, hard-working, two-fisted pastor, friend of Archbishop O'Brien and Mayor Daley." Also a hot-rodder on Emerald Avenue when it was game time at Comiskey Park.

Father Tom McDonough, chaplain of the Calvert Club at the University of Chicago, had taken Father Egan to Florida for some much-needed recuperation after the Our Lady of the Angels fire. Walking and praying through the tragedy. with the mourning families had taken a monstrous toll on the priests involved. "Monsignor Cussen, poor man, never recovered," Father Egan recalls. "He just sat in his rocker and rocked away the rest of his life."

Thanks to McDonough, Jack Egan was ready to participate when Alinsky organizers Nicholas von Hoffman, Ed Chambers, and Joe Vilimas began studying the possibilities for an Organization for the Southwest Community in January, 1959. Egan was Alinsky's liaison to the pastors, vital because he could get their support and bring in the necessary money. "Saul had a fixed rule," Father Egan recalls. "He insisted that the money for a three-year operation be in the bank prior to the first organizing steps. Once the people begin to take sides, and once political pressure comes in on forces that are offering the money, very few people can withstand the pressure. Not only did the Catholic Church contribute to the Organization for the Southwest Community but also Protestant churches, particularly the Presbyterian, and a few foundations."

The organizers' first goal was to set up a neighborhood congress, as inclusive as possible. A congress of delegates from church groups, social and fraternal clubs, neighborhood associations, and local businesses would have status and legitimacy when it adopted a program, elected leaders, and wrote a constitution. Saul Alinsky had done this successfully in Back of the Yards. That neighborhood organization had empowered the people to change conditions in their neighborhood in ways they themselves wanted them changed. This was the hope for the Organization for the Southwest Community. The young Chambers, as an ex-seminarian, was charged with studying the Protestant churches on the Southwest Side, the way Egan and Hunt had studied the Grand Boulevard area only three years before.

The three organizers worked an area fifty blocks long and thirty blocks wide bounded by Sixty-seventh Street, State Street, the city limits, and Western Avenue. They found the bulk of the people moderate in their views and content with the present condition of their neighborhoods. Offsetting the moderates were a passel of ultraconservatives (whose goal was to keep blacks out) and a cluster of liberals who wanted blacks in, integrated in. Von Hoffman and Vilimas slowly gained the confidence of potential allies at the big Catholic parishes, even people who had to be converted like the redoubtable Monsignor Molloy at St. Leo's.

In the spring of 1959, preliminary contacts made, the organizers called together three hundred community leaders from eighty organizations to the Park Manor VFW hall to form the Provisional Organization of Southwest Communities (POSC). There were Catholic pastors there, including Monsignors Patrick Molloy and John McMahon, and a dozen Protestant ministers. There were also representatives from civic and fraternal organizations, and business people in the neighborhood. Each of them had a stake in Saul Alinsky's vision of blacks of a similar class moving into their neighborhoods and being accepted by their parishioners and members and customers.

As the provisional organization worked to stop blockbusting, Egan had a hand in the proceedings. In addition to the liaison he provided from the archdiocese to Southwest Side pastors, he filled in where asked, accepting such responsibilities as reading the cardinal's statement on housing discrimination at hearings of the president's Commission on Civil Rights. Notre Dame's Father Theodore Hesburgh, whom Jack Egan knew from their mutual association with Catholic Action activities, presided at the hearings as the commission's chairperson, listening to witnesses' assessments of discrimination in Chicago.

Chicago neighborhoods were tense with apprehension and the vague need to ascribe blame for what was really simply the city's demographics. The cardinal's statement Jack read did not mention quotas, although Alinsky's did. Even so, the two statements were associated in people's minds (Nick von Hoffman had written them both), and the cardinal was tarred with Alinsky's brush. Reaction from people hungry for a scapegoat was negative and dramatic. Groups such as *We the People* red-baited Saul Alinsky, ignoring his close ties with the Catholic Church. They illogically assumed, or artfully affected to believe, that anyone in favor of any form of integration was a Communist. They asked why the cardinal was abetting a Saul Alinsky?

All through the summer and early fall Alinsky's organizers worked with the Provisional Organization of Southwest Communities to bring participants into the founding convention they were planning for October 24, 1959.

When the beautiful October day came, businessmen and clergymen, union members and bank presidents, blacks and whites surged through the school doors. Shortly after three o'clock that afternoon, there were more than 1,000 delegates packed in the auditorium of Calumet High School: 104 delegates from civic associations, churches, labor unions, neighborhood organizations, and businesses. It was a triumph of organization, especially because it included a delegation from a black Methodist church. The delegates worked until midnight to ratify a constitution, elect officers, and adopt their program. Jack Egan, in the back of the school auditorium watching the unlikely combination of confederates side by side, tingled with hope and pride and humility. It was "one of the thrills of my life," he says, to witness this experiment in democracy engineered by his Alinsky connections and accepted by such disparate pastors as Patrick Molloy and John McMahon. Seeing this outpouring of concern and cooperation, he allowed himself the momentary fancy of a deep dream of peace in the Southwest area of the city as local banker Donald O'Toole was elected OSC president and Monsignor McMahon an OSC vice-president.

During its first year the Organization for the Southwest Community educated its members in four areas: changing neighborhoods, civil rights, block busting, and real estate practices. When they held meetings on these controversial issues in preparation for their first anniversary, speakers represented a wide spectrum: the Church Federation of

Greater Chicago, the Chicago Urban League, and the Chicago Archdiocese.

When the Resolutions committee met, chairman Peter Fitzpatrick announced it was time "to get down to business and come up with a program the community can stand on." The group heard strong pleas for racial equality and an end to discrimination against blacks seeking to move into white neighborhoods. There were few dissenting voices when members were asked to keep an open door policy with regard to blacks and to demand that local business owners hire employees on the basis of ability alone, without regard to race, creed, or national origin.

The chairman of the real estate practices committee asked support for a six-point program to pinpoint the minority segment of real estate dealers who profited from their exploitation of neighborhood changes. Jack Egan strongly applauded the proposed code of ethics the committee wanted real estate dealers to sign, agreeing it should be implemented to the letter.

The Organization for the Southwest Community was an energetic and valiant rear-ditch effort to stem developments demographics made inevitable. But it couldn't hold the people in the neighborhoods (although it did have other good effects) once Saul Alinsky pulled out his trained organizers. As Jack Egan says, "The first convention is always dramatic, magnificent. This was the first time a black church was represented in an area where so many people were racist. It was a great victory for Monsignor McMahon. Unfortunately, the Organization for the Southwest Community needed a top-notch organizer to keep that thing moving. Saul did a disastrous thing in pulling his two key organizers out of OSC shortly after the first convention.

"The organization fell apart. The neighborhood didn't have the strong leaders to integrate the community. There was no one to evaluate and train the leaders they had. White people were panicked by the real estate people, and there was no force to prevent real estate people from panicking them. Putting up a For Sale sign down the block. Telling people, 'If you don't get out now, you won't be able to sell your house.'"

There were bitter days. Monsignor McMahon, considered saintly by many in the neighborhood, carefully visited every black family that moved into his parish and welcomed each child into the parish school. The majority of his white parishioners loyally held on to their homes until a seventeen-year-old white boy was shot at Seventy-eighth and Racine Avenue as he was talking with his friends across the street from St. Sabina's community center. A black boy held the gun.

It is hard to see how any Alinsky organizing team could have held the parish together once everyone's subliminal nightmare was played out on Seventy-eighth Street. Immediately, families began to look for new homes, a thousand in 1965, another thousand in 1966. As Monsignor John McMahon, who'd given his life for his people, told Jack Egan, "The saddest thing that ever happened to me, Jack, was having my finest parishioners move out in the night without ever saying goodbye." Jack Egan shakes his head and grieves, "It broke his heart."

As Monsignor Harry Koenig summed up the situation in the archdiocesan history of Monsignor Molloy's St. Leo the Great Church, "The parish was caught in a web of hatred, tension, frustration, and misunderstanding. Unscrupulous real estate agents used 'blockbusting' tactics to pressure whites to sell their homes. These buildings were resold to black families at inflated prices." Twenty years later, St. Leo the Great was a flourishing black parish. Of the 700 registered families in 1978, 350 had close ties to the parish school where 550 students were enrolled.

A fringe benefit salvaged from the OSC work was increased understanding and regard between clergypersons. Methodist minister Jim Reed told Alinsky biographer Sandy Horwitt that he would say "that was the first time I had a sense of Protestant and Catholic clergy actually sitting down together and talking about issues." Reflecting attitudes from the past, some Presbyterians warned one of the ministers he "could be defrocked" for working with Saul Alinsky and his Catholic allies. He gamely took that chance. Cardinal Meyer (he was raised to the red hat November 16, 1959, a year to the day after he was installed as archbishop) risked unrest in his church when he told pastors of Roman Catholic parishes in the OSC area, "United we stand, divided we fall."

The risk paid off ecumenically. The Organization for the Southwest Community failed its main goal of integrating the community. Yet it tempered the bitterness of inevitable change. It also convinced many clergypersons that they could work profitably together, a change no one would have called inevitable. This could have had enormous effect in a city where people so identified with their churches if only church members had kept pace with their leaders—and death hadn't intervened as it did so tragically in just a few years.

Before that disappointing denouement, the Interreligious Council on Urban Affairs, that Jack Egan initiated under the nose of Mayor Daley, united in 1959 to expose the city's failure to house its people adequately. More than 250 rabbis and other clergymen met at the Saddle and Sirloin Club to plan a city-wide conference on "Religion, Community Life, and Chicago's Housing."

Mayor Richard M. Daley, as luncheon speaker, defended Chicago as "one of the nation's leaders in the rebuilding of its city." Not true, insisted the religious leaders. Jack Egan boldly countered the mayor's chauvinism by describing some neighborhoods as "eaten away with physical deterioration because, among other things, the building department lacks an imaginative and forceful policy and because our municipal courts, with a few notable exceptions, treat the pernicious slum landlords with gentle continuances and petty fines."

Dr. Alvin Pitcher of the federated theological faculty of the University of Chicago, agreed. He told morning sessions that the Chicago City Council, the Chicago Housing Authority, the Chicago Dwellings Association, the Community Conservation Board, and the Land Clearance Commission had "not provided the needed leadership." He was very strong in his condemnation, saying that "we have permitted the situation to drift without leadership to a point where we are sitting on a keg of dynamite." Rabbi Jacob Weinstein stoutly warned that clergypersons must take the leadership in inducing members of their congregations to remain and help their Chicago neighborhoods instead of fleeing to the suburbs.

It would be hard to recapture now the lightheadedness members of the clergy experienced when the walls between churches were breached in the 1960s. Four years before, the gently restrained Cardinal Stritch pecked at his typewriter in his imposing, multi-chimneyed residence on North State Parkway, choosing the appropriate words to forbid any Roman Catholic from attending meetings of the World Council of Churches in nearby Evanston. Now his successor was telling public meetings how important was "the need to work and cooperate with churches of other faiths in regard to problems affecting the welfare of all."

Here was a major shift. Here was reward for disappointment toler-
ated and frustration swallowed. There were many clergy who risked
their theology, their sociology, their brave new hearts, their bracing
dedication (Saul Alinsky said of ministers he trained, "They burn with a
pure white flame.") on this common cause. They shared in the marvelous enterprise Jack Egan calls "the Golden Age of community organizing."

They did not achieve the impossible goals they set for making
straight the topsy-turvy ways of their city. Too many indigestible lumps
had been added to its boiling civic broth as one immigrant group after
another pushed on its predecessors. But none of those clergypersons has
forgotten the esprit de corps that made it wonderful to wake up in the
morning during those hopeful, frenetic, stormy, baffling—and exalted—
days.

13

"Jack Was Starting Everybody's Fire"

If the Church is the Mystical Body, as St. Paul taught—"And you are Christ's body, organs of it depending on each other"—some people would class Jack Egan as the endorphins. Like those chemicals in the blood that give runners their high, he gets into people's blood and provokes euphoria and change.

For transplanted Chicagoan Nina Polcyn Moore, Father Egan was such an agent of change. She first felt this force in him in 1955 when her boss, Archbishop Bernard J. Sheil, peremptorily resigned as head of the large assortment of enterprises he controlled under the umbrella of the CYO (Catholic Youth Organization). Nina was connected to the bishop's Sheil School. She'd been hired away from her Milwaukee schoolteaching in 1942 by the founder of Friendship House (and friend of the bishop), Baroness Catherine de Hueck. Recruiting apostolic types for the bishop, the Baroness invited Nina to Chicago "to change the world," in the no-small-plans parlance of the apostolates. She was to be assistant director of the bishop's adult education effort. In time, Nina had slipped over to the other cultural arm of the CYO, St. Benet's Library and Book Shop. The storied atmosphere there was more to her liking.

"I was vastly more interested in the St. Benet operation than in the Sheil School," Nina says. She saw at St. Benet's "tremendous possibilities, the germ, the gem of an idea that could blossom out into a cultural oasis, something that could vivify what was happening in the Church world."

In the fruit-basket-upset following Sheil's resignation, Cardinal Stritch and his officers at the chancery office sorted out the many parts of Bishop Sheil's empire. Monsignor Edward J. Kelly was responsible

132

for the disposition of St. Benet's. Kelly—"a priest who wore white socks," according to Nina—was a "very practical man who in this instance proved his impracticality," according to Jack Egan. Approached by Jack, he agreed that Nina Polcyn should have St. Benet's "so long as she keeps the rental library operating." Jack was "dumfounded, speechless, because within that store there was at least $25,000 to $45,000 worth of merchandise." And it was Nina's—lock, stock and book inventory.

The lending library was widely cherished as a resource for Chicago's Catholic community. First organized in her bedroom at a South Side residential hotel by St. Benet founder Sara Benedicta O'Neill, it might have passed for the cultural bargain of the century even by the Depression standards of its beginnings. "A card issued by Miss O'Neill cost twenty-five cents," according to Nina Polcyn, "and you could take out books for life." Nina assesses Miss O'Neill's business arrangements as "totally unrealistic but beautifully generous."

Card in hand, any comer was welcomed to a bookshop haunted by Catholic writers Chesterton, Belloc, Mauriac, Greene, and Nina's friends Dorothy Day (with whom she went to the Soviet Union), and Peter Maurin, as well as the French authors who told stories of worker priests and lay apostles. "We thought we were quite liberal to be carrying the complete Mauriac, Waugh, and Graham Greene. And we had a good laugh when one of our readers felt these books should be made available only to qualified members of the Altar and Rosary sodalities. At St. Benet's every day was a rich adventure."

Today magazine called the shop the Chicago Catholic counterpart of Ciro's or the Stork Club, New York centers for people-in-the-know: "If you want to meet anyone active in the apostolate—whether it be Father Reinhold who hails from the state of Washington or Maisie Sheed, a New Yorker, or England's Donald Attwater or just a girl who has found her apostolate jerking sodas at Walgreen's—the thing to do is camp at St. Benet's." It was a pleasant thing to do. As well as a clearing house, St. Benet's was the place to track what was avant-garde in Catholic Chicago, where to find the classical Tenebrae service, the best Easter vigil, the most astute confessor, the latest in the liturgy. Catholic novelist Joe Dever dropped in daily. "At the height of the Thomas Merton trend," Nina recalls, "he'd shout loudly at the door, 'Got any *Seeds of Concupiscence*?'"

Over the years, benefactors charmed by Miss O'Neill's discriminating contribution to the intellectual respectability of the city's Catholic population, including Bishop Sheil, upgraded her location several times. As the operation grew more sophisticated, Miss O'Neill gave over the book shop to Bishop Sheil to run as part of the Sheil School. He paid the (meager) salaries. She poured the tea and bought the books.

When Jack Egan engineered Nina's takeover, he gave her the keys to 300 South Wabash, a corner location with considerable potential. He then waved his plenipotentiary wand to turn her into "merchant princess and trafficker in crucifixes," in her words. As he had a vision for the Church and for the city, Jack Egan had a vision for St. Benet's as a "jewel box" from whose cache the people in the movements could draw the support and sustenance of the best of Catholic literature and art. The shop was an actual physical haven for traveling Catholic eminences caught between trains at a time when every cross-country traveler had to change trains in the City of the Big Shoulders. Sara O'Neill, in her day, cosseted patrons with tea on Saturday afternoons (or thimble-sized glasses of Benedictine brandy and "high-class crackers" in the back room for "visiting firemen of note"), community Compline, and the chance to join her weekly Saturday evening dinner group at the Congress Hotel—Dutch treat.

To fortify the hesitant, idealistic young Nina Polcyn's ability to build on the success of Sara Benedicta O'Neill, Jack Egan rallied a top-flight board of trustees, including Cana board president Art Schaefer and early board member Bob Podesta; CFM pioneer John Clark; Jim Tobin, president of Wieboldt's Department Store; Jack's lawyer friend Jim O'Shaughnessy; banker Roy Andersen, and an advertising man. Jack served as board chairperson. Explaining the high quality of the board members' experience, Nina shrugs. "Jack knew everybody who could do anything," she says, adding, "You could see the fine Italian hand of whatever the Cana Conference or CFM had been in people's lives" in their willingness to use their talents for whatever was asked of them.

It didn't surprise Nina that Jack organized her board out of his cassock pocket, so to speak. "Jack is a real renaissance man," Nina says. "It wasn't enough for him to have just the Cana Conference. He liked nothing better than a new challenge: a fresh file in a fresh folder in a fresh filing cabinet."

The operation showed Jack Egan, in Nina's words, "as a negotiator par excellence, behind the scenes, in front of the scenes, next door and next week." Generous: he engineered the archdiocese's bequest of a going enterprise. Feminist: he advocated a woman owner instead of a woman managing an archdiocesan enterprise. Gregarious: he drew on his wide-ranging acquaintances to arrange a top-of-the-form board of trustees. Enthusiastic: he believed in the shop's potential and Nina's competence. Far-seeing: he knew the importance of an intellectual base for the development of the Church in Chicago.

With Nina and St. Benet's preserved, he'd secured "the thrill of the browse," in Nina's phrase, for the movement people. For her he provided his enthusiasm and his belief that she could do the job. Like Peg Burke in the early CFM group Jack chaplained, however, Nina was aware that Jack expected her to produce quid for his quo. She was required to perform. As she puts it pointedly, "Jack kept a stiletto to my spine." Every meeting of the board was an assessment of her effectiveness.

"If Jack was peddling this vision abroad," she reflects, scrambling her fairy tales, "like Little Red Riding Hood leaving breadcrumbs along the way, you better pick them up because otherwise you're going to be dead, friend. That's his style." If you produced, so did Jack. The Lord Mayor of Dublin addressed the crowd at the gala opening of Nina's St. Benet's. Asked how she lured a lord mayor to her tiny bookstore, Nina waves her hand like a wand. "You know Jack Egan. Three phone calls and the Lord Mayor came."

A reader of books, a giver of books, a believer in books, Jack Egan wanted St. Benet's to succeed. Remembering the intensity of his involvement, Nina reviews the list of people Jack Egan started on their way from the fifteen-year-old Pat Hollahan Judge to Cana chaircouple Art and Virginia Schaefer. "You have to get a vision someplace, you have to get on fire, you have to get ignited to change the face of the earth." From Nina's point of view, Jack "was starting everybody's fire. That's the way he was. You couldn't not do it." As his network grew, he had more people to call on, like the board members he collected for Nina. Whoever he was with, "he would learn from that person." Then he would also "use that person," in the sense that he considered anyone he met a contact, should he need their expertise. Nina stipulates that she doesn't mean "use" in a pejorative sense when she says it of Jack's operation. "People wanted to be useful to him."

Not everybody felt that way. British priest John Fitzsimons, in noting the same quality in Jack, called it manipulation. He suggested that some people would say that Jack was a manipulator admiringly. Others "would say it meanly." He said it with admiration.

Asked if Jack Egan had ever manipulated him, Father Fitzsimons answered quickly, "Oh, no." Then he thought back and smiled wryly, "At least I don't think so. That's the subtlety of it. You're anesthetized." He explained the mechanism of that anesthetization. "One way, after a time you so respect him as an operator that you say to yourself, 'That must be the best way; Jack knows.' The other is, he will add a bit of flattery so you think if I do this, I will please Jack, so you do it."

Father Fitzsimons would have agreed that Jack Egan never shied away from change as many contemporaries in the Church did. Rather, he galvanized it. In the early 1960s, change was the coin of the realm, hope the currency of movers and shakers. John Kennedy in the White House was drawing on young people's idealism to lure them to the Peace Corps. Pope John XXIII was opening a window to give the Holy Spirit a chance to blow out some of the calcified curial cobwebs holding back modulations in the Church's course. Adam Clayton Powell was organizing the blacks in Harlem to improve their working conditions. Religious people of all faiths shared a sense that they could be part of the changes fumbling for expression.

For his part, Jack Egan was pressing out from his new base as head of the archdiocesan Office of Urban Affairs into Protestant circles, Jewish circles, black circles, community organizations. He drew into those circles people from his own Church who'd been marking time, scrabbling for ways to spark changes they saw necessary. As at Cana, some of the people he drew in were lay, some clerical. Many were nuns. The mixed board of activists he chose for the Office of Urban Affairs were people ready to experience change even as they tried to effect it.

They, in turn, affected others. Groups of laypeople and Sisters formed. Jack Egan was instrumental in helping Sister Mary William, a Daughter of Charity at Marillac House, and Benedictine Sister Mary Benet McKinney organize the Urban Apostolate of the Sisters to train and support fellow religious in their difficult job of teaching and ministering in the inner city. Sister Mary Benet caught the spirit of those changing times—and changing Sisters—when she described a very young, beautiful Holy Family of Nazareth Sister, "in full habit as most of us were in those days, wide-eyed, eager, discovering a whole new world." For this young Sister, the new world was the Organization for the Southwest Community.

One afternoon, Sister Mary Benet was meeting with ten or twelve women who'd been in community organization for about six months to find out what problems they'd encountered, what support they needed. "We sat in a circle," she remembers. "The question was very simply put to them: 'How are you feeling about the six months of working on the street?'"

When the question got to the young Holy Family of Nazareth Sister, Sister Benet recalls how totally alive she looked, eyes sparkling, cheeks aglow. "Well," she said, "it has really been something! I have gone from a community where our motto is 'Oh, my Jesus, all for thee' to this community where the motto is, 'We don't take no shit from no one.'"

Somehow that remark captured the reality of the city. So long as that Sister, and hundreds like her, quietly plied flash cards before first graders, they were no threat to the status quo. Once they confronted the trauma their first-graders faced on the streets, the Sisters menaced the city's tranquillity as surely as Martin Luther King, Jr., disturbed the peace of the racists in the South. For what those Sisters were trying to do was empower the powerless of the city.

If blacks had no power in Chicago, they also had no history in Chicago. At least as far as the power structure was concerned. Newspaper men of that era routinely screened out stories about blacks. Black accomplishments were not news any more than black deaths were. Even as their numbers increased they remained invisible—in Ralph Ellison's sense—to city residents. In 1910 they lived in thirteen of the city's thirty-five wards, their highest concentration even then in the Second and Third Wards between Twenty-second and Thirty-ninth Streets and from State Street east to the lake. As the black population increased from 44,103 in 1910 to 233,903 in 1930, the Black Belt firmed up: Thirty-first Street to Fifty-fifth Street along State Street and Federal Street.

At the turn of the century blacks worshipped in the basement of St. Mary's Church on Wabash Avenue, "but they were made welcome at any of the other churches," according to the archdiocesan history. That may be true. But their priest John Augustine Tolton, the first Negro priest to be ordained for the United States, was forced to study at the Sacred College of the Propaganda in Rome. He was refused admittance to any American seminary.

By 1930, in spite of resistance to change in the neighborhoods, there were many more preeminently black parishes and others on the verge of going black. Monsignor Koenig tells in his archdiocesan history how organizations like the Woodlawn Property Owners' League promoted racially restrictive agreements to keep blacks from buying property in white neighborhoods. About ninety-five percent of the homes in the Washington Park subdivision in the western edge of Holy Cross Parish in the Woodlawn area of the South Side, for instance, were "covenanted." They couldn't be sold to persons of "one eighth part or more negro blood." This practice was widespread. During the thirties, half of city residences were traded under such restrictive arrangements.

Finally, not even covenants could stem the inevitable. In spite of them, the Washington Park subdivision did go black between 1938 and 1940. St. Anselm, to the west of Holy Cross, was designated a black parish in 1932. The area east of Cottage Grove Avenue changed in the 1950s as the black population of Woodlawn increased from 31,329 in 1950 to 72,397 in 1960.

Father Martin Farrell, assigned as pastor of Holy Cross Church in July 1956, ("another wonderful priest" cut to the Monsignor John McMahon mold, according to Jack Egan) saw his black parishioners at Holy Cross put upon by the city. How could he help them help themselves? The co-pastors of the First Presbyterian Church in Woodlawn wrestled with the same ugly reality. Dr. Ulysses B. Blakeley summed up the situation: "We were watching a community dying for lack of leaders, a community that had lost hope in the decency of things and people."

If the people had lost hope, Dr. Blakeley hadn't lost hope in them. He told Jane Jacobs for an article in the May 1962 *Architectural Forum* that he and the other religious leaders didn't look at Woodlawn as a kind of zoo or jungle as outsiders did. "Such people may mean well, but they choke us." Local leaders thought that any "effort would be futile unless our own people could direct it, choose their own goals and work for them, grow in the process and have a sense again of the rightness of things."

Imaginatively, they turned to Saul Alinsky. "Woodlawn itself is the most disorganized community in the United States," Father Farrell wrote him. "There is no leadership. On the other hand, I have found many ordinary people in the community waiting for somebody to lead them to effective democratic organization according to American and

Alinsky principles." About the time Saul heard from Father Farrell, he was also hearing from Jack Egan. Saul had organized a changing community in Chicago. Now would he organize a black community and a poor, ethnic community?

Father Farrell was pressuring Father Egan, almost daily, as well as Monsignor Vincent Cooke at Catholic Charities. Saul was resisting the notion of organizing Woodlawn, as was organizer Nick von Hoffman who had no desire to tangle once again with the University of Chicago looming on Woodlawn's northern border.

But Father Farrell was not easily deterred. Once he got seed money, a promise of fifty thousand dollars contingent on his raising the other money he needed, from his friend Monsignor Cooke at Catholic Charities, he called a meeting. A year after Cardinal Meyer blessed OSC's start at Monsignor Patrick Gleeson's Christ the King rectory, Father Martin Farrell was hosting in his rectory a group including Dr. Blakeley and his co-minister Dr. Charles Leber of the First Presbyterian Church in Woodlawn. They launched a new community organization, the Temporary Woodlawn Organization.

Archdiocesan support for this enterprise was as crucial as recruiting Saul Alinsky. They managed both. "It was a miraculous thing," Jack says. "I was alone with the cardinal and Saul Alinsky. The cardinal made a commitment for $150,000 for three years, $50,000 a year. I'll never forget the scene. It was something that impressed me very, very much. They didn't sign any contract. The cardinal had confidence in Saul. Saul always prided himself that a handshake was his contract. That was his bond. That was his word. He would fulfill what he had promised."

"I was standing there quietly when they shook hands," Jack recalls. The five foot eleven Saul Alinsky looked up at the six foot six cardinal. "Now, Your Eminence," Alinsky said, "I hope you realize there will be conflict and controversy when we do this work. We'll have to take on the Daley machine which is just ripping this neighborhood apart, and some other bureaucracies."

As Jack remembers the seminal meeting, the cardinal replied with the same gentle determination that served him unwaveringly at the Vatican Council in Rome five years later. "Mr. Alinsky, if the work is worthwhile, it doesn't make any difference to me whether there is conflict or controversy. Even though you and I don't share the same faith,

Mr. Alinsky, there is nothing more controversial than a Man hanging on a cross."

Thus was the stage readied for a second engagement between the Alinsky/Churches coalition and the University of Chicago. Woodlawn bordered the university. Nicholas von Hoffman was aware that the university was already buying up land in Woodlawn for what officials called the new South Campus project, another barrier reef to separate the scholastic community from the ghetto to the south. Muggings and robberies were becoming more common on the Midway, the grassy moat between the university and the Woodlawn neighborhood. From the university's point of view, a barrier was absolutely necessary. From von Hoffman's point of view, any gain for the university would be at the expense of the poor to the south who stood to lose some of their few amenities if the university preempted the grassy area of the Midway used as a park by the people of Woodlawn, as well as considerable housing stock.

What was needed, as local clergypersons saw it, was a powerful black community group to counterbalance the university's acknowledged power. A united group could withstand the urban renewal pattern of reserving the new residential stock for the middle class and dumping blacks into ever more deplorable housing. A strong organization would provide, in time, what Saul called "a regenerative force" to improve conditions for all the people living in Woodlawn. Saul believed, as he told the Field Foundation, that "if even one substantial and powerful Negro organization were in existence now on the city's South Side, interracial cooperation could become a reality. Then, once men and women of both races are working together and getting to know each other as persons, we can only hope that people will judge each other as individuals, not as faceless members of groups." That was a powerful argument for a neighborhood organization, one that religious leaders could support.

Young Presbyterian professionals like Douglas Still of the Church Federation; David Ramage, head of the urban-church department of the Presbytery, and Chuck Leber of the First Woodlawn Church, garnered a Presbyterian contribution of $22,000 to augment the archdiocesan funding. When the Schwarzhaupt Foundation provided another $69,000, Saul Alinsky had his "money in the bank." The Temporary Woodlawn Organization was born on January 5, 1961, with a name, temporary officers, and an issue around which to unite the community. Father

Farrell would be a vice president of TWO as Monsignor John McMahon was of OSC.

Sandy Horwitt likens the organizing process to magic. He quotes Nicholas von Hoffman in *Let Them Call Me Rebel*:

It's a very strange thing. You go somewhere, and you know nobody. You drive up in a car, and you know nobody, and you've got to organize it into something that it's never been before . . . You don't have much going for you. You don't have prestige, you don't have muscle, you've got no money to give away. All you have are your wits, charm, and whatever you can put together. So you had better form a very accurate picture of what is going on, and you had better not bring in too many a priori maps (because) if you do, you're just not going to get anywhere.

The area abounded in organizations, churches, block clubs, according to Father Egan, all headed up by people with some native flair as Pied Pipers. To observers who thought of poorer neighborhoods as unorganized, it was surprising how many natural groupings there were. Alinsky's organizers found some of the most promising leaders in pool hall, barber shop, and beauty salon operators. Natural organizers, "they all had twenty-five, maybe fifty, people who listened to them," Egan says admiringly.

A great part of an organizer's skill is putting aside any such conventional wisdom as the notion a poor neighborhood doesn't have its own leaders. A good organizer seeks out the leaders who are there. He or she also encourages potentially unifying issues to rise to the surface like air bubbles through an aquarium. Talking to people in Woodlawn, von Hoffman, Richard Harmon and Bob Squires found that, in addition to the threat of imminent dispossession if the university succeeded in another urban renewal coup, the people in Woodlawn suffered other indignities. There was a pattern, for instance, of local merchants cheating their customers through short weights, overcharging, and hidden interest charges. Could one of these issues motivate community involvement to the flash point needed to fuse them into an irresistible force? asked TWO organizers looking for a spark to ignite the community.

In another part of the country, groups of blacks and whites were working together to effect even more startling change. Freedom Riders, blacks and whites together, were traveling through the South on buses to test compliance with a new Supreme Court decision. Segregation was now outlawed on interstate transportation. Until that decision, blacks traveling from North to South had had to go to the back of the bus when the wheels rolled over the invisible—but mutually under-stood—Mason and Dixon line.

Now there were black riders courageously cleaving to the front of the bus as interstate buses rolled into Southern cities. Whites accompanied them for moral support, as witnesses, and, where it was possible, protection.

Jack Egan and the people organizing Woodlawn rejoiced in the entries into Southern cities that were peaceful. They heard about other cities where Freedom Riders were met by crowds flailing chains and axes. A TWO volunteer who'd left Chicago to ride the buses with an interracial group sponsored by the Congress of Racial Equality was one of the riders attacked. Hospitalized, he called Nick von Hoffman. Could Nick organize a public meeting to make Chicago aware of what was going on? The Freedom Riders needed support.

Nick told Sandy Horwitt that he personally doubted that TWO could mount an effective rally for the Freedom Riders. However, the TWO executive committee wanted to go ahead. They believed their people were looking for an opportunity to show their support. They were right. Hundreds of people turned up, filling not only the big gymnasium at St. Cyril's Church, but also the foyer and even the stairs. Von Hoffman may have hesitated initially rather than embarrass the embryo TWO organization. But he could hear when the people spoke with their bodies. At three in the morning after the rally, he called Saul Alinsky and suggested they should drop their current plans and "work on the premise that this is the whirlwind." Alinsky, sleepy maybe but equally responsive, immediately agreed with his lieutenant on the scene. They'd found their issue in the gut of those galvanized Woodlawn residents. Now they had leaders and rallying point.

Freedom in the North was not represented by riding at the front of the bus. In Chicago freedom was electing candidates truly representative of their constituents, a freedom not yet in place for the blacks of Woodlawn. That process began with voting. In 1961, through a political fluke, every voter in Illinois had to re-register. Why not organize their own Freedom Ride to register the blacks of Woodlawn en masse? TWO organizers wondered. The city's power structure would be forced to take notice. Up to this time, the city's administration had had nothing to fear from black voters. According to Harvard Professor James Q. Wilson, co-author of *City Politics*, there had been "no Negro organizations, or no group of Negro leaders, in a position to . . . force larger issues by mounting a massive, vocal, and sustained demand for race goals."

It was important for the city's power structure to experience the potential power of the city's hitherto powerless. It was equally important for the people of Woodlawn to get a sense of their own power. It wasn't that there wasn't black representation in the city. However, black power broker Congressman William Dawson, committeeman of the Second Ward, kept his place in Mayor Daley's inner circle by defusing any of his constituents' demands that might disrupt the city's equilibrium. As some people saw it, he didn't press for social change, nor did he want anyone else doing it. He kept fair employment, open housing, and other efforts toward real institutional improvement off his docket.

Not surprisingly for such a canny manipulator, he had his troops on the spot when TWO organized an impressively large bus caravan to link into the Freedom Riding buses in the South. Woodlawn voters would ride their buses for a freedom, too, theirs the freedom to vote. To make a strong showing, TWO needed organizers to go from door to door explaining their strategy and recruiting their freedom riders. They had to raise money to hire the buses. They needed money for the signs advertising their goals—"Better Housing." "Vote." "Jobs."

A key commandment in Alinsky's decalogue decreed that an organizer never does for a group what it can do for itself. If the TWO Freedom Ride was to be successful, then the people themselves would have to raise the funds to hire the busses. As Nicholas von Hoffman told Sandy Horwitt, "We had these endless fund-raisers for the busses. At one apartment house after another. We had chicken dinners, barbecues, we even had hookers running fund-raisers."

That Saturday morning event when twenty-five hundred black voters boarded forty-six yellow buses on the Midway south of the University of Chicago exuded that same combination of exultation and latent fear that makes a crowd tense at a Cape Canaveral shuttle launch. The black pastor at the Pentecostal Apostolic Church of God, the Reverend Arthur Brazier, remembers riding in that registration caravan as "one of the most exhilarating experiences of my life."

Congressman Dawson's people stood at the buses cautioning those boarding that they were forfeiting the favors regularly dispensed by the

Democratic machine. Vainly. The people of Woodlawn no longer wanted to be given favors like children. This was a first step in creating a world in which they could manage their own futures. Arthur Brazier explains how imperative a call that was: "You have to remember that the black people in Chicago were practically powerless at that time. Plantation politics were played in the city, and of course we were part of the plantation. We had no entrée into the power structure of the city."

Ordinarily, the voter registration office would have closed at noon. But Mayor Daley gave out the word that the offices should remain open until every person on those forty buses was duly registered. The organizers had banked on this political astuteness on Daley's part. They knew he didn't want the papers headlining stories of potential voters stymied by the political process. The blacks in the city, no longer willing to be invisible, were creating what Charles Silberman calls in *Crisis in Black and White* "the first successful attempt anywhere in the United States to mobilize the residents of a Negro slum into a large and effective organization."

Once it was organized, TWO went on to address other issues. Ministers worked with local businessmen to create a Code of Business Ethics. After they'd introduced the code with a big parade, they set up a registered scale at a local Catholic church one Sunday morning. Shoppers brought packages purchased at suspect markets along with their sales slips. When proof of cheating was established, it was publicized. Merchants who didn't want to go out of business signed a "Square Deal" agreement with TWO.

To get action on the broken windows, burst pipes, and temperamental boilers they'd complained about perennially with no relief, Woodlawn residents organized rent strikes. When pickets carried signs in front of their landlords' suburban homes proclaiming, "Your Neighbor Is a Slumlord," many landlords agreed to make long-postponed repairs.

What worried Woodlawn parents most was the quality of their children's education. They knew their neighborhood schools were inferior. Clergymen, including Jack Egan, walked in the protest marches when the Superintendent of Schools refused to deal with the irate parents. A delegation of eighteen local pastors, Protestant and Catholic, organized a sit-in at Inland Steel where the president of the school board was an executive.

Reverend Arthur Brazier was elected president of The Woodlawn Organization at its founding meeting in the Southmoor Hotel in March 1962. Disciplined and dependable, this seasoned preacher had the necessary confidence to understand that whites still had a role to fill in this complicated urban quadrille he'd been elected to dance in. White leaders like Jack Egan were necessary buffers between the blacks getting the feel of autonomy and the white power structure of the city. Brazier remembers an occasion when Saul Alinsky, Chuck Leber, "and any number of men and women," met for lunch at the Chicago Athletic Association on Michigan Avenue. "I was the only black. We sat an hour without anyone serving us." When they asked what was going on, the maitre d' informed the group that blacks were not served in the CAA dining room. "We ended up having our lunch in the basement. I raise that point," Bishop Brazier says, "to show that Jack Egan could move in circles black people could not move in, and he would be able to defend what TWO was doing."

When asked whether TWO could have been organized equally successfully without him, Jack Egan minimizes his role, suggesting that Father Farrell was the indispensable Catholic presence. "I wasn't that essential. I served as a buffer, a mediator, between the chancery office and The Woodlawn Organization. My role was to attend meetings, to give support, to interpret, to walk beside. They looked at me as the voice of the cardinal in The Woodlawn Organization."

From Arthur Brazier's place at that table in the CAA basement, Jack looked like a unique asset for the people of Woodlawn. "He has consistently been on the side of the oppressed people, the dispossessed people, the poor, the people the system took advantage of," he insists. Unlike a Congressman Dawson who used his black power base for his own ends, Egan "has had a tremendous effect on the conscience of the city," according to Brazier, "because he has tried to bring his influence to bear on the power structure of the city." Brazier observes pointedly that Jack didn't look to gain power himself, but only to gain power for the people themselves.

"He has worked on people to (further their own concerns) rather than try to make a personal impact as a Catholic priest on the power structure. He has used his intelligence, his influence, his immense capabilities, to work with people so that they can find the power they need to have some effect on their own lives.

"You have to remember," Brazier emphasizes, "that black people were practically powerless in the sixties." As they began to understand some of the dynamics of power, the people of Woodlawn began to be less fearful of what the power structure could do to them. As they were speaking for the mass of the people, not for a' local improvement association, their fear of reprisals began to diminish. It was daunting to agitate for change when it meant losing your job or your apartment or your welfare check. That couldn't happen to a whole community. The federal poverty program accelerated that confidence because those monies were not dependent on local clout. However, because the poverty program was undermining local power, Brazier points out that forces friendly to local power soon started to emasculate the poverty program.

From Brazier's point of view, the residents in The Woodlawn Organization needed what might be called front men, "people like Jack who had presence in the city, who had respect in the city." Otherwise Woodlawn activists could be destroyed by rumormongers always willing to brand as Communist any persons willing to take up cudgels for the poor, the powerless. That happened to TWO. As soon as TWO began to achieve some success fighting the endemic problems of the ghetto, the members were attacked severely as Communists, as a hate group opposed to the expansion of the University of Chicago into Woodlawn. These were very serious tags in a country that had just come through the McCarthy era of the fifties. People reacted automatically, blindly, to any charge of Communism. Although Brazier insists that Monsignor Jack Egan never traded on his Roman collar, this was the moment when a Roman collar was an excellent cover.

"We were called a hate group because we were doing so many things that were out of the ordinary," Brazier says, "because we were against 'Negro removal,' moving black people out of the area to be taken over by the university." But with Monsignor Jack Egan out in front of the Woodlawn people, it would have taken Superglue to make the accusations stick.

As Brazier puts it, "It's pretty hard to call a Catholic monsignor (with a ready grin, a record of perfect obedience, and an Irish moniker) a Communist, or a supporter of a hate group."

14

"A Beautiful Mosaic of Community Organizations"

In the view of Bishop Arthur Brazier of the Pentecostal Apostolic Church of God, "A Jack Egan comes along once in a lifetime." In an effort to describe Monsignor Egan's unique role vis-a-vis The Woodlawn Organization, Reverend Brazier tries different formulations. "He was a priest and he wasn't a priest." "It wasn't, 'Monsignor this,' or 'Monsignor that.'"

Finally, he zeroes in on his analysis: "When you get to working with people, they cease to be black or white." Father Egan ceased to be set apart as a priest or monsignor when you worked with him. He didn't trade on his skin. He didn't trade on his collar. He didn't trade on his title. He was simply Jack. That's how he introduced himself. He'd thrust out his hand and say, "I'm Jack Egan," in a friendly, yet forceful, growl. Lest he be misunderstood, Reverend Brazier carefully qualifies his characterization, "But he never forgot who he was."

Often in his Cana days, Jack Egan was heard to say, "No amount of money could pay me to do what I'm doing." Brazier understood that sentiment. "He could have been doing something else. The man sacrificed to make the people of Chicago his career."

If meetings are the hairshirts of the twentieth century, as Alexian Brother Louis Roncoli contends, then driving to meetings is the scourge of the twentieth century. Both exercises take a toll on physical health, however elevating they are to the spirit and necessary to the body politic. Jack Egan was literally beating up on his body as he slipped behind a steering wheel day after day to begin the rounds of community meetings he was making a career of. Before long, that toll was going to tell. Meanwhile, he was energized by a sense that he was the right man in the right place. As the only clergyperson released full-time to serve the city, Jack Egan was the point man not only for the Roman Catholic Church, but also for the Interreligious Council on Urban Affairs, the inter-church group he'd organized with Edgar Chandler and Rabbi Rosenbaum to attend area-wide concerns.

The Cana Conference had been a challenging assignment for a young priest four years out of the seminary. He'd had to create a structure for the search for a marriage theology that truly supported contemporary couples in their contemporary world. But that project was limited, limited to one area of life.

In the role of "clergyman as citizen," Jack Egan was taking on the city for a project, a city whose intractable problems had a century of history and inexact, unfixed boundaries. He'd made a success of the Cana Conference. He wanted another success—for the city's sake, but also for Jack Egan's. He was driven by his empathy with the powerless, for the men he'd met without jobs and the women without proper living quarters, and also by an ambition he couldn't stopper. "Maybe the 'little man complex' Berenice O'Brien (co-chair of Cana in the 1950s) teases me about," Jack says.

Kris Ronnow, IRCUA executive director, recalls Jack Egan's pastoral concern. "Father Egan was instrumental in gathering together a growing interreligious group of clergy with a healthy presence of laity who began to articulate . . . a better way to rebuild the city." They saw "the inner core of the city as the birthplace and the deathplace of the urban poor, living out their lives without dignity, without skills, without hope." They saw the outer ring as "the final target at which the middle and upper classes are aiming, where they can live out their lives in abundance, indifference, and social distance." How could IRCUA connect these two cores for the good of each?

At the time, Jack Egan told the Board of National Missions of the United Presbyterian Church, USA, that the role of clergyman as citizen—the role the cardinal had assigned him—was to address that inherent conflict between inner and outer core, and build community within and between these isolated communities. Clearly, Jack needed "confreres"—his word—to share the task. Increasingly, he analyzed ministry as a cooperative, consultative means of replacing indifference with service. "It was always on my mind that anything we (in the Catholic Church) did relating to human questions should always be done in consort with others and to have that inclusiveness as wide as possible."

Twenty years later, those words could roll easily off many tongues. But before the Vatican Council in the 1960s, bitterness and distrust characterized many relationships between Jews, Protestants and Catholics. The young Presbyterian minister who was a major force in the Organization for the Southwest Community leadership admitted to author Sanford Horwitt that he'd come out of McCormick Seminary in 1954 with the "standard middle 1950s Protestant point of view that, you know, Catholics fought Martin Luther, they played bingo, they had confession, and they weren't intellectually respectable." Many Jews knew "good Catholics" as people who didn't think for themselves.

According to Kris Ronnow, once the coalition of religious leaders that Jack Egan aligned got to working together, the members learned "that what was individually frustrating could be overcome when clergy of various faiths spoke with a united voice. Father Egan was instrumental in helping people of faith work together and (learn) that it was far more difficult for those in power to challenge or dispute a united voice calling for justice." For Jack, it was "a question of brothers and sisters created by God who are working to bring peace and justice to the world."

"Whether it is the Community Renewal Society, the Methodist Church, or the Muslims, or the Urban League, no matter who it may be," he reflects on this period in his life, "I can't help but feel that there is one God who has created all of us. I have based the last thirty years of my life on the premise that there are no Catholic problems, no Presbyterian issues, no Jewish concerns in the city of Chicago. There are human questions and we all better get together to try to cope with them and to bring about a solution." To minister to real human needs, Jack would work with any organization, "whoever they may be, to bring about the amelioration of human suffering. So the Chicago Food Depository, for example, will get my full support."

Jack wanted to strengthen local organizations by his presence. Ronnow says Jack did that. "With Jewish and Protestant support, Father Egan brought a sense of legitimacy to local community struggles and affirmed the right of people to organize and participate in the democratic process."

To Ronnow, those groups that "struggl(ed) on picket lines and community meetings" were "a beautiful mosaic of community organizations." He credits the evident spirit and cooperation in large part to "the genius of Jack Egan," who was "able to say it was all right for people of different faiths and backgrounds to come and struggle together." Jack Egan could also be relied on for the mechanics of daily organization. When a group needed a parish hall, Jack got the permission. When another wanted announcements in local pulpits, Jack made the phone calls. He put at IRCUA's call the persuasiveness he'd learned as he ingratiated himself in the city's rectories on Cana's behalf.

All the time that Jack busied himself stroking and nurturing reluctant pastors of various religious persuasions, as Ronnow puts it, Jack was haunted by shadows on his efforts. One was cast by Monsignor Hillenbrand's old criticism of Jack's interference in the University of Chicago's urban renewal plans. Jack was working out of Hillenbrand's vision of ministry without Hillenbrand's blessing. The other goad he pushed against was the charge that he was usurping the function of the layperson. Even as he poured his energy into the interreligious package, Jack juggled his chronic need to justify his entire dynamic.

He felt firmly fixed in the Church, his two feet like metaphysical poet John Donne's compass, one steady, one circling. Donne described how "thy soul the fixt foot/makes no show to move/but doth/if the other do." Jack found the foot he was keeping in the Church was indeed moving "if the other do," however much he tried to keep it "fixt." At times he questioned this movement because no one seemed to be following.

"I am quite sure that I show up at affairs that other priests wouldn't be caught dead at," he admits. These are places where he feels he "should be present as part of my ministry. But I have never, never once disobeyed an order from my superior. Nor would I ever do so. I keep the cardinal informed on everything I do."

To show his priestly credentials, Jack underscores his faithfulness to pastoral rubrics. He's a good confessor. He prepares pertinent homilies. He takes his turns on call and baptisms and standing out front after Mass of a Sunday. He likes pastoral work, participating in the sacramental life of parishioners. Yet he also needs an over-arching involvement "in affairs that affect the lives of people," the whole community.

Brazier, as president of The Woodlawn Organization, appreciated Jack's involvement, especially because Father Egan had the sense to root from the wings. He let the TWO officers take center stage. The point was that Jack Egan was present. By his presence, he symbolized the unity in relation to social questions he saw as necessary among religious groups. "Otherwise, I don't understand Jesus's words that we must all be one as He and the Father are one," he says.

"We go to God with others," he repeats as often as anyone will listen. "Who are the others?" he asks, knowing that in his own mind he's including Buddhists and Muslims and Hindus and people from every group found in Chicago in increasing numbers. This realization causes him to inveigh, occasionally, against the provincialism of his own Church. "When we talk of ministry, I feel we make mistakes in centering it too much around the altar. That is the center of our ministry, what gives us life and the word to go forth out into the world. But the ministry is to be carried on in the world."

Jack Egan has never forgot an encounter Monsignor Hillenbrand described to his seminarians. Hillenbrand and a priest friend were pulled up in a large Oldsmobile next to one of the concrete islands on which the city's working class collected in the days when streetcars traveled Chicago's streets, "the kind of island against which drivers killed themselves every Saturday night," Jack says parenthetically.

This was a summer afternoon. The car windows were open. A construction worker sweated on the island, hugging his lunch pail, observing the pair of priests resting comfortably against their plush upholstery in their pressed black suits and Roman collars.

The light changed. The Oldsmobile was ready to move, but the streetcar the workman awaited was still far down the tracks. Before the clerical duo could drive away, the working man pronounced his verdict. "Figures!" he summed up their diverse circumstances. "Fathers, I don't know how the hell you can afford a car like that, but after all, I support you, huh?"

Whether it stemmed from Hillenbrand's story or whether the story activated a latent outrage, Jack Egan confesses a lifelong distaste for clerical display of material difference or any arrogance that indicates spiritual superiority over lay people. "God, we're in this ball game together and most of the help I received as a priest didn't come from priests. It came from lay people."

That's not to say that Jack Egan hasn't benefitted from his own clerical connections. "I've been thirty-two years a monsignor," he says, "because I had a friend in the chancery office who thought I was doing a good job. A lot of people he didn't like were on a list to be made monsignor that came across his desk, so he added my name. It's been useful many ways, especially calling Italian and Polish parishes." He adds that while being a monsignor has opened a lot of doors for the work of Jesus, it has opened many doors for Jack Egan, too.

Jack also acknowledges that he likes keeping his "one foot in the Church" at Holy Name Cathedral on Chicago's near North Side. His classmate Bishop Timothy Lyne ("who's done a superb job in parish work for forty-six years") was rector there when Jack came back to Chicago. "He has as much interest as I in the race question, ecumenical work, life in the world. He's respected by many organizations—but they are Roman Catholic organizations." As Jack sees the Church's situation, Bishop Lyne represents "one dimension of Church we better have. Mine is another."

When Jack Egan tapped into the Golden Age of community organizing and interreligious relations in 1958 (he cites as many "Golden Ages" as he does "historic moments"), he was acting on a principle made explicit by the Catholic bishops at their 1971 synod on Justice in the World: "Action on behalf of justice and participation in the transformation of the world fully appear to us as a constitutive dimension of the preaching of the Gospel." When his colleague Father Larry Kelly heard the bishops' statement quoted at the March 1971 CCUM meeting at Moreau Seminary, he told Father Egan with some satisfaction, "Jack, listen, we were right all along."

Although he had the influence of Monsignor Hillenbrand's teaching and the Church's encyclicals, and Monsignor Daniel Cantwell and the hard workers at the Catholic Interracial Council and Friendship House who interpreted the scene as he did, Egan felt very much alone in the Church in 1958. He felt on the outside, "a particular person outside the ordinary ministry of the Church." If he'd felt on the inside, as one of the clerical guys, Jack Egan would not have had to do such extensive soul-searching. He could see trauma ahead for the city. His friend Father Farrell was convinced change was inevitable. Certainly Monsignor McMahon was convinced. But there were many in the city who thought they could resist the implacable drive of demographics. Jack felt like a twentieth century circuit rider calling out his alerts.

Mary Louise Schniedwind, his secretary/assistant at the Office of Urban Affairs, observed how Jack involved everybody with a stake in his plans for the city: blacks, whites, churches, businesses, local organizations. He believed, she says, that when the inevitable inflow of blacks and outflow of whites occurred, fighting and riots could be prevented only by strong structures. Blacks active in community organizations would have the same concern for neighborhood preservation as the whites.

"Eventually," Schniedwind continues her analysis, "as whites became a minority or disappeared from the area, blacks would have a good organization to help themselves. The Catholic Church (which would participate in the transition) would still be there . . . and help stabilize the community." Schniedwind found Jack's ability to "organize pastors, who probably never would have done it without his leadership, remarkable." She saw what great sacrifices the changeover was asking of parish leaders, how hard it was for them to contribute money and ask their parishioners to contribute. She describes Jack as "outgoing, uncomplicated, without affectation, open, and able to make everybody feel comfortable." At times he made her uncomfortable when he publicly made the case for the opposition better than the opposition voices could do it for themselves.

She watched Jack empower organization people. Where he thought another could function better than he could, he was quick to seek that person out. Community organizer Tom Gaudette, commenting wryly on this knack of Jack's for gaining compliance from his prey, says he is "an awful man because he decides he wants you to do something and you can't resist." Schniedwind observed in amazement: "With every movement he created, with every organization he created, he found the right people." As much as she admired his political acuity, she couldn't help being amused when she'd arrive with Monsignor Egan at a public function being recorded for television. "I'd stand at the door and say to someone, 'Watch Jack position himself for the camera.' Then we'd observe as Jack surveyed the site, found some important personage near the camera and strode across to him or her to say, 'How do you do, Joe Blow, Mr. Mayor, or whatever.' Jack thought that was good for the Church, a Catholic priest being seen at the right place with the right people."

Monsignor Egan put his political skills to work as he made the circuit of the, maybe, seventy-five community organizations at various stages of development stretched throughout the city, each an opportunity. Jack Egan clocked miles as religiously as his parents' generation had trickled rosary beads. In his Cana days he'd spun the odometer hurtling from rectory to rectory, Cana Conference to Cana Conference. In 1961, his rotation was bringing him from meeting to meeting to meeting. Out Archer Avenue to the Organization for the Southwest Community. Across Division Street to ring rectory doorbells to beg funds for the Northwest Community Organization. South down Ashland to Woodlawn to encourage Father Farrell. Down Jeffrey to the South Shore Temple.

In some sense he was pastor to the city. He saw his job as liaison between the cardinal and the city's community organizations. The job both freed him up and tied him down. He was spared full-time parish duties, but, being Jack, he felt responsible for legitimizing and educating—as well as inspiriting—community organizations in the city and suburbs. He tried to turn up at all regular meetings. When he was asked to say a few words, he'd have a speech ready, often written by Nicholas von Hoffman. "Nick was my brains," Jack says. "I was getting an education. I didn't mind getting an education from a young guy like Nick because I needed it. Nick had a profound understanding of the meaning of democracy."

As director of the Office of Urban Affairs, Jack preached the goal of service to congregations, neighborhoods, and the metropolis. He'd tell audiences how the political process created community. Then he'd work the room to create a little community of his own as he assured people of his faith in them, his awareness of their dignity, and their importance to the civic health of the city. They scarcely noticed how quickly he pressed from one hand to the next for experiencing the intensity of his personal concern. He never left a person's side without asking what the archbishop of Chicago could do for him or her.

He told parish priests they should be out walking around, studying their territory, cataloging the rotting outside staircases on firetrap buildings and the smelly hallways in once well-kept apartment buildings. "You'll find opportunities for service," he said, if you develop what writer Michael Harrington called "social eyes," the faculty of seeing many individual misfortunes in poverty instead of a city-wide, indeed a national, catastrophe.

When he talked about ridding the city of its growing slums and replacing them with decent housing, he warned against developers who "get approval for eminent domain as quietly as (they) can, and then move in as fast as (they) can before the people wake up and know what's going on." He told stories of a pastor who waked to find a superhighway built between his church and his school, and another who found all the homes in the vicinity of his parish torn down so the land could lay idle five years.

Jack Egan gave community groups facts they could work with. He would quote a Chicago consultant's estimate that 25,000 dwelling units (home to more than 100,000 people) were demolished in Chicago between 1950 and 1958, that another 25,000 would be a memory by 1961. He could dramatize those figures with the saga of Sandburg Village, "the biggest and the richest of the land grabs. The quaintness of the name would both beguile you and numb you to what was really going on beneath your very eyes."

Jack suggests there were enough lies told about how this project would bring together wealthy, near wealthy, the middle class and the poor, black and white, people of different cultures, that even the most honorable people would think this would be the spiritual Taj Mahal or Parthenon of Chicago. The Land Clearance Commission used eminent domain to vacate the land and demolish the old buildings on LaSalle and Clark from Division Street to North Avenue. Helped by the most powerful City Hall alderman ("a man of brilliance and renown who later spent some time in the federal penitentiary for mail fraud," according to Jack), the firm of Arthur Rubloff made a bid for the land now cleared of old, tired mansions and the poor people who'd had rooms in them.

"Representing the Office of Urban Affairs of the archdiocese, I appeared before the Housing and Planning Committee of the City Council to protest this giveaway," Jack says, "particularly since there was no room allotted for the poor and lower income groups." Loud roars of disapproval came from the voices of the vice presidents of Arthur Rubloff Company (after Jack's testimony). "But a knowing man, Alderman Seymour Simon, later a distinguished judge, spoke up in a phrase I shall never forget. Said he, 'There is a smell of money in this room.' It was more than a smell. It was a dirty, dishonest deal and the taxpayers suffered again. The rents went up and up, and are still going up. There was no room in Sandburg Village for lower income people, to say nothing of the poor."

Jack instructed neighborhood people to take the initiative. Your job, he told them, is to represent the views and needs of your neighborhood to the rest of the city. You are the mechanism by which "neighborhood citizens can formulate the goals and needs of their neighborhood and defend and promote them both to the area planners and to the city at large. Don't think you can do this without raising a little heat," he advised, but be "prepared to accept a measure of heat as a necessary adjunct to a vital community life. Your job is to open up issues so the political process can resolve them, and to fight hard to get what you need. You must be true to yourself, cantankerous and tough."

Jack asked tough questions of the community organizations. How many of them had pressed for more street lighting, garbage collection, and police protection? How many had launched programs for support of increased municipal budgets in their areas? How many community groups, organized in the face of the expanding Negro ghetto, had supported realistic programs to open up housing opportunities for middle income Negroes and take the pressure off the ghetto frontier? How many neighborhood organizations had taken the time and effort to develop a workable and realistic rehabilitation program—one of the city's greatest needs—and to sell the plan to the property owners and the financial interests? How many had left the entire job, because it is so difficult, to the Department of Urban Renewal?

As Peg Burke and Nina Polcyn had found out, Jack Egan could be tough when he expected performance. He could sound cantankerous when he spoke the truth. When a young acquaintance asked him to speak to a community group at the American Legion Hall at Sixty-ninth Street and Paulina, Jack pulled no punches. He outlined his enthusiasm for the possibilities inherent in a generous attitude toward change. In that Southwest Side neighborhood, change had only one meaning. That audience was not about to participate in the political process by enlarging their vision of city as a place where the stranger becomes the neighbor. When Jack used the word, "integration," he lanced a pustule. His audience had no tolerance for that concept when it referred to strangers—blacks—buying into their neighborhoods.

Saul Alinsky and Jack Egan were already being called Communists by people of that area who had organized block clubs to keep the blacks out. Jack had felt sure that a group on Sixty-ninth Street, so near St. Justin Martyr, must know he was no Communist. "I talked to them on the race question and this was, God, in hostile territory." When the young man who had invited Father Egan to address the group realized that Father Egan was advocating integration, "he went to the bathroom and," as Father Egan drew on his best skills to soften the audience's resistance to change, "you could hear him retching. He knew he would probably be fired."

Father Egan hadn't thought his suggestion of using community organization to achieve an integrated neighborhood was "that dramatic. But it was the last thing they wanted to hear." Four burly guys—"fellows I'd married or baptized their children"—escorted Jack Egan to his car and warned, "You better get out the neighborhood, Father." Although they resented his interfering, they didn't want him to come to any harm. "Otherwise," he smiles ruefully, "if I'd been totally foreign, it would have been a good bit worse." Jack got out of the neighborhood.

When the talk was reported in the press. Bill Berry, director of the Urban League, admitted, "One thing about Jack Egan: he says the same thing in the white areas that he does in the black areas." Jack was no Lyndon Johnson, telling one story in Texas' rural areas and another at the Petroleum Club in Dallas. That may have made Jack a hero to Bill Berry. In the guys at the Sixty-ninth Street American Legion Hall, it prompted suspicion that the sunny young assistant who'd always smiled when he shook their hands after Mass had turned into a Communist— Roman collar or no Roman collar.

For over three years now, since Cardinal Meyer had given him the city as his parish, Jack Egan had run up against this mentality as he pushed his body to perform. "I was rushing around, the Cana Conference, YCS, YCW, community organizing and· everything else, running to meetings morning, noon, and night. I was trying to live three lives at once." His schedule was no different the March day in 1962 when he told his secretary Fran Hearn, "I'm not feeling that well." Although he was due at a meeting, he had the sense to lie down on his couch at his Seven-twenty North Rush office.

After a few minutes, he lectured himself. "Oh, come on, Jack, what the heck. Stop babying yourself. You'll be all right." Late now for the interfaith social action meeting at the Chicago Board of Rabbis office with several rabbis and CIC's John McDermott and the city's director of human relations, Edward Marciniak, Jack jumped in a cab, directing the Chinese driver to Eleventh and State. By this time he knew he was having a heart attack. "It felt like a Mack truck was running over me. Instead of being smart and going to a hospital, I go down to the meeting, I pay the cabbie, I go upstairs to the seventh floor to where the meeting was, and I walk in and collapse. They put me on the couch and called the fire department. No one thought of calling a priest."

The firemen were prompt. They asked Jack, "When did you eat last?" He answered, "Seven this morning," through his pain as they bundled him up for the rush trip to Mercy Hospital. "Apparently, I was very grey and not expected to live." Jack recalls heads shaking over him as firemen brought him into the emergency room. Cardinal Meyer and Bishop Cletus O'Donnell, visiting the hospitalized vicar general, floated briefly through the room where the doctors were wiring Jack to an electrocardiograph.

That was the cardinal's last chance for many days. As Jack says, "Not even my mother was allowed to see me for ten days." A cadre of fellow priests, co-workers, and friends sat guard outside his door around the clock for several weeks, denying entrance to anyone but nurses and doctors. Cautioned that any exertion on Jack's part could precipitate a fatal paroxysm, they meant to save his life. "They did save my life," Jack says, years later, of the guard that included his brother Jim, Father Imbiorski of the Cana Conference, Tom Gaudette (an Alinsky-trained organizer), and a dozen others. "I was in Mercy Hospital thirty-two days recovering." Gaudette characteristically remembers the "guards" making book on which of them would officiate when the cardinal was first denied admittance to Jack's room. "I was it," Gaudette recalls with satisfaction.

The ever-gracious Cardinal Meyer nodded approval of the policy, saying mildly, "I think that's a good idea." On his way to the elevator, he passed another priest of the archdiocese marching down the corridor to the door defended by Gaudette. Without pressing the call button, Cardinal Meyer lingered at the elevator door, watching a reenactment of his rebuff. When Jack's second visitor of the hour joined the cardinal at the elevator stacks, the prelate smiled gently. "Me, too," he confided companionably.

It was April 8 before hospital personnel reported to callers that Monsignor Egan was no longer in critical condition. The hospital had to put an extra person on the switch board for the rash of phone calls and messages. Mail and packages were collected in special large boxes. The public relations officer worked overtime to satisfy the media. Even after Jack left the hospital, visitors were rationed.

At forty-five, Jack Egan was too young for a heart attack. He'd prodded his body too far and too fast, pushed his father's work ethic to the extreme, to serve his city. Once his doctor relented he was back in the Chevy again, only slightly chastened. "My heart attack did slow me down a little bit," he admits. Only a little bit. The city needed him.

15

"A Theology of Care for the Public Realm"

As Jack Egan resumed his junkets across Division Street, along Cottage Grove, through the underpass that blocked blacks from Back of the Yards, he tried to take it easy. Slowing down went against his nature. He had this sense that the fate of the city rode on the seat next to him, urging him on. If only he could make people see that they could save their city by working for the common good and uniting for the requisite clout!

Alternatives to generosity and community-building were frightening. The remedy to the impasse in the city, as Jack saw it, was viewing the city's plight in the light of the Gospel. Neighbors must work through their tension and fears instead of ducking and running.

Jack Egan struggled to formulate a theology of care for the public realm. Ten years earlier, he'd gone to France to find a theology of care in the conjugal realm. Now he worked at gathering a coalition of churches to develop, and then support, structures within which the city's people could reach out to each other. Could he capitalize on C. T. Vivian's perception that the country might be repenting of its repression of Negroes? As Martin Luther King, Jr.'s aide would put it some years later, "A person really does have to repent of sins to be saved. And that's true of a nation, too. What happened in the 1960s was that this entire country took just a few steps toward admitting it had been wrong on race, and the result was an explosion of creativity and humanity in all directions. We moved temporarily toward becoming a more humane society for everyone."

Trying to take advantage of that explosion of creativity and humanity in his town had brought Jack to Saul Alinsky and Nicholas von Hoffman. Now, could they capitalize on the humanity that was funding

159

the Freedom Riders, pastors like Arthur Brazier and Chuck Leber and John McMahon and Martin Farrell, groups planning interracial functions, churches studying race questions, politicians equally sympathetic to whites and blacks?

Could the Church's teaching on race call forth the generosity toward the black population that the Church's teaching on marriage had elicited in Cana people? Large sections of the area facing inevitable change were heavily Catholic. Studies showed much latent good will. In 1990, an astute social commentator would verify Jack Egan's experience: "An often-ignored message of the 1960s is that many, many white people, under the impact of the African-American movement, really did break with the patterns of four hundred years of history and aligned themselves, four-square, with the movement against racism."

That subtle change plus the movement of plain people without money, prestige, or power to organize for their own purposes were the hopes of the sixties. Jack Egan preached those hopes as he went from meeting to meeting. He described the power of community organization to a South Shore Leadership Conference in April of 1963 as "strong enough and broad enough to control the panic operations of real estate men—both white and colored. (An organized community) will prevent overcrowding by taking vigilant steps to see that building and housing codes are enforced; will work against the abuses of absentee landlords and of contract selling, and will have a positive program to prevent increasing blight and deterioration."

Jack doggedly pursued his course. Saul Alinsky wasn't around; he spent much of his time in California. The brilliant, volatile Nick von Hoffman was a challenging, but not a soothing, colleague. Jack Egan rated von Hoffman the finest organizer he'd ever seen—for his first year on a project. He'd work like hell, Jack says, until the first convention. After that, he'd grow bored with any follow-up. He had no patience for the hack work Jack did, tackling one testy audience after another, night in and night out, from Rogers Park to Beverly. "What I had to do was keep parishes happy," Jack assesses his role. With von Hoffman and Ed Chambers gone from the Organization for the Southwest Community—a move that troubled Monsignor McMahon—Jack filled in as liaison between the archdiocese and OSC, as well as between the Industrial Areas Foundation and OSC.

Jack was encouraged at how well work at the Interreligious Council on Urban Affairs was going. He characterizes IRCUA efforts as "intelligently active, because we used the best research we could get from urban planners at Northwestern University and the University of Chicago. We did our homework well."

This first permanent interfaith group to work on social questions in Chicago took issue with the city on matters relating to housing, neighborhood development, relocation of families, and the development of community organizations. "Always in concert," Jack says, "because we realized that never again would the mayor of the city, or any other force, separate us in our endeavor to attack any social problem.

"Within a couple of years," Jack recalls, "we got enough of a budget to hire H. Kris Ronnow (social welfare consultant for The Church Federation of Greater Chicago at the time) as executive director. IRCUA was doing superb work in community organizing. We (individual churches) did nothing alone." Jack passes easily over that statement, but Ronnow recalls the situation with respectful amazement. "We had to convince Catholic pastors, who had a high discomfort level with Protestant clergy, that we were not the devil incarnate." He recalls one especially uncomfortable session in a Northwest Side rectory which lightened up into congeniality only when the pastor opened sliding doors to reveal an excellently stocked liquor cabinet. "I found out what the levelers were!"

IRCUA staff worked with eleven city agencies. When Jack addressed neighborhood associations, he could assure them that a) they were legitimate, and b) the churches were behind them. With that backup, it was up to them to "work out their own destiny." Looking back, Jack assesses IRCUA's presence as making "a significant difference in community organizing and civil rights in the city."

That support made a difference to The Woodlawn Organization. By the spring of 1963, many blacks were agitating for their civil rights in the country, and many whites were resisting their advances. Birmingham's Public Safety Commissioner, in his straw hat and shirtsleeves, was sending his police dogs against Dr. Martin Luther King, Jr., and his colleagues in the Southern Christian Leadership Conference. Along with King and the Reverend Ralph Abernathy, fifty SCLC marchers went to jail. In May, Birmingham police arrested 959 children marching in a children's crusade for freedom.

Blacks were enraged by the arrest of the children. Birmingham's white leaders, frightened by the threat of violence, agreed to desegregate all facilities. Segregationists retaliated by bombing the black protest headquarters and the home of Dr. King's brother. At the University of Alabama, Governor George Wallace blocked the entrance to black students. Threatened by an open accommodations act, Wallace accused President John Kennedy of inflaming Negroes and encouraging street demonstrations. He suggested a president "who sponsors legislation such as the Civil Rights Act of 1963 should be retired from public life." Wallace went on to describe his resentment over "the fawning and pawing over such people as Martin Luther King and his pro-Communist friends and associates." That same year, civil rights leader Medgar Evers was shot in front of his home in Jackson, Mississippi.

The issue in Chicago was still the University of Chicago's intention to move into Woodlawn, tear down houses, and proceed with what Arthur Brazier calls "Negro removal." The university was adamant about its plans, moving ahead as if the blacks were mice in the way of a bulldozer—as would have been the case if TWO had not existed. But The Woodlawn Organization had used busses to good effect once. They organized to do it again.

TWO organizers disdained Mayor Richard Daley's offer to arrange a meeting on the University of Chicago's South Campus plan. Instead, they brought ten busloads of people from Woodlawn to City Hall. Six hundred people were a reminder to the mayor that 2,500 had ridden similar busses to register to vote. Six hundred people were less likely to be overwhelmed by any opposition than a small contingent in a packed meeting. Some of those bus-riding TWO people picketed outside City Hall. Others sat-in inside City Hall.

It was only at a second meeting that Brazier, increasingly less intimidated, got fired up enough to demand concessions from the mayor. And he got them. The mayor agreed that TWO would have input in any decision concerning urban renewal in the Woodlawn area. In an interview almost thirty years later, Reverend Arthur Brazier relishes that memory. He leans his long, lanky body back into a comfortable position as he re-experiences the sense of power the TWO people felt "because we blocked the (university's) expansion program." Then he leans forward to emphasize the significance of credits from the federal government in the amount of some $13-15 million. "These credits could be taken over by the University of Chicago to do whatever the city wanted to do. We protested against the university's movement into Woodlawn because there was no conservation committee set-up."

Bishop Brazier is sketching out the decline of plantation politics. Here was a group of citizens once voiceless in the disposition of any city funds suddenly having "a big row with Mayor Daley on how the Woodlawn conservation committee would be formulated," Brazier recalls. Savoring the recollection, he describes exacting an "agreement that we could build 500 units of subsidized housing." In return, TWO agreed to end opposition to the university's expansion, "an expansion we weren't against per se." What the representatives of TWO wanted was respect and fairness. "We did not feel the university could expand, move black people out, the city get $13-15 million to do whatever they wanted with it, and the community just be sitting there looking at the expansion," Brazier says.

The city took some of the money, cleared out dilapidated business structures on both sides of Cottage Grove from Sixtieth to Sixty-third, and sold the land back to a development corporation the blacks formed to "build 540 units of 221(d)3 housing."

"This was a winner," the former TWO president says with impressive satisfaction. "Tremendous. A great victory because we knew there was no way we could stop the university. By the time we worked out the agreement, they owned three-quarters of the land anyway." According to the *Chicago Tribune*, the university owned more than thirty acres south of the Midway, but they agreed that this area which had provided recreational space, including playing fields, for Woodlawn's residents would continue to be available for such recreation—a stipulation that Nicholas von Hoffman had asked Saul Alinsky to engineer in his first recommendations.

Assessing the forces that made their triumph possible in 1963, Bishop Brazier carefully analyzes Monsignor Egan's role. "There are a lot of people like Jack Egan, but they are not Jack Egan." Brazier understands that true leaders know when to negotiate and when to keep struggling. "The sixties and seventies were times of cataclysmic change and we needed people who understood strategy and who had the courage to keep going when they were told to quit." Brazier recalls that there were people who stood to benefit from the University of Chicago plan, even people in Jack Egan's community, who "were not happy with what he was doing.

"Now you're talking to someone on the outside," Brazier cautions, "but a lot of people on the outside, outside the power structure, felt that Jack got punished for standing with the poor people. I know his department was abolished. I know Jack was shoveled off into a parish. I know eventually he was gone from Chicago." Rev. Brazier shrugs and dismisses the subject with a wry smile. "Maybe these were all promotions."

Jack Egan had admitted that the University of Chicago "creamed" him when he suggested in 1958 that their urban renewal should include new housing for the people evacuated by their plan. He'd pointed out then that the Chicago City Planning Department estimated that 25,000 units, housing 100,000 people, had been razed by government action in the past eight years. Now, five years later, TWO had won concessions that specified that "the demolition for the South Campus should be delayed . . . until new units of low-cost . . . housing have been built so that the people can be relocated out of the old housing on South Campus into the new." It was TWO's victory, not Jack Egan's. But he wouldn't have been human if he hadn't enjoyed it.

The TWO action was only one of the shifts shaking the city of Chicago, and the country. As Arthur Brazier's group brought pressure on the city, other demonstrators were sitting in at school board offices at 228 N. La Salle Street. In a pushing, shoving, and kicking melee, the *Chicago Tribune* reported, four policemen and a girl of ten were hurt outside the entrance, and three persons arrested. Concurrently, Alderman Leon Despres was defending an open occupancy proposal that sparked a furor in the city council, according to the *Trib*. And the mayor, responding to pressure, was promising equality in the building trades as Governor Otto Kerner was making his promise that public accommodations in Illinois should be open to all races.

With all that going on, the TWO action still stood out as unique, according to Sanford Horwitt's assessment. "The seven-point agreement . . . was extraordinary—almost certainly the first time that a black community in Chicago had, through sheer political power, won a major role in shaping an important urban-renewal program."

Even as he was forced to deal with them, Mayor Daley could never understand why community organizations were necessary. Weren't the people in city government elected by the people? Didn't they serve as the people's representatives? "Mayor Daley and I talked about that," Jack reflects mildly. "I explained that community organizations don't substitute for a political system. They help keep the political system honest. They help (elected officials) do their work."

Whether Mayor Daley felt that community organizations were any help to him in his work, Jack Egan had been persuaded by Saul Alinsky that the evaluation and accountability they provided were necessary to the body politic. (And all other bodies, including the Church of which Jack was a member.)

"It wasn't until I met Saul Alinsky that he helped me see that unless people are organized, they're not going to accomplish the social justice that should be a part of our lives. He used to say that Gandhi brought down the British Empire when he saw the Indians sitting on the ground all over India, and said to them, 'Let's all get together and sit on the ground.'" Jack chuckles at the picture that story evokes, no matter how many times he tells it. "In the neighborhood, it's the same thing." Jack continues to quote his mentor. "In the neighborhoods of great cities, particularly where poor people are living, there must be organization according to certain rules. It must be mass-based. It must be responsible and responsive to needs of people. It must be a continuation of the finest tradition of democracy." He could be referring to TWO.

He tried to explain to the mayor. "Those who represent the people sought office. It is the right of the people to demand that they do their job well, and their job is one of service. As Dr. Martin Luther King, Jr., used to say, 'You could give me the Nobel prize, or any prize, but they are not as important as my trying to be a drum major for justice.'"

Jack himself had been evaluated and held accountable by the master during the summers of 1956 and 1957 when he underwent "the most rigorous training of my life" under Saul Alinsky. He'd learned that evaluation and accountability were "two of the most Christian words I've ever encountered." For Jack Egan, as for Parker Palmer in *The Company of Strangers*, "public life is the area of spiritual experience, a setting in which God speaks to us and forms our hearts with words we cannot hear in the private realm . . . without public experience we cannot experience the fullness of God's word for our lives."

Parker could have been describing Woodlawn in 1960 when he wrote: "In a society which lacks a healthy public life, both private and political life will suffer. In the absence of a public which knows and cares about itself, private life tends to become obsessive and fearful, while political institutions become centralized, overweening, and even totalitarian. If we want authentic privacy and authentic politics, we must cultivate the public life on which both depend."

Alexis de Tocqueville observed in the early nineteenth century that the success of democracy depended on the health of voluntary organizations. Saul Alinsky taught Tocqueville's principles to Jack Egan in 1956. Together with Saul Alinsky and Nick von Hoffman and their other organizers, Jack Egan tried to teach the people of Woodlawn in the early 1960s. Why couldn't everyone see how basic this concept was for the health of the city?

Chicago tossing in the slipstream of forward movement made the 1960s "the most exciting possible years" to Jack. The TWO triumph was major excitement. There were breakthroughs in ecumenism. After 400 years of distrust and bad feeling, the beginnings of rapprochement between churches and synagogues amazed and unsettled all believers. Suddenly, it was no longer a sin for a Catholic to enter a Protestant church. The euphoria released by interfaith and interracial action was intensified by the totally unexpected gesture of Pope John XXIII in convening the Vatican Council that began in Rome, October 11, 1962. It produced, according to Robert Blair Kaiser, correspondent in Rome for *Time* magazine that year, "the most accelerated change in the history of the church.

"I watched two popes, more than 2,000 bishops and almost as many theologians begin to rethink everything that generations of Catholics had taken for granted, then work out, after four years of debate in the Second Vatican Ecumenical Council, a new chapter that would return the people of God to a more primitive Christianity and get them ready as well for the new kind of world that obviously lay ahead," he wrote in *The Politics of Sex and Religion.*

For Jack, home in Chicago, the changes he read about in *The New York Times* "were so positive, so healthy. For the first time it was the total Church gathered in Rome." In councils called before the advent of jet travel, foreigners had represented the Church of deep Africa and the Far East. Now the Church had the benefit of bishops from widely different cultures.

People from whom Jack had gained extraordinary insights into the theology of marriage and the dignity of the human person were now council *periti* (experts). They were instructing his archbishop, Cardinal Meyer, and bishops from the farthest reaches of earth, that the Church couldn't stand still, that it must take advantage of the window Pope John XXIII—an amazing phenomenon himself after the autocratic, stiff Pius XII—had opened. To the amazement of much of the world—especially the Catholic world—the bishops were not so straitlaced as might have been expected. "We can no longer say that the church is afraid to admit her narrowness, her shortcomings, or even her Manicheanism," a French reporter wrote for *Le Monde*. "To recognize one's errors is to grow; thus, the church grew on Thursday at Vatican II . . . Christianity, the religion of love, carried the day over the Catholicism which catalogued prohibitions like a counting machine."

Jack Egan craved an opportunity to observe the action. "This was the most important thing that was going to happen in my life and I was not going to miss it. I saved my money." He spent his three-week vacations in 1963, 1964, and 1965 at a small *pensione* in Rome where his friends, Monsignor George Higgins, Monsignor John Quinn, and Bishop Ernest Primeau kept a room available for him.

The best minds in the Roman Catholic Church were in Rome for the Vatican Council, Jack remembers, "and a number of *periti* including Jesuit theologian John Courtney Murray" lived in the *pensione* where Jack was staying. "A marvelous, marvelous group of brilliant individuals." Jack was the little mouse under the chair, "polite enough to keep my mouth shut and listen" when around eight o'clock each night they would assemble in the common room for a drink and then a conversation that would go on to midnight. Gregory Baum "would come over, Hans Kung would come over, Malachy Martin—God forgive him—always politicking about a million things, knew the inside of what was happening, what the German bishops were doing, what kind of vote was coming up."

John Courtney Murray, a quiet and reflective man, would "sit there with his very, very dry martini, listening, until someone, turning, would ask him, 'What do you think?'" He was only one of the many official *periti* who had had trouble with the Curia or the Holy Office, men like Hans Kung, Godfrey Diekmann, and Gustave Weigel. Only the year before the council started, this trio (together with Murray) had been denied permission to speak at the Catholic University campus in Washington, D.C. Now they were teaching the bishops, *mirabile dictu.*

Conversation was the soul of the council, in some sense. As Protestant observer Robert McAfee Brown put it, "one can sometimes learn more in the coffee bar than by listening to the speeches." At his *pensione*, Jack heard, he recalls, "magnificent discussions and fights over all the questions raised during the day in the *aula* at St. Peter's." Then his friends got him a pass so he could walk through the bronze doors of

St. Peter's Basilica that had been scraped of five centuries of silt and mounted on ball bearings for the council. Perched in the *aula* on one of the lateral platforms erected for the three thousand participants, including 2,500 Council Fathers, he was positioned so he could watch Chicago artist Franklin McMahon draw the extraordinary churchscape of cardinals, bishops, *periti*, and separated brethren intent on a simultaneous translation of "a Syrian bishop speaking Latin through his beard."

For Jack Egan the atmosphere was an intoxicating magnification of the "Chicago moment." He felt a part of history. Not bashful at being a learner, he inhaled the breath of scholarship and the aspiration of holy men as he sat at the feet of the great in St. Peter's. "I was willing to learn from anyone." And everyone. And everyone was there. In Rome, in the early sixties, all the great minds of the Church, many of them Jack Egan's friends, those people he had sought out to teach his Cana people or his CCUM people or his YCW people, were doing their thinking in Latin in the *aula* during the day, and then in English over Scotch at night in the *pensione*. Monsignor George Higgins from Jack's seminary days who'd urged him to fight injustice wherever he found it. Father Stanislaus de Lestapis, the French Jesuit theologian whom Jack had sought out in France in the fifties, here on the birth control commission. His beloved Albert Cardinal Meyer, who'd had faith in Jack from the start, a hero of the council fight for religious liberty. Cardinal Dearden, who'd make a valiant try to bring the council insights to bear on the American church.

Vatican II was a moving—and movable—feast for all those who cared as much as Jack did. It was hard to believe, there on the scene, caught in the updraft of *aggiornamento*, that the bishops' determination to go from a church of rules to a church of service would not prevail. Anyone who read the Pastoral Constitution on the Church in the Modern World (happily called *Gaudium et Spes*) would expect that the Chicago moment, catalyzed by this world-wide affirmation of its rightness, would grow from pockets of renewal to a whole new habit for the U.S. Church. And for the world Church, as well. The schema was a new charter for the Church aimed at turning it from a church of laws, looking inward, as Robert Kaiser wrote, "to a church of love, looking out." In the document, marriage was defined not as a remedy for concupiscence, an outdated notion, but as a "community of life and love," a Cana notion.

As the council progressed, the bishops battened against a rising conservative pressure from the Curia, the Church's administrative arm. Jack Egan was at dinner the night that Cardinal Meyer, one of the four presidents of the council, was instructed by John Courtney Murray on the fine points of the doctrine of religious liberty. This was a groundbreaking document with many enemies. For the cardinal to defend it, he needed expert instruction because the document ran directly counter to an 1864 papal encyclical *Quanta Cura* which called religious liberty, even in the civil arena, a delirium.

No one ducked out early for the coffee bars the day Richard Cardinal Cushing of Boston introduced the document on religious liberty. As Bishop Robert E. Tracy put it, *cappuccinos* went untasted and tired joints went unlimbered as most of the Fathers held to their seats to hear the mighty Alfredo Cardinal Ottaviani sum up the position of the Curia, "Religious truth, this I can understand. But religious liberty, this I cannot understand at all."

The minority managed to have the vote postponed into the fourth session. As French journalist Henri Fesquet condensed the action: "Once again the Church of yesterday plotted against the Church of today." The conservative forces in Spain and Western Europe had managed to delay the vote. According to Jack Egan, "They incurred the ire of Cardinal Meyer and it was very difficult to incur. He then led the fight to see that it was kept on the agenda. That's the only time I ever saw the cardinal exercised." Despite the extraordinary fury of its enemies, the Declaration on Religious Liberty passed in the fourth session with only 249 negative votes out of 2,216 votes. It followed up on Pope John XXIII's ratification of liberty in *Pacem in Terris*, when he affirmed that "the dignity of the human person demands that man enjoy freedom of action." Its passage removed one of the principal obstacles to ecumenism.

With the bishops busy at committee meetings in the afternoon, Jack Egan was alone in the common room reading the *Herald Tribune* on the afternoon the committee voted on the final draft of the document on religious liberty. He was having a hard time concentrating. He knew how much the future of the Church coasted on the outcome of this vote. He looked up as he heard footsteps. Then the door pushed open, and the large ascetic form of Father John Courtney Murray burst into the room.

Jack was taken aback. He had been in groups with Father Murray, but they were by no means close friends. What did it mean that he was returning to the *pensione* alone at such an hour? Had something gone amiss? John Courtney Murray's grinning face belied any such interpretation. He stood before Jack Egan, arms thrown out, as if to embrace the whole world, the whole future. He looked happy, expansive, gratified, welcoming.

At that moment he also looked immense to Jack who stood almost a foot under Courtney Murray's six and a half feet of exulting jubilation. Jack hesitated momentarily. John Courtney Murray grinned at this friend of Chicago's Cardinal Meyer, this quiet priest who'd been spending his days listening intently to the *periti's* analyses of every document. Finally, Father Murray gave his triumph voice. "Jack," he exulted, "we won. We won."

Jack bounded across the room, dropping the *Herald Tribune*, and embraced this priest who had endured so much suffering to bring to his beloved Church a truth that his beloved country lived. The two men sat down to rehash the final hours of the committee meeting. Courtney Murray told Jack how respectful Cardinal Ottaviani had been, and how difficult Cardinal Browne was, who had spoken up for the document, who feared it. They sat in silence a minute, respecting the unlikeliness of the whole episode. Religious liberty in the Church! The integrity of religious conviction! "If I am not mistaken," Jack recalls, "the vote was eighteen to five in committee, or thirteen to five. Then later, of course, when it was presented to the whole council, it passed." Jack Egan will never forget that afternoon. "It was one of the great moments of my life."

On another night, Jack Egan found himself in the common room with Fathers Courtney Murray, Hans Kung, and Gregory Baum after everyone else had gone to bed. "Their whole life was the Church," he says of the theologians who were on this evening deep into discourse about the birth control issue. "Obviously," Jack clarifies, "this was before 1968 and the publication of *Humanae Vitae*. I listened very, very, carefully to these fine, fine theological minds and here they were giving a probable opinion." (In theology, a probable opinion is one that a person can act on.)

"Gentlemen," he asked when there was a pause, "I want to understand what you are saying. Are you saying the practice of birth control is to be determined by the prayer and the conscience of the individual couple and in doing so that they are living under the canons of the best of traditional theology?" They turned as one and said to Jack, "That's absolutely right."

Jack read the questioning looks on their faces to mean, "Haven't you been listening to us?" They pointed out that they'd gone through all the theological developments from St. Thomas on, and "it's certainly right that the couple is the final determinant in their own conscience, with prayer, and if necessary, consultation, to make the decision to practice birth control."

Jack was startled at what was, for him, an absolutely new concept. When he'd been ordained, no less a nabob than the vicar general of the archdiocese had instructed the seminarians that "we were to ask any person who was coming to Confession and had been away from Confession for more than six months, whether they were practicing birth control." And now it was the couples' business, not the priest's? What wonders this council had wrought! (Twenty-five years later, Jack still saw the birth control question as not fully resolved even though Pope John Paul II was holding fast to the position of Pope Paul VI.)

Jack Egan is a great believer in expressing gratitude. He's forever listing the "funders" who have made his life what it is. Before he left Rome on one of his council forays, he had a chance to thank a benefactor who'd exerted himself at a particularly sensitive time in Jack's life. When Monsignor George Higgins first invited Jack to a reception for the Protestant observers, Jack demurred. "George, I don't belong there." Monsignor Higgins importuned, insisting that it was an open affair. So Jack went. As soon as he saw Francis Cardinal Spellman across the room, Jack was glad of his decision.

Going up to the cardinal, Jack introduced himself as a priest of the archdiocese of Chicago. Then he delivered a message he'd been saving in his "when-I-get-the-opportunity-pouch" since 1958. "Your Eminence," he said, "I was a priest living at Our Lady of Angels in Chicago at the time of the fire. I was in the sacristy when you came in and embraced Cardinal Meyer. We were all practically in tears.

"This was a time of unbelievable grief for Cardinal Meyer. He had been in the diocese only two weeks. I will never forget your kindness to all of us in coming out, and being with us, and sharing our sorrow. I just wanted to thank you." Cardinal Spellman had done what Jack Egan would have done had the circumstances been reversed. Jack Egan wanted him to know that he appreciated the gesture—and its cost. No other American bishop had come to share that unforgettably tragic moment.

16

"I Understand There Are Troublemakers in This City"

Like Martin Luther King in 1965, the movement priests in Chicago had been to the mountaintop. They were exultant. Vatican II gains were beyond their expectation. The Chicago moment had towered into the American moment. Again, like Dr. King, they would suffer grievous reverses.

Twenty years later, Jack Egan would designate the beginning of the Golden Age of the American Church to 1940, about the time Monsignor Hillenbrand's first seminarians were ordained. He'd date the Golden Age's termination to that time in 1965 when the Vatican Council ended. But that's hindsight. From their mountaintop in 1965, no Chicago priests would have guessed how quick their fall would be. Their general euphoria had boded a New Age, not a Dark Age.

When Cardinal Meyer returned from Rome after the passage of the decree on religious liberty, Chicago priests greeted him with a sustained ovation at the Resurrection Parish Hall. America's lived experience of religious liberty was now Church doctrine. The Holy Spirit had worked through American Catholics (probably the lay people best prepared for the Council, according to Jack Egan's observation), their priests, and then through their bishops.

"The future enters into us, in order to transform itself in us, long before it happens." Poet Rainer Maria Rilke could have been describing Chicago's priests—especially those on the leading wedge of change— who considered themselves vessels, in Rilke's sense, of the Vatican II transformation. The document on the Church in the modern world validated their work. Their insights on marriage. Their ecumenical contacts. Their experiments in human relations. Their explorations of liturgical change. Their actions for justice. They shared a gratified feeling that

173

Chicago had been a model, a workshop, for the Council. Hadn't they tried out many of the initiatives that the bishops had debated? Would the Council have been the same if Chicago hadn't been open to the future entering into it?

What possibilities were there in that future whose transformation they'd shared in making? How willing was the Church to embrace the world? How high could they climb? Where could they go from the mountain top? At that peak moment, few of them would have answered, "Down."

It was not unexpected that curial forces in Rome jockeyed to recapture control of the Church once the world's bishops jetted back to their flocks. As Jack Egan came home with the priest friend who'd sustained him after the Our Lady of the Angels fire, Father Tom McDonough predicted chillingly that the Curia would get on with its running of the Church, dismissing the Council as "those bishops putting out some— not very important—papers." Jack Egan preferred John Courtney Murray's assessment. On the one occasion when the four priests forbidden to lecture together at Catholic University *did* get together, the author of the religious liberty document spoke hopefully. He looked forward to, maybe, fifteen years of confusion after Vatican II. "Then," he assured the thirty-two priests gathered to say goodbye to their Roman carnival, "I think we are going to see the development of a glorious Church."

Courtney Murray saw green lights ahead. So did Chicago's priests. They'd grown used to their cardinals as a visible—and whole-hearted— means of support. What with episcopal encouragement and the Council's breakthroughs, future Church seemed close as the next intersection.

It wasn't going to work out that way. In surprisingly short order (so much does traffic turn on the traffic manager), the Church in Chicago went into shock. On March 16, 1965, Cardinal Meyer survived a four hour and twenty minute operation to remove a malignant tumor on the right side of his brain. The sixty-two-year-old Cardinal died at Mercy Hospital on April 9, 1965, months before the wind-up of the Vatican Council at which he'd made history. The chronicle of Holy Name parish notes that his untimely death "was looked upon as a severe loss not only for the people of the Church of Chicago, but for the people of the Church Universal." Chicago priests would have reason to mourn that loss.

On June 15, 1965, the Most Reverend John Patrick Cody was appointed Archbishop of Chicago. He was installed August 24, 1965, as head of a diocese with 447 parishes, 278 in the city of Chicago and 169 in the suburbs of Lake and Cook counties. Forty-one percent of the combined population of those two counties were Catholics, making Chicago the largest diocese in the country at that time. Rumors about changes abounded—the clerical rumor mill is always spinning—as the city awaited the new archbishop busy in Rome as the Vatican Council wound down.

As archbishop in New Orleans, Cody had gained a reputation as an able administrator and a staunch upholder of civil rights. He'd directed the integration of the Catholic schools. According to the Chicago archdiocesan history, "his unequivocal stand on racial justice was a model for educators throughout the Deep South."

Nonetheless, to the priests of the archdiocese, the mode of governance Archbishop Cody manifested in both Kansas City and New Orleans, and replicated when he arrived in Chicago, was not in keeping with the finest of the traditions of Vatican II. "That may be unkind," Jack Egan admits, "but that was the impression we had. He would have been a great archbishop in the thirties, but after two bishops who were encouraging, cooperative, permissive, progressive . . ." Jack's voice slows and limps away like an disheartened runner.

Mary Louise Schniedwind, who manned the Office of Urban Affairs office, puts the case more bluntly. She calls Cody's ascension to the Chicago archbishopric a tragedy. "We'd laid some good groundwork," she says. "There seemed to be hope for the city. But Cardinal Cody proceeded to destroy what anybody else had created up to that point. If he didn't think it up or if he wasn't in charge, it was no good." Unfortunately, the new archbishop had not thought up the Interreligious Council on Urban Affairs which Mary Louise characterizes as "a powerful voice making statements in City Hall."

Jack had reason to take an interest in Archbishop Cody's governance, because Archbishop Cody, once home from the Council at the end of November, thought he had reason to take an interest in Jack Egan. The archbishop's first priority was appointing Father John Fahey pastor of St. Luke's Church in River Forest so that influential parish would have a priest for Christmas. Through the clerical pipeline—Fahey to McDonough to Egan—Jack learned he was next. "I understand there are some troublemakers in the city and I should go to work and put them in their proper place," the archbishop told Father Fahey. The "troublemakers" were Rynie's boys with familiar names: Jack Egan, Jake Killgallon, Gerry WebeWr, Bill Quinn, and Dan Cantwell. They were all to get large, poor, black parishes to keep them from troubling their new archbishop.

Jack Egan got the first phone call—as fateful in its way as the life-changing call bidding him visit Cardinal Stritch almost twenty years before—from Monsignor Francis Byrne, Chancellor of the Archdiocese. It was January, 1966. "The archbishop would like to see you." Assuming the appointment would be for the following day, Jack asked the time. "The archbishop wants to see you right now," Monsignor Byrne advised. Jack headed out immediately for the Chancery Office, newly located in the American Dental Building, 211 E. Chicago, "where I waited two hours to see Archbishop Cody."

The archbishop, his jowly face unresponsive, didn't glance up from the letters he was signing when Jack was shown into his office. He seemed incurious at this first encounter with one of the city's most controversial priests. Jack remembers Archbishop Cody must have "signed about twenty letters while I was sitting there, commenting as he did, 'Well, people will have to get used to this signature.'"

When the archbishop finally raised his eyes from his task, Jack rose to his feet to shake his hand. The pleasantries were minimal. "Monsignor, sit down," Archbishop Cody directed. "Monsignor McCarthy at Presentation is resigning and I would like you to accept the pastorship of that parish. Is that all right with you?"

"Your Eminence, is that what you want?" Jack asked.

"Yes, it is."

"Then it's perfectly acceptable to me." Jack spoke out of a lifetime habit of obedience. Nonetheless, he felt compelled to express his loyalty to the work he was doing. "What happens to the Office of Urban Affairs?"

"Well, you can keep that job," the archbishop said, dismissing any importance it might have to Jack Egan by adding, "I understand there's not much going on in that office anyway."

Jack saw his interfaith work ground underfoot like a cigarette butt under a private's heel. "I don't know where you got that information," he insisted stoutly, "but that is not true. We are doing a lot of things."

Archbishop Cody was unmoved. "Well, we are going to have to double up on a lot of things in the Archdiocese of Chicago. I think you'll be able to do both jobs." The archbishop's sardonic dismissal indicated a disrespect for Presentation as well as the Office of Urban Affairs. The archbishop was asking Jack Egan to continue as the OUA director, already an exhausting responsibility. Additionally, Jack was to function as pastor of a church changed from completely white to completely black in a decade and a half. Jack was to be only the third pastor of a church described by Monsignor Koenig in the archdiocesan history as once "a source of protection, strength and love for all those who claim it as their parish." That's when it was "a bon ton Irish immigrant parish," in the words of the priest then acting pastor, "if those aren't contradictory concepts." Established in 1898 to serve West Side Irish Catholics, its 1,574 families were less than one percent black in 1950. By the time Monsignor John J. Egan got his appointment as pastor from Archbishop Cody in January, 1966, the area was almost 100 percent black. Only 400 families were coming to Mass of a Sunday in the heavily ornate Spanish Renaissance style church.

The city of Chicago immediately served notice that giving two draining jobs to a priest who'd had a near-fatal heart attack four years before would not go unnoticed. When the archdiocesan newspaper, *The New World*, carried a routine announcement that the Very Reverend John Joseph Egan, *formerly* director of the Office of Urban Affairs, was transferred to Presentation Parish, the city's blood boiled. Jack confronted the archbishop about the "formerly" at a Palmer House luncheon celebrating Monsignor Malachy Foley's retirement as seminary rector. Archbishop Cody was unabashed. "Apparently there are people in this town who just don't get the message straight," he said. "We'll have to make some adjustments."

It was too late. Even Jack Egan was taken aback by the uproar provoked by his transfer. "And I think Archbishop Cody was, too. He was just overwhelmed to read articles, with pictures, three days in a row in the *Chicago Daily News*." The religion editor, Dave Meade, posed Chicago's question: "To Pastor or to Pasture?" Meade speculated on the possibility that the Church was pulling back on interfaith and interracial cooperation. "People deeply involved in the sensitive work of urban renewal, race relations, and interreligious action—at least those willing to talk—are of the opinion that Monsignor Egan's pastoral appointment is the first step in 'phasing out' the influential archdiocesan Office of Urban Affairs," Meade wrote.

He quoted two religious leaders shaken by the news. Rabbi Robert Marx, director of the Great Lakes Region and Chicago Federation of the Union of American Hebrew Congregations, looked for reassurance that the appointment did "not mean the end of the work of the Office of Urban Affairs, which has been such an asset to the city." The Rev. Edgar H. S. Chandler, executive director of the Church Federation of Greater Chicago, noting Egan's "unique competence, vast knowledge and great commitment," expressed his hope that "his appointment will not be the last of his tremendous leadership in urban affairs."

Immediately, there were repercussions in the neighborhoods. The Austin Community Organization steering committee discussed disbanding because several local priests reneged on pledges of funds to the ACO because "they regarded the recent reassignment of the outspoken urban affairs specialist, Msgr. Egan, as a policy shift on the part of the archdiocese." The Austin Organization would get the $22,000 Father Egan had committed before Archbishop Cody's appointment (although the archbishop fought that disposition of the funds). However, that was the last hurrah, "the last money the archdiocese as an archdiocese ever gave to a community organization," according to Jack Egan.

The letters began to rumble in from Jack's friends, from community organization people, and from the interfaith network. "I think Archbishop Cody got five or six hundred letters," Jack recalls, from people as exercised as Tom Gaudette who wanted to throw a picket line around the archbishop's residence when he heard the news. Jack Egan nixed that notion on the grounds that he was not going to protest his bishop's decision. However, Jack did protest when his archbishop pelted the stacks of letters back at him with a note suggesting that, since he, Jack, had organized the letter-writing campaign, he could very well answer the letters.

"I was hurt very, very much," Jack admits. "I wrapped them up and sent them back with a note of my own, disavowing any campaigning on my part." These were "sent to you by the citizens of Chicago," Jack wrote the archbishop. "They are yours to answer." Looking back, he realizes that Archbishop Cody probably threw them away because nobody got any answers. "I should have kept them for a mailing list."

It was obvious that prior to Archbishop Cody's move into the Victorian manse on North State, Father Egan was already something of a symbol in the archdiocese. He was the priest in the front lines of integration. Widely quoted, he was known for his ringing denunciations of "chicanery with numbers" or "calculated obfuscations." He disparaged the "ruthless renewal" urged by a city planner like Robert Moses. He lashed out at the Hyde Park plan. He upbraided the real estate industry for its opposition to open housing. He opposed the Chicago Housing Authority's "high-rise row." He called attention to the suburbs' lack of compassion for the city. He campaigned for the participation of the poor in policy planning. He was a rallying point for those working for the poor in the city. And an irritant to those who profited from the status quo.

In the black community Jack Egan was credited for standing beside the Reverend Ralph Abernathy at Selma, Alabama, at the turning point in the civil rights struggle. The Civil Rights Act of 1964 on the books, blacks were pushing for a Voting Rights Act. Out of 15,000 blacks of voting age in Dallas county (Selma was the county seat), only 333 were eligible to vote.

On March 7, 1965, television viewers across the country witnessed Alabama state troopers beating Hosea Williams and hundreds of marchers at the Edmund Pettus bridge. Jack Egan watched from Sea Island, Georgia, where Dr. Robert and Marion McCready, long-time friends from the Cana Conference, had taken him for much needed rest. Jack felt personally summoned by Dr. Martin Luther King, Jr.'s nation-wide call to ministers of all races and religions to come to Selma. Always careful to stay within his superior's sanction, Jack Egan called first for Cardinal Meyer's blessing on his mission, then apologized to his gracious hosts, and took off. In spite of his doctor's warning not to take part in stressful activities after his 1962 heart attack, Jack flew to Montgomery, Alabama, rented a car, and drove to Selma with his damaged heart in his mouth. "I was scared. I was all alone and going down the streets of Selma with the rednecks standing on each side and me with the Roman collar on."

Once he'd found Mathew Ahmann, director of the National Catholic Conference for Interracial Justice, at a local Catholic rectory, the two began phoning contacts from the coast of Maine to Los Angeles. They stayed up all night, entreating, "Come, please come to Selma." At the time, Dr. King was keeping vigil at the hospital bed of a Unitarian minister from Boston, James Reeb, who'd sustained massive head injuries from a single blow of a club when he and two other white ministers were attacked on a dark street in Selma walking past a Klan-infested juke joint. Taking Dr. King's place, the Rev. Ralph D. Abernathy called for an immediate march, although marches were illegal at night. "I'll never forget it," Jack says. "Abernathy said tonight priests and ministers and religious will march and the lay people will follow behind us, and we'll confront the authorities down the street."

Abernathy continued the instructions: "On my right hand will be a confrere of Jim Reeb who is dying in Birmingham, and on my left hand will be Monsignor John Egan of Chicago." As the march began, another priest offered to take Jack's place, saying, "I know you've had a heart attack." Jack rejoined, "No, you won't," as they marched out of Brown Chapel, down the street and perhaps five hundred yards to confront Wilson Baker, Selma's newly hired director of public safety; two hundred troops, and photographers from all over the country.

"Behind the two hundred troops were about two thousand rednecks, and we were there all night, face to face, with Abernathy talking to Baker, Baker talking to Abernathy, we kneeling down and praying, we standing up and singing. Then it began to rain. We were all arm in arm, C. T. Vivian on my left, Dr. Abernathy on my right. As some of my classmates say, 'They were holding you up, Jack.'"

Jack claims his paramount contribution was getting his picture sent out by the wire services. When it arrived at the *Chicago Daily News* office at five or six that morning, "some reporter recognized me and sent someone to St. Angela's to get Father O'Brien to identify me. They put the picture on the front page and that opened the door. 'If Jack Egan can be there then I can be there,' people said. Remember it was 1965, the Council was still on, there was all that fear we wouldn't have today, the question of whether we could participate." Once fellow religious saw Jack Egan was at Selma, buses and planes were mobilized. Jack's picture was all the imprimatur civil rights sympathizers needed. By the time they started to arrive, Jack Egan was on his way home. He'd done his part toward making the voting rights act a reality.

All but the most committed racists admired the courage of the rabbis, ministers, nuns, priests, and lay people converged at Selma, including this white Chicago priest who marched into an ambush of Alabama state troopers arm in arm with King lieutenants, Reverend Ralph Abernathy and the Reverend C. T. Vivian. At the time, Jack told a *Sun-Times* reporter that Selma was the "first time that I'd been afraid, wearing a Roman collar, to walk through a white neighborhood. It's the first time I've ever seen hate in the eyes of my fellow brothers, or heard a policeman say, 'I'd like to put my club through that priest's skull.'"

Impressed by the "restraint and real love shown by the Negro people there," Jack Egan expressed the hope that, "a steady stream of priests, ministers, and rabbis" would join the Selma marchers. And that happened. As newspapers across the country picked up the wire service picture of the Chicago priest with Abernathy and Vivian and New England ministers Edward Blackman of Boston and Frank Anderson of Braintree, Massachusetts, at the head of the march, religious from across the country converged on Selma to support the blacks demonstrating for the opportunity to vote.

Selma was a success. Four days after the Unitarian minister from Boston died from blows inflicted by Selma racists, President Lyndon Johnson delivered a voting rights bill to Congress. On August 6, President Johnson signed the Voting Rights Act of 1965.

Chicagoans reacted strongly to Jack Egan's being sent to pasture in 1966 because, as Jack says, "they have never forgotten Selma." Widespread knowledge of the seriousness of his 1962 heart attack was also a factor. Archbishop Cody, a connoisseur of power, even the power of popular opinion, was forced into a gesture of reconciliation. Within two weeks of his Presentation appointment, Jack received a letter appointing him a consultor of the archdiocese for three years. "In those days," Jack Egan says, "the consultors were very, very powerful men. There were only twelve of them. Canon law demanded that the archbishop couldn't make any important decisions without consulting them." Whether he wanted to or not, the archbishop was forced to share his power. Sharing power, however, was another thing from allowing underlings to have separate power bases. That Archbishop Cody could not tolerate.

As Jack Egan puts it, "We had a new bishop who found it difficult to deal with anyone with a power base. He did many wonderful things in the city of Chicago. He led the way in seminary development. But he had to exercise control over any organization under the Church's name, particularly those which got financial support." Jack saw Archbishop Cody's strength, and also his weakness, in his ambition and his total distrust of anyone. Evidently with his disposition of the troublemakers into parishes subject to failing boilers and dependent on his generosity

("I am your banker," as he once told a North Shore parish), Archbishop Cody felt safe. Activist priests wouldn't have the energy for creating mischief in the social action sphere if they had to fill in often enough as janitor. Jack smiles ruefully. "Archbishop Cody had an unbelievable power of underestimating people. I think he underestimated the people he put in those five jobs. We were Chicagoans. We understood power. We were survivors."

Looking back, Jack Egan relishes the turn of events. "I'm living with black people for the first time in my life. Archbishop Cody couldn't have given me a greater gift. I don't think he thought of it that way. I think he thought he was getting rid of me."

The archbishop assumed that Father Egan would be dependent on the archdiocese for supplementary support. Although he may not have had the exact figures in hand, he probably had a fair picture of Jack's predicament: a payroll coming up, a school to maintain, the usual monthly bills, and an uncertain boiler. The former pastor Monsignor McCarthy had watched his parish dwindle and his budget careen through the difficult years of change from healthy Irish parish to impoverished ghetto parish. He left behind a cash balance of about three hundred and eighty-two dollars, according to the new pastor.

What Jack Egan had in his "bank" was not money, but people willing to rally round. Volunteer Ann Coe Pugliese, whom Jack Egan knew from the Adult Education Center at Twenty-one West Superior, rallied around the money issue. She suggested to Jack a fund-raising program called Friends of Presentation. A monthly newsletter, a 1966 version of *Just-in Passing*, would alert the fifteen hundred people on Jack's mailing list (and another several hundred from his associates' lists) to the needs of Presentation Parish, the needs of its boiler, its school, its people. The suggested monthly response was two dollars to take care of those needs. No more. Jack would accept more, but he didn't ask more. Who could refuse two dollars?

Jack Egan got volunteers from outside the parish ("who didn't have the home responsibilities of our people") to print, address, and mail the newsletter. Their efforts reaped an average four thousand dollars a month. That was sufficient—along with the generous support of Presentation's four hundred families—to run the parish, but it was never enough to replace the boiler. That megalosaur was a constant concern. When it went out, as it regularly did, the school got cold, the church got cold, the rectory and the convent got cold. "When the hell are you going to get that boiler fixed?" his brother Jim wrote Jack Egan from Darien, Connecticut, months into *The Perils of Dyspeptic Boilers* saga.

Volunteers from city and suburbs came regularly to aid the "wonderful" (Jack's assessment) BVM Sisters in Presentation School. When Gertrude Snodgrass from the neighborhood alerted Jack to neighbors' need for clothing, Jack alerted his contacts. Clothes pelted in. "Good clothes," Jack says. "My friends always did well by our people." Mrs. Snodgrass set up a clothing shop in the church basement tended by the "finest women in the parish," according to Jack. She herself was one of "those people of every age and race who reduce you to silence in their presence because of their natural goodness," Jack adds. When her husband grew ill and she had to take care of him at home, she opened a food pantry from her house. "I just couldn't stand people being hungry. That's why I did it," she said. She helped found the Greater Chicago Food Depository in 1979. Another appeal brought in books along with Mary Louise O'Shaugnessy and Betty Boyle to set up a library.

For personnel, Father Egan visited six seminaries, promising rectors that any of their students bussed to Presentation every Saturday morning at nine o'clock would get an inner city church experience. Jack assigned each of the sixty weekly seminarian/volunteers his own "parish," a square city block for which he was responsible. They called the program Operation Saturation. Privy as he was to the value of person-to-person contact, Jack Egan coached the seminarians on their responsibilities. "You're to get to know every person in every house or apartment. You're to find out who is ill. Who is out of work. Who has housing problems. Whose kids aren't in school. At the end of the day you're to report to me on every problem you uncover. We'll discuss then what we are going to do about it."

Word got around that something was happening at Presentation. Religious from around the country appeared on the doorstep. Jack welcomed them all, promising free board for two nights, and then a farewell handshake for anyone not prepared to work. For Jack Egan, "work" meant visiting all those troubled, impoverished, sickly, people inventoried by the Saturday seminarians.

There were some surprises for Jack, even in himself. "I'll never forget the first night. I went up to (Father) Jack Gilligan's room. Father Tom Millea and Father Jack Hill were there. I can't imagine myself doing this or saying this. They were having a drink and there was a bottle of Scotch on the top of the dresser. Now we're on the third floor of the rectory and here's the new pastor, saying, 'Fellows, do you think we should have a bottle out in public like this?' I turned them off. I remember them looking at one another, thinking who the hell let him in. They had just got rid of Monsignor McCarthy, an old conservative, and now this guy comes along, Jack Egan, whom they know!"

Jack describes his reversion to prototype domineering Irish tyrant as "a certain type of rigorism that did occupy my life when I was given positions of authority up to the time I was at Presentation. I think I've lost it, I hope I've lost it," he says now. He had exploded at his surprised young associates in their own rooms on their own time. "Here was a man trained in YCS, YCW, the Christian Family Movement, and in community organization all through the fifties and sixties. Now I go into that parish as a pastor. I practically forget all my training. Why? Because I was scared," Jack admits. He was scared by the huge responsibility he'd been given. Driven by that fear and by his gut hankering to succeed, he momentarily parodied himself. But he didn't please himself. His bona fide style was eliciting cooperation, not demanding conformity. Jack Hill, now resigned from the priesthood, doesn't remember the Scotch story. He remembers Father Egan greeting his new associates, "Well, guys, I'm home."

Jack had another compulsion: to clean out the storehouse/basement. Calling a chaplain friend at the Great Lakes Naval Station, he recruited a busload of sailors to heave out generations of junk furniture and scrub down the boiler. Later, that reamed-out basement would house Presentation's most dynamic program, the Contract Buyers League.

Jack Egan advertised his mecca all over the city, knowing from his experiences with Cana and community organizing how many people in the city craved the opportunity to serve the city. The notice he put up at Mundelein College on the city's North Side drew Kathy Pelletier, then a young BVM Sister in training. From her point of view, her community hadn't yet responded forcefully enough to the race question in the city. When she saw an ad suggesting that she could learn something, be useful, and have simultaneously a great weekend, she turned up at Presentation.

"It was like an ad for Florida," she recalls. "We need your talents, your competence, your compassion. Come, live with us, and learn from the people. Let your self be touched and let your heart be opened. Feel the deep joy here." The young Sisters and their students read the job descriptions: cleaning streets, sweeping basements, painting doors. Nonetheless, Kathy says, "when I heard that rallying cry, I was going to go."

She was initially put off by Jack's growly, "Hey, you missed something over here," as she was sweeping up glass in front of the church. "I turned around. Father Egan looked very stern. He had a briefcase in one hand. He was pointing to weeds coming up between the cracked concrete." Kathy thought he was crazy. There was glass everywhere. What was he fussing about? "With that, he gave me this big grin. He grabbed me, gave me a hug, and said, 'Welcome to the team. I'm glad you're here. I'm Jack Egan.'"

That night at dinner Kathy had her first experience of the exciting community that Jack Egan had already drawn to Presentation. "There were twenty or twenty-five of us," representing the two realities of Presentation. First, that community of people energized by the ferment of the times to donate their talents to Chicago's West Side. Second, the residents of the Lawndale neighborhood where, "I don't think there was a day that went by there wasn't shooting," according to former Presentation principal Mary Dowling.

Kathy Pelletier describes changes Jack made. "Before Jack came, there was this tight little group of white people who had this exclusive community. Some privileged black people came in to go to school. Some came to go to church." But the rectory "was an island unto itself. It operated by itself," as far as the black community was concerned. When Jack came, he opened the windows. He opened the doors. He planted flowers. He pulled down the wrought iron fence with the gate that intimidated visitors. To Kathy the mix of people that streamed in from the neighborhood and from all over the country was phenomenal. "From PhDs to Willie Nelson down the street." The dynamic was: "once you got there you wanted to come back, you wanted to stay there. It was a family in the sense that you argued—there were a lot of people you would never choose to live with—fought, disagreed. There was a lot of learning from the people in the neighborhood. All fall and summer, it was like a lid had just popped off something."

The realities were daunting. Streets and parkways littered with old paper and broken glass. Apartments with no screens on windows or screen doors. Sick children. Rats. Housing inadequate in every aspect. Hundreds of high school dropouts. Fifty percent of the residents crowded into the area under fifteen years old. Abandoned buildings.

Joblessness. Kathy Pelletier describes a parish worker bringing groceries into a kitchen with what he thought was one dark wall. When he
switched on the electricity, the "darkness" wriggled to life. It was a
whole wall of cockroaches. Kathy had no trouble believing his horrified
story because she'd encountered similar moving walls of insects.
"Landlords simply weren't taking care of places," she says.

At first, Kathy remembers, tenants were hesitant about letting this
army of white people into their homes. "There was reluctance to talk,"
she adds. Yet, in the end, "there weren't very many people told they
couldn't come in." And the effort did bring in a corps of people from
the neighborhood. What was disheartening was the enormousness and
enormity of the problems. It's Kathy Pelletier's sense that Presentation
teams made "only a tiny beginning" on using the information they
culled in Operation Saturation. The results were limited.

Yet, while it lasted, the Presentation time was electric with excitement. Jack's clarion command was, "If we're going to do it, let's have
fun while we're doing it." Jack would expect everyone to work hard, to
do his or her best, Kathy Pelletier recalls. "There was no fooling
around about that." But they had to laugh to get through the day. "Just
looking at the devastation around us. The suffering. The incredible
hardship. The institutional violence. We had to make fun of ourselves
and each other or we'd all be crazy. We couldn't take ourselves too
seriously because we knew our efforts were pitiful" against the need.

It was Kathy's job for Caravan: Operation Balloon to get a daily
tank of helium donated so she could put on her blue "Presentation" tee
shirt, gas up the Presentation van, and set up at a vacant lot near the
church. The kids attracted by her helium balloons were set to work at
art projects or organized into volleyball and baseball games. Every
morning and afternoon thirty of them boarded the Presentation bus for a
field trip to a museum, the beach, maybe the Garfield Park swimming
pool. Many of these kids had never before run through Lake Michigan
sand or splashed in the water. Another worker was back at the rectory
phoning around for free instruments for the drum and bugle corps.
Some teachers were doing remedial work with kids who needed it. Others were painting the schoolrooms bright orange, blue, yellow, and
green with paint they paid for from their own pockets, and hanging up
huge murals of Martin Luther King.

In the evenings, there were educational opportunities for adults,
GED courses for those who wanted to pass high school equivalency

tests. A volunteer taught boys carpentry. Neighbor Sam Flowers taught others the tool and die trade, and then tried to get them jobs.

The people who lived and worked at Presentation, like principal Mary Dowling, were attracted to the West Side because—in a country up for grabs—"everything important going on in the country was re-flected on the West Side of Chicago, civil rights, peace." Mary Dowling had "never seen anything like this, a parish where things were happen-ing." Politically active in college a few years before, she felt she was "coming home" to these politically and socially active people.

To her and Kathy Pelletier, the eye of the storm was the rectory dining room. Meals meant "ideas feeding off ideas." People hardly knew what wonderful victuals Maria Jones was feeding them in their hunger for new understanding of the world about them. Many of them were in personal identity and power struggles with their religious or-ders. "The first year there were nine Sisters in the convent. The next year there were a couple of old Sisters. The rest paid rent to live in the convent, and kept the same jobs, but they weren't nuns any more." They hung around Presentation because they were committed to poor people and to education. They quit their communities and set up their own structures because they were not allowed to serve poor people and education as Sisters under the dominion of Cardinal Cody. When they tried to respond to people's needs as they saw them, Cardinal Cody got in the way, a "consecrated obstruction," as English economist Walter Bagehot said of King George III. For instance, when Martin Luther King, Jr., brought his campaign to empower blacks into Chicago, the Sisters who supported him took responsibility for rounding up local people for a big King rally at Soldier Field. The cardinal insisted they desist. They rallied participants, anyway. Then the cardinal forbade the Sisters themselves to attend. How could they show solidarity with the people of Lawndale if they stayed away?

Father Egan assured his associates struggling with personal decisions that they could still provide their expertise to the people of Lawndale. And they did, sometimes in extravagant ways. To make the Easter lit-urgy meaningful one year, those in charge strung a garden hose up the center aisle of the nave and forty feet into the air to create a fantastic fountain sprinkling water and new life. Jack Egan's teasing protest that he couldn't read the Gospel because his glasses were all wet was the only complaint. What people talked about was the compelling force of the wonderful old Negro spirituals of resurrection sung under this incredible symbol of new life that Father George Fleming and Father Jack Hill had Rube-Goldberged together. "Who would expect that wonder in the middle of Lawndale?" Kathy Pelletier asks. "Or the restraint and respect and taste with which it was created?"

Rectory dinners were like ping pong matches. "We'd all tease and go after each other. Then we'd talk about how good it all was." After the Holy Saturday garden hose liturgy, everyone repaired back to the rectory for good talk until two in the morning. That was expected. At times like these, Kathy Pelletier began to examine "the familiar, the values my family had passed on, what I had learned in school, and the fragile beliefs that had not yet been tested at the age of twenty-one—all in the light of what I was seeing, hearing, doing, and thinking in the Lawndale community on the West Side of Chicago right after Selma and right before Martin Luther King's assassination. The sense I have of that time at Presentation is that I was in some way 'broken into.'"

One of Mary Dowling's first surprises was the wall in the common room signed by all the guests who'd come to share Maria's coq au vin. As she studied the signatures, Mary realized, "Everybody I'd read about in college had sat on that sofa." Jack Egan liked to recall the night he invited Dorothy Day and Saul Alinsky for one of Maria Jones' conveniently stretchable meals. He warned the other guests to hush their tongues and listen to these two great advocates for the poor. "You'll learn a lot," he told the regulars, reminding them of his trip with Saul Alinsky to a Bakersfield, California, rally of the United Farm Workers where Jack met Cesar Chavez. Pressed by Jack Egan about his motivation for getting into community organizing, Alinsky had told Jack "almost in a whisper, as if he didn't want anyone else to hear, 'Jack, I got in it and stayed in it because it was fun, and also because I hate to see people get pushed around—by government, by big business, or even by your big Church.'" The questers hanging around Presentation, wrestling with authority problems, easily related to that view.

Exciting as things were in the rectory, and devastating as they were in the neighborhood, neither was preparation for the incredible destruction to come. Helium balloons, rap sessions at the rectory, and garden hose fountains could not contain the breakdown after the assassination of Dr. Martin Luther King, Jr. But before that breakdown, a former priest at Presentation, John Hill, remembers Jack Egan keeping "a light of hope shining for a few years in an otherwise bleak ghetto. Specific programs didn't fulfill their promise, but they gave a bit of hope to a population sorely in need of it." Hill adds that during those years the liturgy "was appreciably better." More important, he told Father Egan, "in you many black families met the one white person they could call a lasting friend."

Father Egan, once he'd leapfrogged over the "no Scotch in your rooms" hurdle, gave his associates and parishioners a lot of respect. He subscribed to Leon-Joseph Cardinal Suenens' exhortation to the Council Fathers that Baptism gives charisms "of vital importance" to each and every Christian, "lettered or unlettered." Suenens said, "It is the duty of pastors to listen carefully and with an open heart to laymen and repeatedly to engage in a living dialogue with them. For each and every layman has been given his own gifts and charisms, and more often than not has greater experience than the clergy in daily life in the world."

Jack Hill was amazed how carefully, with what an open heart, Jack Egan listened not only to his associate priests, but also to lay parishioners. He truly shared responsibility. "Jack acquitted himself very well at Presentation," Hill says. "He was sort of like an equal of us." Egan gave Hill the impression "that he thought it was going to be a good ride and he wanted to be there for it. Smack dab in the middle of the sixties," Hill says, the idea of team ministry, "the idea that a pastor would sit down and talk things over," was novel. "The idea that you bring laypersons on parish councils and let them make decisions was even more novel.

"This wasn't a do-gooder thing," Hill add. "Jack didn't call parishioners by their first names. He treated all parishioners with respect. They respected him and loved him." Hill doesn't prettify the difficulties. "It was a time of emotional and pastoral chaos, but it was creative. I look back at it fondly."

Cardinal Suenens could counsel open-hearted listening and shared decision-making. He didn't describe the wear and tear on pastors inspired by his ideas, the pastors who faced up to need. At Presentation, more than anywhere Jack Egan had been, the needs in the rectory, in the Church, in the school, and in the neighborhood, were overwhelming. Although needs were Jack Egan's shtick, the needs he found at Presentation came close to overwhelming him.

17

"The Worst Kept Secret in Chicago"

The nurses had dosed Jack Egan for a good night's rest prior to his 1980 heart valve surgery at Rush-Presbyterian-St. Luke's Medical Center. Groggy and scared, he was courting sleep's blessed release when he heard a rustle at his bedside. "I sort of had tears in my eyes thinking about what was going to happen to me the next morning," Jack says, explaining why he didn't immediately recognize the black face looking down at him.

"You don't remember me, do you?" the after-hours visitor said, identifying himself as Rutherford Maynard. "Oh, my God." Jack was more alert now. "You have grown up. You're so good-looking. Tell me what you've been doing." And Maynard told the story he wanted Father Egan to hear before he had his life-threatening surgery. His voice flowed as he sketched a playground scene of a Father pastor counseling a black youngster sweaty and tuckered after a parking lot basketball game, exhorting the boy to finish high school, to stay out of gangs and away from dope because he had a great future. "You encouraged me to go to high school," Maynard said, "and then to the University of Illinois where I became an architect. You got me an entry level job at Skidmore, Owings, and Merrill where I studied under Bruce Graham. Now I'm starting my own firm."

Rutherford Maynard's was a heart-warming success story out of Presentation. But Presentation was not a clear success story. No pastor could have "succeeded" at Presentation in 1965. What Jack Egan could do—and tried to do—was accept people like Rutherford Maynard where they were in their lives and preach to them, as he persistently did, the "dignity of their person, the dignity of their work, and their calling to a life of holiness and therefore a life of happiness."

What was chastening was the result of his efforts. Jack Egan had few available models for empowering the oppressed. No matter how sound priests were theoretically, practically they found it extremely difficult to share power. It was their trade-off, in some sense, for their sacrifice of the rewards of home and family. Jack's mentor, Monsignor Hillenbrand, was so admired that Jack Egan's associate John Hill used poet Edwin Arlington Robinson's expression that he "glittered when he walked" to describe him. Yet Hillenbrand could not share his power with the young followers who had once stood in clusters, their faces "fairly glistening," in Hill's words, with admiration for him. When one of those followers took a lonely position on the Hyde Park-Kenwood project, Monsignor Hillenbrand couldn't translate his belief in Jack Egan's inherent dignity into respect for Jack Egan's course of action.

Rutherford Maynard's coming in the night bears out John Hill's contention that many black people found a friend in Father Egan. Yet Hill counts few structural improvements. A look at Jack's years at Presentation shows how heavy the issues were. Maintenance of old buildings. Support of the school and the summer programs. Organization of the volunteers energized by need and Vatican II initiatives. Curtailment of the Office of Urban Affairs. The waning of the Interreligious Council on Urban Affairs. The rise of the Association of Chicago Priests. And, pervasively, the restless, turbulent tremors of the national friction over civil rights.

Dr. Martin Luther King, Jr., and the Southern Christian Leadership Conference had parleyed resistance to that Southern racism incarnated in Eugene "Bull" Connor and Sheriff Jim Clark into the Civil Rights Act of 1964 and the Voting Rights Act of 1965. It was time in 1966, by their lights, to throw their weight against the racism in northern cities. Encouraged by reports about the supportive religious community in Chicago, Dr. King rented a four-room, $90 month apartment in an aging building at 1550 S. Hamlin Avenue, down the street from Presentation Church. He moved in with his wife Coretta on January 26, 1966.

King found himself butting a wall of putty in Chicago instead of the wall of granite his co-marchers grazed against in Birmingham and Selma. Mayor Richard J. Daley was as adept at dodging empathy-mobilizing confrontation as Bull Connor had been lead-footed in creating it. The mayor's Director of Human Relations, Edward Marciniak, had met Dr. King at the airport the previous July. The Mayor himself gave orders that Dr. King's neighborhood should be spruced up. Mayor Daley carefully acknowledged the worries of ghetto dwellers and promised to remedy any evils brought to his attention.

Typically, Jack walked down to welcome his new neighbor to Lawndale soon after Dr. King arrived. He accomplished more for Dr. King's
movement, however, as an archdiocesan consultor than as a neighbor.
As a consultor, Jack Egan harried Archbishop Cody into agreeing to
take a part, however removed from the scene, at Dr. King's July 10,
1966, rally. This gathering at Soldier Field was planned as the kickoff
of the Chicago movement's action phase, an attempt to call attention to
urban segregation and make Chicago an "open city." Dr. King pledged
a peaceful campaign. "I'm trying to keep the movement nonviolent," he
told a questioner, "but I can't keep it nonviolent by myself. Much of
the responsibility is on the white power structure to give meaningful
concessions to Negroes."

To get any concessions, King had to forge alliances. Churches were
his natural allies. The Catholic Church in Chicago, indigenous and influential, was indispensable. Jack Egan knew that. He pressed the case
for supporting King even though he was aware of opposition, even
within the Church. Citing the bishops' 1958 statement on race, he told
his archbishop, "You don't have to be (at the Soldier Field rally), but
you'll endanger the city if you don't support Dr. King." John Hill remembers Archbishop Cody as ticked off at Martin Luther King, Jr.
("Remember how he vilified King?" he reminded Jack Egan. "The FBI
fed him some stuff.")

Hill believes the speech Jack Egan wrote, and persuaded the archbishop to have Bishop Aloysius Wycislo read in the archbishop's name
at Soldier Field, strengthened Dr. King's position. "If Cody had sat on
his hands," Hill surmises, "all those Catholics who were racists would
have said he supported them. And the gains made in Church/black community relations by Friendship House and people like (Monsignor) Dan
Cantwell and (Father) Doc Farrell would have been rolled back. King's
influence in Chicago would certainly have been affected."

Blacks recognized the importance of the archbishop's statement that
Jack Egan wrote. Disappointed when the rally turnout fell short of their
projected one hundred thousand, they were heartened by "a surprisingly
strong message of support from Archbishop Cody," according to David
Garrow in *Bearing the Cross*. Some people in the Chicago religious
community were proving to be supportive, as blacks had hoped.

But not supportive enough. By August 10, Archbishop Cody was
advising King to suspend the marches designed to demonstrate the injustices of residential segregation. What the marches were bringing to

the surface was the white/black rift in the city. Black leaders, for their part, thought Archbishop Cody should be addressing racist real estate professionals, not the marchers.

At the time, Michael Schiltz of the National Opinion Research Center faulted not so much Archbishop Cody as the Catholic pastoral ministry that "took no steps of any consequence, during the migration and resettlement of the fifties, to help its flock separate the class aspects of their experience from the race aspects, nor to preach, 'in and out of season,' understanding and charity." He ascribed the ugliness that accompanied Dr. King's marches into segregated areas when "mobs of loyal Catholics in Gage Park turned not only on the Chicago Freedom marchers but on their parish priests and pastors" as symptomatic of "a growing moral cancer of the fifties." Schiltz also lamented Archbishop Cody "could find no space" in the Chancery Office for men like Monsignor Jack Egan and Monsignor Dan Cantwell who'd been in constant touch with the civil rights struggle.

About this time, Chicagoan Peggy Roach, who'd been spearheading social action issues at the National Council of Catholic Women in Washington, planned a move back to Chicago where her mother had only a few years to live. Like Jack, Peggy had been interested in race issues early on, influenced by Father Martin Carrabine at CISCA and Summer Schools of Catholic Action at the Morrison Hotel. "What Hillenbrand did for seminarians," Peggy suggests, "Carrabine did for lay people," for Chicago students. As a St. Scholastica High School student, Peggy had had to accept her mother's insistence that she couldn't visit Friendship House at Forty-third and Indiana in a black neighborhood all by herself, however strong her interest in exploring black/white relationships.

Later, Baroness de Hueck initiated a Friendship House Outer Circle that met at that battered old schoolhouse at Three East Chicago Avenue where Peggy's sister Jane would later scrub floors as a Young Christian Student. ("She never has time to scrub them at home," was Mrs. Roach's—"everymother's"—comment about her daughter's apostolic activities.) When Peggy still couldn't find a friend to accompany her, Mrs. Roach agreed to a series of monthly treks to hear the Baroness boom out the story of her spiritual journey. An ample matron of forceful mien, hair drawn up in a bun, the Baroness romanced her impressionable listeners with tales of her pilgrimage from privileged child in Russia to advocate for North American blacks. Peggy was impressed, although she didn't take up the Baroness' cause during her early work years after graduation from Mundelein College.

Wherever Peggy was working, however, at Mundelein in alumnae relations, with Nina Polcyn at St. Benet Book Shop, at the naval station at Glenview, she was part of the activist John A. Ryan Forum group. Founded by Monsignor Cantwell as a fund-raiser for the Catholic Labor Alliance, the John A. Ryan Forums were the *ne plus ultra* of the Chicago movement. Four times a year a speaker, perhaps a Walter Reuther out of labor circles, would preach to Chicago's converted and catalyze transactions between Chicago's Catholic Action "Four Hundred," those who shared the action and passion of their times with no risk of never having lived. These were the live wires of the Catholic Church's electric moment in the city.

Peggy had been part of that circle as executive secretary of the Archdiocesan Council of Catholic Women before she went to Washington. Drumming up volunteer slots for ACCW members, she'd come to know the people at the city's social service agencies.

Peggy got directly into race relations at the Catholic Interracial Council where she organized the fund raisers honoring Sargent Shriver one year and Lyndon Johnson the next, fund raisers that provided sixty percent of the CIC budget. The CIC was on the third floor of Twenty-one West Superior, above Matt Ahmann's National Catholic Conference for Interracial Justice on the first floor of that Catholic Action axis. When Russ Barta, a major force on the Catholic scene as director of Archdiocesan Adult Education, got a query from Margaret Mealey, executive director of the National Council of Catholic Women, about a staff opening for a social action and legislation person, he told Mealey, "You need a Peggy Roach." Margaret Mealey wooed Peggy to Washington. Without Matt Ahmann's advice to look up NCCW member Hope Brophy, however, Peggy might not have made the NCCW commitment. Hope persuaded Peggy that only someone with her CIC background could "raise awareness of Catholic women over the country about race. Only if we get someone out of a CIC can we get that to happen." Peggy went to Washington hoping that she could raise the social consciousness of the thousands of NCCW women in the country.

Only a saving remnant of NCCW women, women like Hope Brophy, were ready to move as fast as Peggy. Hope, who couldn't go herself, paid Peggy's airfare to the Selma march when Matt Ahmann called for volunteers. Peggy went with the Chicago NCCIJ group. In an all-night session with her Selma host family, Peggy got "the greatest education of my life" from the three black couples responsible for billeting her and other members of the group. Their personal stories exposed the subtleties and horrors of segregation. Their openness didn't make it any easier to face the clustered rednecks the next day. "I was frightened to death," Peggy admits. "You didn't know what you were in for," even though the marshals put women in the middle of the line.

Peggy's Selma experience jolted her into her more strenuous efforts on behalf of the Civil Rights Bill. "People were so afraid of what was in it." Peggy had a difficult time persuading Margaret Mealey, NCCW executive director, to spend ten cents a member to mail out the text. "Isn't justice worth ten cents?" Peggy demanded of Mealey, who finally agreed. After the Civil Rights Bill passed, Peggy and Jane O'Grady of the AFL/CIO were crying tears of joy when Monsignor Frank Hurley, assistant general secretary of the National Catholic Welfare Conference, called. The three of them arranged an impromptu Mass of thanksgiving at the NCWC chapel. Later over a celebratory drink in Peggy's studio apartment, Monsignor Hurley removed a small package from his pocket. "When I was at the White House today, I got pens used to sign HR 7165. I wasn't the one who worked on it. You were," he said, giving Peggy a little box holding a pen. (Peggy carried that significant memento in her purse for ten years until President Richard Nixon sacked Father Theodore Hesburgh as head of his Civil Rights Commission. Then she thought Hesburgh should have it.)

When the charge Peggy got from her Selma experience and her participation in a "Wednesdays in Mississippi" program that introduced her to the problems of women in the Deep South proved too galvanizing for the basically conservative NCCW ranks, Peggy returned to Chicago. She joined Matt Ahmann at the National Catholic Conference for Interracial Justice at 1307 S. Wabash in Chicago. Matt, who was setting up national programs for addressing specific black/white issues, assigned Peggy to health care. Temporarily disoriented after four years away, Peggy looked for the action that she'd associated with the John A. Ryan Forum group in the past.

Like Mary Dowling, Presentation's principal, she perceived the West Side as the nexus of the big social issues of race and peace. The Sunday liturgy at her home parish, Queen of All Saints in the Sauganash area, seemed regressive by the standards of her Washington experience. Joining the Presentation community at the noon Sunday Mass in Lawndale was an effective intake mechanism into the community as well as an alternative for the Sauganash rite. Peggy had known Jack Egan since he'd burst into her office at the Archdiocesan Council of Catholic Women years before, announcing typically, "I'm Jack Egan. May I use your phone?" They'd got to be friends as part of the John Ryan Forum network. Any time Jack had let her know he'd be in Washington, Peggy had crowded ten or twelve activists privy to D.C. developments into her tiny apartment to bring him up to date.

Now that she was back in Chicago, Jack couldn't afford to hire Peggy as the secretary he desperately needed. Nevertheless, he was busy as the ants in a colony newly spaded up, trying to keep up his interreligious and city contacts, his work with IRCUA and the Association of Chicago Priests, without slighting his parish. At the invitation of Archbishop Paul Hallinan of Atlanta, he'd additionally agreed to chair a group to research the "Pastoral Ministry and Life of the Priest" for the Episcopal Committee on Pastoral Research and Practice of the National Conference of Catholic Bishops. This meant circulating an original draft to stimulate response and then collating and analyzing the response from a wide sample of priests, religious, laity, and non-Catholics who "share a concern for the life of the Church."

If Jack couldn't afford to hire Peggy, he'd had a lot of success suggesting people volunteer to aid his worthy schemes. Peggy was a natural for that kind of appeal. Peggy knew he needed someone like her. As she said of him, "He was sort of taking care of the world." Or trying to.

Peggy's whole career had been service over and above the call of duty. When Jack adverted to the piles of correspondence in his room, she agreed to have a look, happy to have a role in the action. "Jack had an idea that coping with his correspondence was impossible," Peggy recalls. "He answered everything. He still does." In effect, he was throwing up his hands—and they full of letters.

Peggy promptly displayed the coping-with-Jack mechanisms that caused the Reverend Theodore Hesburgh, president of the University of Notre Dame, to call Jack and Peggy "the most symbiotic pair he'd ever met." She told Jack simply, "If you would organize it, it wouldn't be so bad." Then she proceeded to organize it. "A lot of the letters were one-liners," she recalls. "You can zip those off real quick." He was the steam in the engine, spitting out visionary schemes, subtle maneuvers, political firestorms. Peggy was the steel in the engine that contained the explosion, keeping his drive focused and his projects on track.

Every Saturday morning she rolled down Pulaski Road and over to 758 S. Springfield where Jack would have his correspondence sorted in piles on his office floor. He'd dictate dozens of letters at his breakneck pace. When Peggy came back to Mass the next morning from her parents' home on the Northwest Side, she'd have the typed letters ready for signatures and the envelopes stamped. In some sense, their co-ministry started with that cooperative effort. Jack Egan couldn't have kept up with his "fresh entries in fresh folders in fresh filing cabinets" without Peggy to sift and sort, categorize and systematize. As he added to his portfolios, Peggy made it possible for Jack to continue to be Jack.

Peggy's involvement in Presentation practically took over her life when one of Jack's young Jesuit seminarians initiated the innovative Contract Buyers League. Jack Egan describes Jack Macnamara as very bright, a man always angry for the right reasons. "I want to see you alone," Macnamara told Egan after one of his Operation Saturation sorties to his block "parish" west of Pulaski Road. Macnamara had collided against "something I don't like," he told Jack, a basic injustice strait-jacketing Lawndale residents.

A brave parishioner on his block had confided in Macnamara the terms of the contract governing the sale of his or her house. The Lawndale area was redlined by the local banks, barring blacks moving in from getting regular mortgages. As a result, black buyers were forced to deal with one of five or six real estate speculators who bought properties and then sold them on contract. In a contract sale, interest was high and buyers had no equity in their property until they had made the last payment. A payment missed because of illness or job loss could put a family on the street. "That is the worst kept secret in Chicago," Egan told Macnamara. "City Hall knows about it. Real estate firms know about it. The Chicago Title and Trust knows about it. The people involved know about it. But no one is saying anything about it because the power behind contract buying is so great some people have been killed who have tried to correct the situation. I'd like you to talk to Saul Alinsky about it."

Alinsky was equally direct. "If I were you I would leave it alone. You're not going to do anything about it," he told Macnamara, adding a friend of his had died trying. When Macnamara still stubbornly insisted he wanted to challenge the lenders, Alinsky warned him their practice was legal. "What they are doing may be legal," Macnamara retorted, "but it is immoral." Alinsky persisted, "You can't win on a single issue if it's legal." Macnamara made it clear he was going to try.

18

"Very Close to an Economic Miracle"

"In that case," Jack Egan assured a Macnamara determined to organize contract buyers, "I will wholeheartedly support you." Immediately, Macnamara set up what would become the Contract Buyers League in the dining room of his apartment in Lawndale. Along with Joe Putnick, another Jesuit seminarian, Macnamara researched at the County Building the status of homes recently purchased in Lawndale. They carefully copied out names of former owners, sale price, resale price, terms of deal. Their case studies showed a pattern of homes unloaded by frightened white sellers at low prices and resold to blacks for high prices, on contract. Because redlining insurance companies would not insure them, the new "owners" also bought their insurance from their contract-holders.

Macnamara invited all local residents who'd bought their homes on contract to a Wednesday night meeting in the Presentation Church basement. He laid out for them the facts he and Putnick had collected at Chicago Title and Trust and the Cook County Recorder of Deeds. Lawndale residents were as aware as Father Egan that there'd be consequences if they took any action, and as leery as he was. Asked to rise and protest the grievances Macnamara and Putnick had documented, they slunk in their seats. No one wanted to admit that he or she'd been taken. Finally, a brave black woman rose majestically from her hard folding chair and broke the damn choking Macnamara and Putnick's next move. Ruth Wells, who would be known as the Rosa Parks of Presentation, took that first step of the legendary thousand mile journey. She admitted she'd been victimized. "And I'm willing to do something about it," she added staunchly. With her declaration, the Contract Buyers League could be born. Other contract buyers were prompted to say, "If Ruth Wells can fight this setup, then I can, too." Pretty soon there were three, four, five hundred people coming faithfully every Wednesday night to the school basement. One by one, they rose to share their stories and shore up their self-confidence from the well of their common concern.

Macnamara and Putnick had organized their information according to the pattern of sellers. According to Peggy Roach (who left her NCCIJ niche to provide the same kind of backup as office manager to Macnamara and Putnick during the week that she was giving Jack Egan on the weekend), they'd found "that twenty-five contract buyers would have bought from this guy, thirty from that guy. With that information, the CBL people could go after the holder of a whole group of contracts at one time." The first move was on Ruth Wells' contract-holder. Ruth Wells, Jack Macnamara, and Monsignor Egan appeared at the appointed hour to ask her contract-holder to renegotiate her contract into a standard mortgage. The office setting overwhelmed the black woman unused to corporate Loop offices. As Peggy reports, "Ruth Wells was absolutely scared to death." But she held her chin firm as her contract-holder tentatively assured her, "You got a very good deal here." Ruth Wells was in command enough to observe that she wasn't the only one threatened by the circumstances. Later, she reported to the two Jacks about her contract holder, "When I saw his hand shaking, I knew I had him. He's scared because he knows he's wrong."

Gradually, the Contract Buyers League honed its techniques. The first move would be a group visit to the offices of the contracts holder. If refused admittance, the group would picket on the street outside. If they got no satisfaction from this action, they would travel to the suburban homes of the contract holders. There they'd pace the pavement, disporting their signs. Neighbors' shades would flutter as they peeked out to read charges that, "Your Neighbor Is a Slumlord." According to Peggy Roach, "That invasion of neighborhoods really made (the holders of the contracts) mad."

By March, 1968, the *Chicago Sun-Times* was calling CBL successes "very close to an economic miracle." They credited the 30-year-old Macnamara, six white college students, and several hundred Negro home-owners for reducing "the high cost of being black." CBL had just reported to the U.S. Commission on Civil Rights "an agreement by an investment firm to renegotiate the terms under which some 300 Lawndale residents were paying for their homes."

The paper credited Macnamara and his college team for digging up evidence that many Lawndale home-owners paid an average of $20,000 more for their property than whites with access to conventional mortgages buying in a real estate market that wasn't racially inflated. The newspaper account made a point of blacks' fear of losing all they had paid into their homes because they lacked equity.

For the hard cases, CBL escalated the action to rent strikes both on the West Side and on the South Side where CBL had helped families initiate a second CBL chapter. Instead of paying their rent to the contract holder each month, strikers made out money orders to themselves and deposited them at CBL in escrow against the day when the contract holders would negotiate. Some of the contract holders went to Sheriff Joseph Woods who sent his police to evict CBL members for nonpayment of rent. Macnamara contacted the newspapers who sent photographers to cover the evictions.

Chicago realtor/author Dempsey Travis notes in *An Autobiography of Black Chicago* that about four hundred and thirty families withheld their payments. He watched Cook County Sheriff's Police carry out the belongings of twelve families on South Eggleston Avenue. "The sidewalk and streets became filled with rocking horses, beheaded dolls, baby carriages, rolled-up bedding, dining room tables, refrigerators, sofas and television sets. There were also paintings of Dr. Martin Luther King and Robert Kennedy heaped up in the mud and unseasonable snow of April 1970. The watching crowd, kept back by burly police officers, added their tears to those of the ex-homeowners." Travis helped negotiate new mortgage packages with lending institutions.

Jack Egan involved religious cohorts from the Interreligious Council on Urban Affairs in both the contract buyers dispute and in appeals to local groups to accept neighborhood integration. "I can't believe the courage it took for you, an urban priest, a member of the establishment, to go into churches where people were terrified of losing their homes and preach integration," Rabbi Robert Marx told Jack Egan over dinner one evening at Marx's home. "I remember you and me and Edgar Chandler [Church Federation of Greater Chicago] spending countless evenings going as a team into churches, mostly Catholic, and telling them how life could be beautiful in a society where all people were equal. You took the lead in doing that."

Rabbi Marx, Jack Egan's loyal IRCUA ally, remembers first meeting Monsignor Egan at an IRCUA session shortly after Marx arrived in

Chicago in 1962 as the head of the Union of American Hebrew Congregations. "There was this dynamic Catholic priest—bald even in those days—talking about community organizations." As a result of Jack Egan's work, Rabbi Marx "got into something which was to change my life directly." When Saul Alinsky called the attention of the Merrill Trust to the fine work Rabbi Marx was doing in The Woodlawn Organization, a vice president of the trust came to Marx's door with free good-doing grant money for the rabbi.

As Marx tells it, only minutes after the Merrill Trust vice president handed over the $15,000 check made out to Rabbi Robert Marx, Marx's phone rang. At the Jewish Federation office, a former professor of political science at the University of Wisconsin was asking about a job. "In that moment." Rabbi Marx says, "the Jewish Council on Urban Affairs was created. We used the $15,000 to hire the bearded scholar Lew Kreinberg, an esoteric human being, and set him to work on housing with the Northwest Community Organization." (In 1990, John McCarron would call Kreinberg "a man of a million causes," in the *Chicago Tribune*.)

The first complaint JCUA handled, Marx says, "related to a slum landlord who happened to be Jewish." Called into Marx's office, he agreed to remove housing code violations. "We had our first successful resolution of a problem related to the Jewish Council on Urban Affairs," Marx reports. As a man who has given much thought to the situation of Jews in society, Rabbi Marx saw how easy it was to focus on the role of the Jews holding blacks' contracts in Lawndale. While it was true there was "a group of unscrupulous businessmen, I'm sorry to say most of them Jewish, who went around Lawndale, which was primarily a Jewish neighborhood in the early sixties, saying 'The blacks are coming,'" there were other contributing groups. The mortgage houses, the banks, the insurers, all had redlined Lawndale.

John McKnight, Midwest Director of the U.S. Commission on Civil Rights, suggested that the Federal Housing Authority was "one of the leading villains in ghetto land deals. When the FHA pulled out of older inner-city neighborhoods and financial institutions followed, the vacuum was filled by speculators who gutted the area and robbed the people," McKnight told the *Chicago Sun-Times*. "As far as I'm concerned, the white racist institutions—particularly the old FHA—are even guiltier than the speculators. They created the conditions."

It's Marx's view that Monsignor Egan brought the Jewish Council into the Contract Buyers League "because he didn't want it to be an anti-Semitic issue." They both remember a bitter January day when, Jewish rabbi and Catholic priest together, they helped cart furniture of evicted CBL families back into homes it had just been carted out of. An unsafe practice in Lawndale in 1967. Marx recalls the armed guards hired by the realty companies "in the basement of the home. There was gunfire. Looking back twenty-two years later, we could have been killed."

Some of the families, thoroughly frightened, took their money out of escrow and paid their fees to escape eviction. By this time, the Contract Buyers League had filed a class action suit against the sellers on the grounds the buyers' civil rights had been violated. The CBL clients were getting good advice from lawyers like Tom Boodell who never missed a Wednesday night opportunity to update the contract buyers on the progress of their cases. Tom Sullivan of Jenner and Block, one of the city's most prestigious firms, worked alongside the contract buyers. The CBL case gained more weight all the time. It was a page one story in the *Chicago Sun-Times* on July 9, 1968, when U.S. Attorney Thomas A. Foran announced that he would seek federal indictments of ten local real estate firms and savings and loan companies.

According to the *Sun-Times*, the companies were to be charged with misapplication of funds and misrepresentation in selling homes in Lawndale and large tracts of vacant land in the suburbs. "There is no racial discrimination when a quick profit could be made," Foran said. "They exploited everybody—white and black." Foran may have disagreed with Egan on urban renewal, "but I was all the way with Jack on CBL."

The pressure built until one night a discouraged Jack Macnamara got a request to meet a seller at a coffee shop on the North Side about 9:30 or 10 o'clock. Across the table from Macnamara, a man who had sold overpriced homes at exorbitant interest rates to some of the city's poorest people broke down. "I had no idea," he said, "that people were so hurt by what I was doing. I just thought it was a good business deal, buying for fourteen and selling for thirty. But being confronted with that husband and wife who both work two jobs to meet the payments, realizing they leave their kids unsupervised, I knew that I had to meet with them and renegotiate the package and get them on a mortgage."

When Jack Macnamara saw Peggy Roach the next morning, the Jesuit seminarian couldn't wait to tell her, "I think I've just heard my first confession."

In the end, the Contract Buyers League renegotiated contracts to save Lawndale buyers six million dollars. "Local efforts like CBL," Peggy Roach adds, "helped legislators see the need for federal regulation to outlaw redlining. They also undergirded efforts to achieve the Community Reinvestment Act (spearheaded locally by Gail Cincotta) stipulating that any bank taking money from a community must plow a certain amount back into the community from which it came."

Jack Macnamara and the other seminarians responded to the contract buyers' plight out of a sensitivity sown by community organizer Tom Gaudette. When Jack Egan brought Gaudette in to teach the seminarians how to make communities out of their blocks, Gaudette drilled them on two main techniques: listen to the community and confirm community involvement. The people of the community had to venture their own capital, even if it wasn't money.

After Gaudette's sensitivization, Jack Macnamara and the other seminarians who surveyed their block/parishes were conditioned to *hear* the cry of the contract buyer when they got out on the streets. By Macnamara's lights, Jack Egan functioned as a CBL enabler "for activities, particularly organizing activities, which would never have happened if it wasn't for his initiative." Egan provided a base at Presentation. He reassured the Jesuit provincial of the legitimacy of the seminarians' activism. He introduced the seminarians "to scores of people who could be helpful because they were funding sources, political allies, etc. At every turn, he brought in new supporters including such notables as U.S. Attorney Tom Foran and Midas International President Gordon Sherman who proved to be a steady backer."

John McKnight arranged the dinner meeting when Monsignor Egan met Gordon Sherman. It'd been a wearing day for Jack, "the kind of day you wanted to end quickly." Jack's mind was blank as he fought traffic, rushing downtown. He and Tom Gaudette had stood on their heads all day to convince some thirty Jesuit scholastics that community organization was fundamental to the common weal. When Father Egan got to the Standard Club at six p.m., he looked small, fragile, and pale to Gordon Sherman.

Jack was "so bushed"—his phrase—he didn't know whom he was supposed to be meeting. "I was tired. I just wanted to get out of there and get home." Then John McKnight, Midwest director of the U.S. Civil Rights Commission, beckoned him across the nearly empty dining room. "Well, what is it you want of me?" Father Egan abruptly and uncharacteristically challenged the president of Midas Muffler when he was introduced. Gordon Sherman told Jack he was the fourteenth person he'd talked to about putting a quarter of a million where it would do the most good for the people of the city. Jack's mind immediately cleared. Two hundred and fifty thousand dollars! He had an immediate graphic vision of the Lawndale community organized, his people taught to take charge of their own lives, the very vision that had taken him that day to rouse the young Jesuit seminarians. He told Sherman how much he'd like to see Lawndale organized the way Woodlawn was, the work directed by Saul Alinsky. Now Sherman came to attention. "Do you know Saul Alinsky?" Sherman asked eagerly. "He's a dear friend of mine," Jack said.

Jack intended that Alinsky should flesh out Jack Egan's aspirations for the people of Lawndale. He never dreamed that Alinsky would flesh out his own dreams, persuading Gordon Sherman that putting his quarter million in a training institute for community organizers was more desirable than funding a community organization in Lawndale. Egan's sop was the promise—never fulfilled—that he would get the first four black organizers. Initially furious, Jack "felt betrayed, I felt double-crossed." Egan soon forgave Alinsky because he loved the man. He even brought himself to suggest later that, "I knew Saul was right . . . because Alinsky had no black organizers to put in Lawndale. And that was 1969—months after King's death."

Midas Muffler money did flow into the Contract Buyers League. Macnamara found another generous "angel" in the father of a fellow Jesuit seminarian. Peggy Roach describes opening envelopes and catching checks for five or ten thousand dollars from a man who in time (after Jack Macnamara left the seminary) would be Jack Macnamara's father-in-law. That money was a major factor in CBL's successful renegotiation of contracts into regular mortgages to save that six million dollars for Lawndale residents.

Renegotiating those contracts was a structural, not cosmetic, change. It twisted a noose on a monetary practice that was hurtful to some, profitable to others. Somehow the city couldn't tolerate it. Rabbi Robert

Marx is convinced that due to that structural change, "directly as a result of the CBL battle," the three leaders of the Interreligious Council on Urban Affairs were gone from the city within six months. Before Father Egan left Lawndale, the area suffered a paroxysm that overshadowed the CBL contest. In April, 1968, the blocks around Presentation went up in flames. James Earl Ray had assassinated Dr. Martin Luther King, Jr., in Memphis. King had risen above the country's divisions by his personal inner strength and his gift for reaching an audience. When he was killed, there was no holding the dispossessed of the cities.

The morning after the tragedy, the children at Presentation took their seats, sorrowing but calm, as did children at the neighboring schools. Soon surface composure was ruptured by hundreds of black students in nearby high schools leaving their classrooms and taking to the streets. They were soon blocking traffic and breaking store windows on the West Side. The tempo of the rampage accelerated rapidly.

Presentation teachers, trying to help children express their grief, felt the atmosphere slowly changing. "About noon the parents started coming for the kids," says Mary Dowling who lived and taught at Presentation in the 1960s. "Each parent who showed up would have another message of something burning." The people of Presentation were as terrified as the shopkeepers on Madison Street. Parents reported high school kids at Crane and Marshall east of Presentation were provoking riots around their schools.

By the time the last of the Presentation children had been collected by their parents, "the streets were full of people," Mary Dowling remembers. "It was awful, terrible, a blackout situation," as night came on. Shops on Madison Street were looted. Roving bands stopped frightened drivers, smashing their windows. Soon the women in the convent building could see smoke coming from every direction. Coming closer. A *Sun-Times* reporter noted smoke "billowing hundreds of feet in the air in the area of West Madison Street." The teachers were awestruck. "We were actually surrounded by fire within a block all around us." With the electricity out, the only information came from eyeballing the terrain and listening to transistor radios. "We could see a lot of shopping carts pushed by looters. The kids justified the thefts the next day, saying they saw police stealing television sets."

The teachers felt they were in a war zone. None of them slept that night as they watched reflected flames dancing on their bedroom walls and heard helicopters chopping the sky overhead. Nonetheless, they were shocked at Mayor Daley's shoot-to-kill order, as was the rest of the country. All teachers had seen was teenagers without weapons. All the crimes were against property.

By Saturday thirty thousand National Guard troops were patrolling troubled areas. Presentation personnel were relieved to see the National Guard come in. The tanks looked threatening, but the soldiers were friendly, waving to the kids. The fire department had half the city's fire fighting equipment on a two-mile stretch of Madison Street just north of Presentation. The newspapers were calling the street a battleground. "With looters and others milling about them, the firemen battled raging fires and wondered when a rock or something worse might come their way."

Nine civilians were reported dead as looting, fire-bombing, and sniping continued. Ninety police officers were injured, two of them shot by snipers. Police used fire department searchlights to illuminate buildings to locate sharpshooters. Forty-eight civilians were wounded by gunfire. Over three thousand were arrested. Ten thousand plus police worked twelve hour shifts with no days off. The property damage was in the millions, due to one hundred and fifty major fires and two hundred and fifty major cases of looting. Three hundred were newly homeless. Most of the destruction was on Chicago's West Side, within one bus stop of Presentation.

Assuming responsibility for his parishioners as well as the cluster of whites living and working in rectory and convent, Father Egan encouraged all Presentation personnel to walk the streets to reassure the neighbors. He suggested precautions. "That was the only time I ever heard Egan give an order," Mary Dowling recalls. "If we went out, we were to wear veils. I wasn't even a nun, mind you. (Even in the sixties when most nuns went mufti, Father Egan did not lose his belief in the power of symbolic dress.) People sloshing through streets slippery from the hundreds of gallons of water used in firefighting were relieved to talk about their fears with members of the Presentation community.

For decades, those who braved the 1960s at Presentation continued to exchange stories of the heightened experience that was theirs. That need to sift through reminiscences of the turbulent sixties also affects Rabbi Robert Marx whom Jack Egan (who sees himself as an unorthodox priest) characterizes as an unorthodox Rabbi. "The beautiful thing, the sad thing," Marx says of the actions the two men shared in the sixties, "is that our greatest moments of glory have been fighting the institutions we love the most."

People in CBL and Presentation succeeded ultimately in bringing society to some realization of the nastiness of redlining and of denying mortgages to home buyers. They encouraged some hope in Lawndale. They forged some wonderful friendships—always a byproduct of Jack Egan's projects. But structural changes were limited and, as Kathy Pelletier assesses Presentation days in hindsight, "our efforts were pitiful" against the need.

19

"If He Can Do It to Egan,
He Can Do It to Anybody"

When Chicago priests first got word that John Patrick Cody was to be their new archbishop, "a malaise affected the archdiocese," as one activist priest put it. Monsignor Egan heard from his friend Monsignor George Higgins in Washington. He immediately invited "all these great guys who were doing everything in Chicago" (pretty much the old Sunday night group at Annunciation) to Father Tom McDonough's place, the Calvert House at the University of Chicago.

The hope of these priests who wanted to advance the Vatican II agenda was to contain Cody. They knew his reputation as authoritarian. A New Orleans priest had told them, "We are sure glad he is there and not in New Orleans." On the other hand, the bishops in Rome had shown how effective collegiality could be. Working together, they had "contained" the Curia (the Church's entrenched bureaucracy). These Chicago priests thought they had a good chance of making Cody bend their way if they, too, organized. They were to be stopped short, and not by Cody.

"Before a bottle of booze was opened," as they tell the story, sociologist/priest Joe Fichter (of New Orleans whence Cody was coming) was yelling at them from the shower in McDonough's quarters. "Go on home, fellows, forget it. You can't do a thing. Daddy's going to take care . . ." When Fichter walked out, drying himself, into the room where the young priests were gathered for sustenance and strategy, he offered them neither. Having lived in Archbishop Cody's archdiocese and analyzed his operation, sociologist Fichter gave this clerical group a devastating picture of what they could expect from their new ordinary. They realized as they listened how accustomed they were to the permissive style of Cardinal Meyer. How could they possibly retrench to a pre-Vatican II, 1930s, Tridentine autocracy?

"Father Fichter so demoralized us," Father James Killgallon reported, "that we went home without ever having a party." The first effort to implement Vatican II collegiality in the Archdiocese of Chicago had fizzled.

That left Archbishop Cody a clear track when he arrived. Immediately, he replaced existing chancery personnel. He took over decision making. He summarily fired several dozen elderly pastors. He closed several parishes. He took "troublemakers" out of key jobs.

Younger priests, who felt like the junior members of the liberal priestly establishment, initially looked to their seniors like Egan and Killgallon to throw up roadblocks in front of Cody. They waited impatiently, contenting themselves with griping, until Archbishop Cody made his move on the "five troublemakers." For them, that action bared the archbishop's calculated intent to show an iron fist. Around a small card table in the St. Frances Xavier parish hall after Father Gerry Weber's father's funeral on March 27, 1966, Fathers Frank Slobig and Jack Hill shared coffee and the fear their peers were all harboring: "If Cody can do it to Egan (their most visible representative), he can do it to anybody." Their new archbishop was re-instituting the one-man rule voted out of the Church by the bishops at Vatican II. The young priests stared somberly into their coffee cups, ruing the irony of a post-Vatican II archbishop taking them not back to the future, but forward to the past.

Was Fichter right? Was there nothing the priests could do? Jack Hill "couldn't imagine that with the activism bred in them by Reynold Hillenbrand the priests wouldn't take some action, but they didn't, they didn't." He and Slobig brooded about what they could do. Slobig suggested, "Let's expand what we've got here, and get representation from other classes." In their minds, it was time to act. Vatican II had blessed the people as the Church. If Archbishop Cody was not to be an absolute ruler, someone had to organize a countervailing force. Like the people in The Woodlawn Organization, young priests didn't have money or power. Maybe they did have numbers. They wouldn't know until they polled their peers. Possibly, with numbers, they could get a hearing for their agenda, their needs, their complaints, with the archbishop.

Hill had heard the carping: "You guys talk, but you never *do* anything." Challenged, he told Slobig he'd see what he could do. Back at Presentation Parish where he had been the temporary administrator between pastors Monsignor Frank McCarthy and Monsignor Egan, he approached Jack that night. Which of Jack Egan's friends, he asked, would be likely candidates for an organizing luncheon at Madame Galli's on East Chicago Avenue, a clerical hangout next door to the chancery office? Hill figured this was one of those "fresh files in fresh file folders in fresh filing cabinets" Jack Egan relished. (Jack Egan's version differs: "Cardinal Cody felt I was the one who engineered the ACP, but I had nothing to do with the origins of it. I do not remember Jack coming home from that meeting and consulting me. In fact, I felt there was a conspiracy of silence. It wasn't until later that Jack Hill began speaking to me about it.") Jack Hill firmly insists, "I know I asked that question."

The archbishop was right to fix on Presentation as the venue, in any case. Father Patrick O'Malley remembers meeting at 758 South Springfield Avenue often "with the sense it was a 'safe house'—a place where the ideas we were dealing with were met with understanding and acceptance." Jack Egan says, "Jack Hill gave practically his full time to the development of the Association of Chicago Priests that first year, and immediately after that to the development of the National Organization of Priests' Councils."

Thus, Father Gerry Weber's father's funeral ride stirred a group of young priests to launch a historic turnabout. They broke through ingrained clerical barriers in the spirit of Rosa Parks of Montgomery, Alabama, and Ruth Wells of the Contract Buyers League in Lawndale. "That was our Selma, Alabama, the beginning of a movement," one of them said of their first organizing luncheon at Madame Galli's. With that luncheon they opened a window, in Pope John XXIII's parlance. By dividing class lists and getting directly to work, Frank Slobig and John Hill had rallied sixteen like-minded priests for a gathering just one week after Weber's father's funeral—Easter Thursday, 1966.

In spite of the collegiality ordained by the Second Vatican Council, the Church in Chicago was still a patriarchy. Any one of those young priests who sprinkled Parmesan cheese on his spaghetti that day could have suffered the fate of a Jack Egan sent to a parish that could do in a lesser man—and would almost do in Egan—or a Monsignor Hillenbrand dismissed from the rector's seat at one of the world's largest seminaries to a small, if distinguished, parish, without a word of explanation. Any archbishop's decision was law. As Jack Egan was icily informed when he asked Hillenbrand why he lost the Mundelein rectorship, "They never told me, and I never asked." In 1966 in the Archdiocese of Chicago, that story still conveyed the clerical climate. Into that climate had moved an archbishop contemporaries described as mistrustful of priests, an initiative-depressant, a Captain Queeg in both his ability to charm and his knack for vindictiveness.

Ideas flowed with the coffee at Madame Galli's. Were other curates as concerned as they were? Should they try picketing? Father Jake Killgallon suggested using the legitimacy conferred on him and John Barlow as assistant consultors as a legal ploy for assembling associate pastors. The sixteen priests around the table at Madame Galli's appointed Jack Hill and Patrick O'Malley to organize three regional meetings for associate pastors on the North, West and South Sides. Organizing large numbers would be a protection against retribution, they thought, as well as a power base to balance the Corporation Sole (Archbishop Cody's legal status). They'd find out what their peers were thinking. How else could they harness that tide in the affairs of the Chicago Church they believed could lead on to a Vatican II-inspired fortune?

What made the meeting electric, according to Jack Hill (now a resigned priest), "what gave it a charge, was that we were not going to ask permission. If you go back to 1966, that was something. There was an umbilical cord then between the bishop and his priests. (We were like) someone who's always been under the thumb of a tyrant mother or father." Hill describes the fear/hope relationship as umbilical in nature because Archbishop Cody's authoritarian power could land a disobedient priest in the sticks or with some pastor widely acknowledged to be impossible. Conversely, he could "make you a pastor or head of the school board."

Father Peter Shannon, a canon lawyer in the chancery office, expressed the edginess palpable at Madame Galli's, in this haven where clerical conviviality usually eased clerical pain. "If those people upstairs knew where I was, I would be dead." He went on to say that if this was a move to get Cody, he wanted no part of it. "But if this is a move to prevent the development of any more Codys, I'm all for it." The group agreed, and repaired to the chancery office phones to begin the hundreds of phone contacts they'd make to get out the numbers at their regional meetings. They knew they had to work fast. They'd ascertained from Dan Ryan, the archbishop's secretary, that Archbishop Cody would be in Europe. They planned the assistants' meeting before he returned. (Aware of the movement from its inception, Cody called the diocesan editors to suggest they not cover the story of the priests' meetings. "I'll take care of all that when I get back.")

As they started the dialing which would consume much of their free time for the next week, the young priests asked themselves how many curates it would take to make a credible showing at their three meetings. At this point they hesitated to ask pastors. They fixed on a figure of four hundred of the archdiocese's twenty-two hundred priests. By doing what Jack Egan called "a hell of a lot of work" in a very short time, they got out their numbers. Getting the halls alone was a prodigious effort. Jack Hill spent a full Saturday calling rectories. Most of the pastors were friendly, saying, "It's a great idea for you guys to get together." Then they'd float the zinger: "What does the boss think about all this?" All Hill could answer was, "We haven't asked him." It was suppertime before he got a pastor, Monsignor James Hishen at St. Gall Church at 55th and Kedzie, on Chicago's Southwest Side, with enough chutzpa to agree to host a meeting of those disaffected by Cody's arrival. Later, St. Frances Xavier and St. Leonard's were added.

The Madame Galli group were meticulous planners. Aware that the tone set at the first meeting would be extremely influential, the coordinating committee's detailed planning reached even into the bathrooms at the first site, St. Leonard's in Berwyn. They paid the janitor extra "to have the place spotless for that day." Their efforts were rewarded. Again, that first meeting at St. Leonard's was "very electric" because "this was a meeting held without the permission of the ordinary." Several of the young assistants spoke up about their frustrations and fears for the future. John Barlow and Jake Killgallon, as the consultors, promised they would bring the curates' concerns to the archbishop.

Their concerns were two. Feeling, as Jack Hill says, that authoritarianism kept them at an immature level, the young priests proposed an experiment with democracy in the Chicago Church. "We were trying to lateralize the priesthood, make it collegial." The changes they proposed were a personnel board to make future clerical appointments in the archdiocese after consultation with those to be appointed, and a retirement package for older priests. Archbishop Cody had immediately on arrival forced the retirement of some priests who had no resources, nowhere to go.

From the start, the coordinating committee meant to include the archbishop in all their plans (they sent him all their minutes). All they asked was a head start in their organizing so the archbishop could not stamp out their seedling before it sent up shoots. When the two assistant consultors asked for a meeting to bring the priests' views to Archbishop Cody, he suggested a meeting with the entire coordinating committee of the clergy on Saturday night. Fine, Barlow and Killgallon thought, they'd be a stronger force *en force*.

Looking back, those committee members compare the meticulously planned strategies necessary to deal with their archbishop to the intricacies of Chicago ward politics. They told themselves a resistance like this could develop only in Chicago. Part of their strategy was to recruit early some priests not on the radical fringe, including Father George Herdegen, the most popular priest in the archdiocese. "His name blessed everything." His allegiance would help with their first priority for the meeting, "to come out alive," as they put it. If Archbishop Cody forbade any priests' meetings at all, "we couldn't organize against that." That would put off the more conservative priests.

On Saturday night they meant to tell the archbishop about the large meeting of the archdiocesan priests they were planning at McCormick Place, the enormous girdered convention site on Lake Michigan at Twenty-third Street. Meaning always to include him in their post-Vatican II collegiality, they would ask Archbishop Cody to address the gathering.

As they parked their cars at Quigley Seminary and started the warm summer evening ramble through the archbishop's posh neighborhood to 1555 N. State, members of the coordinating committee knew they were breaking a clerical barrier. They allayed their trepidation by reviewing their plans. They'd assigned note-taking in fifteen minute blocks. They wanted to take minutes, but they didn't want to be conspicuous, to scare Archbishop Cody off. They intended to ask that pastors be allowed to join the association.

While they would ask the archbishop to speak at their first big meeting, they had no intention of asking his permission to have the meeting. In fact, they were so paranoid (their word) about the archbishop's intransigence that they couldn't bring themselves to post all the priests' invitations together. They stuffed them into different mailboxes around town. Only when the archbishop's opportunity to forestall delivery of the priests' invitations was scuttled did they hand-deliver the archbishop's bid. They could assure their archbishop that he got his invitation ahead of anyone else. They could reassure themselves that his would not be the only invitation delivered.

Over the strawberry cake and coffee in his handsome residence, Archbishop Cody made light of the meetings his guests were planning, saying they were nothing. Maybe not, they replied, but many of the priests are so afraid that we had hard times finding pastors to host the first meetings. The archbishop was smoothly helpful. "You could have asked me because you could have used the seminaries." As they exited the Gold Coast neighborhood for Quigley and their cars, the committee was exultant. They'd "hoped to come out alive." They'd done better than they hoped. The archbishop had himself suggested pastors be added to their group, and he had offered Quigley North and Quigley South as meeting places. What remained for the committee was the drudge labor of defining a purpose, selecting a name, and writing a constitution. A prodigious task, as it turned out.

Father Peter Shannon had a summer place on the south end of Lake Michigan. There the committee repaired to suggest and reject, pace off and brood over, the building blocks of their constitution. Long summer days faded into spectacular sunsets as they debated the mechanics of organizing the first priests' association in the country. What should it be called? How would they elect officers? What terms would they have? What was the archbishop's role?

Permitted to invite pastors, the group got nine hundred priests to their two Quigley meetings. The big test of the association's viability would be the McCormick Place meeting to which all the priests in the archdiocese, including priests in religious orders, were invited on October 24, 1966. The lures were the possibility of a personnel board and retirement policies. The pastors whom Archbishop Cody had fired since his arrival had got only two weeks notice, a fact which worried priests even though they knew people past their competency shouldn't continue to serve. According to Father Charles Dahm in *Power and Authority in the Catholic Church,* those Archbishop Cody fired had "to find (their) own place(s) to live, at a time when no retirement benefits were yet available."

The archbishop played the reluctant gallant, holding off on any firm commitment to speak until the meeting day itself, suggesting he'd be out of town. Meantime, he belittled organizing efforts as he got wind of them. You won't get five hundred priests, he warned the committee, deprecating—as he had from the start—any possibility that this organization would fly. At the same time, he didn't take any chances on losing his starring role if there was indeed to be an audience for his performance. About nine forty-five on the morning of the meeting, Father Tom Fitzgerald got a call at McCormick Place from one of his friends in the Chancery Office. "How are things going?" came the studiously casual query. "I don't have any time for you," Fitzgerald answered, telling the caller all he wanted to know. "We've got nine hundred chairs and they are all full. I have to find a couple of hundred more chairs before anyone else gets here. Call me back."

Five minutes later, there was another phone call for Fitzgerald. The voice was formal and incisive. "The archbishop has changed his plans. He will be down to speak at the time you asked him." It was clear the archbishop respected numbers. During the day, just short of thirteen hundred of the twenty-one or twenty-two hundred priests in the archdiocese voted on the by-laws. According to Jack Hill, it was "an organizational achievement in that we got everybody, eighty-nine, ninety percent. In each parish one priest stayed home and watched the shop. Everybody else came to the meeting."

Cardinal Cody arrived in time to hear Scripture scholar Father Barnabas Mary Ahern describe a bishop without his priests as powerless, a man without ears, without hands, without feet. These priests who wanted to be Archbishop Cody's hands, his ears, his feet, gave their ordinary a standing ovation when he rose to speak. However, Archbishop Cody did not pick up on Father Barnabas Mary's forceful image, although he did initially express his pride in his priests for implementing the dictates of Vatican II. He called their meeting an "historic gathering" and "epochal," and spoke of himself as *primus inter pares* (first among equals).

Having made these necessary obeisances, however, Cody was "patronizing, discouraging, and dispiriting," according to Jack Hill. "All you have recommended (in your previous meetings), I have already put in the hopper and I intend to act on it." As the committee interpreted their ordinary, his message was, "Fellows, get lost. I don't need you." He deprecated their numbers: "If I had all my priests, I suppose I would need Soldier Field." As far as the priests could tell, he was saying, in effect, *l'eglise, c'est moi* loud and clear. They were not the Church. He was.

The press, held at arm's length by the committee, interpreted the Association of Chicago Priests as a priests' union. At a press conference after the morning session, the organizers quoted Father Barnabas Mary saying the association was not independent, not autonomous, not hostile to superiors, and therefore not like a union. As Jack Hill explained later, "We felt a union would solidify this almost parental/filial relationship between bishops and priests. That had to go. At the ad hoc meetings, there was little talk against Cody. That kind of talk made him responsible. It really was a congress of peers." Hill reflected later that the priests put off the newspeople at the press conference, citing only the positive aspects of Archbishop Cody's remarks, the *primus inter pares* bit. "We who mouthed First Amendment rights manipulated the press. We told them little things that were absolutely true, but truly misleading." He regrets that.

Nonetheless, the press knew a clerical Rubicon had been crossed. The Association of Chicago Priests dominated front pages across the country. After the McCormick Place meeting, the organizers were interviewed on radio and television. Jack Hill related the establishment of the ACP to Vatican II initiatives on the *Today* show. As the priest organizers celebrated at Presentation rectory after their successful October 24, 1966, priests called from all over the country. "Please send us your constitution." Hill estimates forty or fifty dioceses had priests' associations or priests' senates by the end of the year. Once again, as in Cana and CFM, the Chicago archdiocese provided much-needed leadership.

Whether or not it was a union forming in Chicago, Archbishop Cody endured considerable teasing from his fellow bishops. He was having a hard enough time adjusting without that additional indignity. Some of the original ACP board recall an early meeting with the archbishop at the cathedral. Until the third point on the agenda, Cody sat quietly. At that juncture, he announced, "This is what I want." Chairperson Jack Hill thanked his archbishop for expressing his opinion before he turned to ask, "How do you others feel?" Cody's jaw dropped. "I've never seen him so nonplused," a board member remembers. For the first time, a decisive expression by an ordinary was put to the *pares*, those "equals" he was first among.

In some ways, the "equals" found that the archbishop could be brought around. After the priests at McCormick Place voted unanimously for a personnel board, Archbishop Cody announced at the next meeting of the ACP board, "We don't need a personnel board. I know all the priests." Board members looked at one another, trying to intuit their next move. Cody turned to Bishop Cletus O'Donnell, a very popular bishop whom most priests of the archdiocese would have liked to see in Cody's job. "Isn't that true, Bishop O'Donnell?" he asked.

Bishop O'Donnell deflected the question with urbane skill. "I've lived here all my life (Cody had been in Chicago only months) and I don't know all the priests. It would be a great weight off my conscience if we had a personnel board." Cody appeared impressed. "Let's go out to dinner and come back and talk about it." When he came back, "a different man," and asked some lead time to implement a personnel board, the committee members had their opportunity to be gracious and grant the time. A personnel board was established, as well as retirement policies.

Another time, the encounter was less smooth when Father Hill showed Cody a press release on a McCormick Place meeting. Archbishop Cody wanted changes made. "We did not intend you to censor this," Father Hill said. "It's our release. We dropped it off as a matter of courtesy." It was one of the few occasions when Archbishop Cody could not control his irritation: "What the hell do you guys want me to do?" he demanded. "Quit?" Father Hill, determinedly restrained, answered evenly, "I wish you would accept the fact that we are trying very hard to make you look good." A hard pronouncement for a bishop who wanted to be assured his word was law.

Jack Egan credits Archbishop Cody for coming to every single meeting of the ACP board for the first year. The board checked the agenda with the archbishop ahead of time. He got a chance to express his views. Jack Egan was elected member at large to that board for the first two years. He was off the third year, a stipulation of the by-laws. He was elected chairperson for the ACP's fourth year. The group was working on issues of a personnel board, authority in the Church, pensions, sabbaticals, and retirement. "They were interested in things affecting their lives as priests," Father Egan says. "It was the first time they were both allowed and had the inspiration and courage to look into their own lives and to feel they might have something to say about it. That's what the ACP was: an opportunity for priests to have something to say about the life they lived."

20

"How Can They Survive Without the Eucharist?"

Democracy being as messy in the Church as anywhere else, the Association of Chicago Priests early developed its share of problems. Not all the decisions members made were wise. Young priests agitated their new personnel board for raises. Older priests thought raises an inappropriate initiative. Privately, the personnel board collected a list of parishes where they couldn't in conscience send inexperienced associates. Pastors of blacklisted parishes disputed the priests' assessments. The young priests had their own list of difficult pastors. They released theirs to the newspapers. Young priests bargained with the personnel board over grievances in a way that infuriated many older men.

The Young Priests Caucus was formed in the spring of 1969 about the time that Jack Egan was elected ACP president. Jack Egan, always a man of the *via media*, pressed carefully between his ever-deferential respect for authority and an ever-vigilant lookout for opportunities to advance the ACP agenda. He would never bring down his Church to make a point, or to solve a grievance. Nor would he cut off his opponents' only means of saving grace or saving face. He expected the same from the Young Turk curates. They didn't share his skill at circumspection. As high-handed and righteous, in their way, as the student activists of the 1960s, they didn't heed Jack Egan's suggestion that young priests should try to work out conditions they deplored through judicial processes. Egan was quoted as saying that the ACP board thought the young priests were not acting "according to high standards of responsibility and accountability." The personnel board that the ACP had fought for was now under fire. Set up to resolve grievances, it now seemed to give rise to them.

"Even though we were all friends, the Young Priests Caucus put terrible pressure on me," Jack remembers. "Putting out a list of pastors to whom no young associates should be sent! Everything was in the press. Oh, God, they had learned that lesson. We taught them too well. Can you imagine what that did to the morale of the diocese?"

That same age rift operated within the Presentation community where Jack still lived the year he headed the ACP although he shifted his pastoral responsibilities to another administrator. Kathy Pelletier Moriarity looks back on youthful manifestos from her confederates as intemperate then, embarrassing now. She deplores the "lack of judgment. We had such a strong sense of righteousness. Father Egan had brought people together who were searching and questioning, theologically and psychologically." Kathy sees how every life at Presentation was re-examined and changed. "A lot of mistakes are made when you open a place up. Out of all the religious, only one person is still a priest besides Jack Egan. All the Sisters left religious life." In the same way, many of those Young Turk priests eventually resigned from the priesthood.

At both Presentation and the ACP, Jack Egan made a place on his agenda for all those come to queue and question. To his ACP office came the priests who both wanted to leave the priesthood and to be exonerated of guilt for leaving. Jack tried to befriend them, even as he befriended associates at Presentation and the Young Priests Caucus. He shared their perceptions and disquietude. He knew they were a bomb waiting to explode in the Church.

When Jack Egan allows himself to think of his term as president of the Association of Chicago Priests, he calls that penitential season "the most difficult year of my life. Looking back, we can't comprehend what was happening in the Church at that time. We were just coming out of that terrible year 1968, that turning point in history, with assassinations, the end of the civil rights movement, the Vietnam War eating us up, the feminist movement." This was also the year of the great exodus of the clergy from the Church. "While I was chairman, forty-five priests came to tell me they were leaving the priesthood and why." Mistrusting Cardinal Cody, they were reporting to Father Egan as to a commanding officer.

Concurrently, men staying in the priesthood had an intense interest in the questions about their vocation raised by the Vatican Council. A Bishops' Synod was planned for 1971 to consider a) justice in the world, and b) the Roman Catholic priesthood. For the first time priests would have a chance to let their feelings be known. "The major question for Chicago priests," Father Egan remembers, "was optional celibacy. We had many meetings to discuss how we felt about it."

Jack Egan who had survived the loneliness of the torch-bearer in the Hyde Park-Kenwood confrontation, the loss of his beloved interreligious coalition, and now the torching of Lawndale after Dr. King's death, seemed to be witnessing the dissolution of the Church and the city to which he had devoted his life. Yet he felt he had to stay strong for the sake of those who looked to him. As Jack Hill says of Jack at Presentation, "perhaps the most appreciated contribution you made was to your colleagues there. You were kind to them all even though their concerns were a distraction from the programs at Presentation. You provided an accepting atmosphere in which your friends could work out their lives." However, the quiet that Jack brought to those making hard decisions at Presentation brought disquiet to him.

He didn't want to see anyone leave the priesthood or the Church. Yet circumstances forced him into the position of being responsible for creating safe space where people who were leaving could roost while they contemplated awesome life changes. The decisions of some were so painful to Jack that a suburban couple remembers his begging a table full of dinner guests to write Father Walter Imbiorski (who'd succeeded Jack at the Cana Conference) to reconsider his decision to leave the priesthood for marriage. Peggy Roach tells how he left a workshop in the South early, an action that went against his grain, upon hearing a friend was resigning.

His friend, Father Tom McDonough, made it clear to Jack that he didn't have the option many of his friends were taking. Even if Jack Egan flirted with the notion of resigning, "Some people are so symbolic that they simply have to remain in the Church," McDonough counseled his fellow cleric. Jack remembers his own reaction to the resignation of his fellow priests as one of disbelief. "How could they face life without the opportunity to say daily Mass?" Or, if they were leaving the Church, "How could they survive without the Eucharist?"

The turmoil took its toll on every priest, and particularly on those with multiple responsibilities. Parish life was deteriorating at Presentation, from Jack's point of view, under the administrator assigned there to free up time for Jack during his year as chairperson of the Association for Chicago Priests. Jack winced to hear doors slamming shut that he'd struggled to open. Ecumenical structures Jack thought essential were weakening, as *Sun-Times* religion editor Roy Larson would note a few years later. Once the leading diocese in the nation, Chicago was heading into the "backwater" Chicago activists like John McDermott would call it in 1975.

If he had looked "small and fragile and pale" to Gordon Sherman in the spring of 1968, Jack Egan looked transparently ill to the Reverend Theodore Hesburgh, President of the University of Notre Dame, when he met him standing in line for coffee at O'Hare Airport in Chicago in the spring of 1969. Jack had recently been treated for exhaustion in Mercy Hospital. Father Hesburgh, who'd known Jack Egan for years through their YCS, YCW, and CFM associations, was shocked. "Jack, you look like the devil. Are you ill or just very tired?"

When Jack admitted exhaustion, having just left a trying meeting with the ACP board and Cardinal Cody, Father Hesburgh did some quick figuring. "Look," he said, "you have been hitting the ball for twenty-eight years. I know because we were ordained the same year. It's about time you took a sabbatical. Why not come to Notre Dame for a year and rest up? I have a small bit of money that will pay for your expenses, and you can help us with our new program in pastoral theology. You could live with Father Louis Putz at Moreau Seminary and give him a hand with the diocesan seminarians living there. What about it—just for a year?"

Jack wrote Cardinal Cody, asking for an appointment on a strictly personal matter. Would the cardinal surmise he was leaving the priesthood and expedite the arrangements? The cardinal's reply was immediate, and Jack arrived promptly for his appointment the next day. The cardinal took a chair and waved Jack to a couch. "He always brought a number of manila folders," Jack says, reconstructing that seminal scene in his life. "While you were talking, he would be thumbing through the pages of the folders." Jack figured that Cardinal Cody labored under two misapprehensions about the pastor of Presentation. The first, that Jack was bitter. The second, that he was the spirit behind the Association of Chicago Priests. "He also thought I engineered the public outcry when I was sent to Presentation," Jack adds.

In Jack's mind, any disaffection the cardinal harbored against him was no excuse for the folders. Jack didn't appreciate their distraction. "What I'm going to talk to you about is extremely important to me,"

Jack told his superior. "If you'd kindly put that folder away, let's you and I talk. I have a letter I'd like you to read."

The cardinal guardedly brooded over the invitation that Father Egan had received from Notre Dame. Finally, he spoke. "I've been expecting this."

"How could you possible be expecting this? It came only yesterday morning."

"You've been trying to get out of the diocese."

Jack replied fiercely, "Nothing could be further from the truth."

"The answer is absolutely no. I am not going to give you permission," the cardinal announced. "We need you in Chicago. I am going to send you back to Presentation Parish."

The cardinal pointed out that if Jack were to go to Notre Dame, other priests would ask for sabbaticals and increase the shortage of priests. Jack volunteered to serve on weekends in a South Side parish. The cardinal grumbled, "If you go there, I want you to stay there and not bring back any of that 'bum theology.' " He had a further objection: "What will the priests say if you go?" Jack thought his reputation with the priests was secure. The cardinal pressed on. "But what will the people say?" Jack suggested the people at Presentation were quite used to priests being transferred.

Then he bared the nub of his irritation. "But what will the press say? You will get better press than I will." Jack was too embarrassed to respond. By now it was noon. To end the interview, he asked quietly, "What shall I tell Father Hesburgh?"

The cardinal sputtered a surprising volte-face for which Jack was unprepared. "Tell him I will not stand in your way and you go with my permission."

Father Egan could take some satisfaction in his five years at Presentation. The Contract Buyers League (although its success may have contributed to the demise of the Interreligious Council on Urban Affairs, according to Rabbi Marx) was saving Presentation neighbors some six million dollars through negotiation of contracts into mortgages.

Parents were taking responsibility for Presentation School, attending meetings, making decisions for their children. In May 1969, seven eighth graders won full scholarships to Catholic high schools, and three more earned partial scholarships. Those kids had as commencement speaker comedian Dick Gregory, who'd led marches demanding school desegregation from Buckingham Fountain to Mayor Daley's Bridgeport home. A program to start up small businesses was in place at Presentation, as well as a Food Buying Club. Skidmore, Owings and Merrill had done the work-up on turning the unused portion of the convent into a center with a small health clinic, a legal aid bureau, and an adult education center. Jack had repeatedly called attention to the violence in the inner city: the violence of slum landlords, the violence of inequitable political representation, the violence of inadequate health facilities, the violence of poor but expensive housing, the violence of inferior food and merchandise in neighborhood stores.

He was leaving a parish where every night he felt he was opening a Chinese fortune cookie to see what the next day would be like. Splitting his days between Presentation and the office of the Association of Chicago Priests during his year as chairperson, Jack had been forced to look daily at the discrepancy between Lawndale's shortcomings as a environment and the larger metropolitan reality. People in Lawndale still needed homes, jobs, food that was fairly priced, doctors in the community, dentists, a high school, fair rents, to catch up with the rest of the city. He hadn't waved a magic wand.

He was leaving a city where the Interreligious Council on Urban Affairs no longer functioned as it had, where the archdiocesan Office of Urban Affairs was closed, where he no longer operated on a national level because of parish demands. In June 1968, Jack Egan had heard from "some of the finest people in the parish," the early rumblings of the disappointment they would express more forcibly when he left in 1970. "You four priests are our priests. We like you. We want you here at Presentation and in Lawndale. We want to work with you and support you . . . but you don't know us . . . our problems . . . our children . . . our neighborhood. You have rarely been in our homes . . . We know you work hard, but you have not done the most important thing."

Mea culpa, the priests had answered in 1968. They knew it was true that Father Hill had been busy about the affairs of the ACP and the National Federation of Priests' Councils which grew out of the ACP. Fathers George Fleming and Jack Gilligan were on frequent call for Pre-Cana and days of recollection. Father Egan himself served on a raft of local and national boards. The priests had relied on the seminarians and nuns to visit the homes. It seemed that was not enough. The people wanted their own priests to ring their front doorbells, the very thing Jack Egan had done at St. Justin Martyr. It wasn't enough for Father Egan to walk the streets of a Saturday, saying, "Hello, hello, hello."

Fortunately, in June 1968, Father Hill's NFPC organizing work was at an end. Fleming and Gilligan could cut back on Pre-Canas. Jack resigned from six committees and boards, including the Chicago Conference on Religion and Race, the Community Renewal Society, (and for a brief period) the Catholic Community on Urban Ministry and the Interreligious Foundation for Community Organization. All the priests curtailed "whatever small social life we have had," as Jack noted in the Friends of Presentation newsletter. Within months, the cardinal would free up more of Jack's time by cutting funding—and thus cutting the throat—of the Interreligious Council on Urban Affairs. In early January 1969, the cardinal reduced the membership from twelve to three, and the funding from $24,000 yearly to $6,000 yearly.

According to the *Chicago Daily News*, Jack Egan was among the Catholic members dropped. For the cardinal archbishop, IRCUA's proper—and only—function was researching community groups for possible funding by church and synagogue groups. IRCUA leaders like Rabbi Marx, Edgar Chandler, and Jack Egan had envisioned—and taken—a much more active role in the life of the city. "Our job was to be a constructive moral voice in the city," Jack says. "We tried to protect the poor and the middle class from some large business, real estate and development interests that had emerged in Chicago, and that, to this day, (as he later told a reporter for the Notre Dame magazine) are people bent on their own profit. They couldn't care less about the city or its people." Egan saw the community organizations as means to deal with human and physical problems, "everything from getting a traffic light fixed to improving schools to getting rid of merchants who rip off people. Community organizations are watchdogs on city agencies, buffers between the people and the body politic."

IRCUA itself was united Jewish, Protestant, and Catholic voices lobbying for voiceless people. They'd spoken out to halt construction of high-rise public housing in the city. "They were vertical slums," Jack Egan insists, deriding high-rises as inhuman. "There's no way a mother can raise children on the seventeenth floor of one of those buildings." He points out that Mayor Daley quietly halted their continued construction after IRCUA's testimony. IRCUA also worked to modify the haphazard relocation procedure for families caught in the path of urban renewal. Jack admits that IRCUA's stands were controversial. "But I think we raised the consciousness of the people of Chicago so that they looked at the moral implications of what city agencies were doing."

With the cardinal's budget cut, IRCUA's voice for the people was stilled. Jack rues his docility in the face of Cardinal Cody's decision. "In the last analysis," Jack Egan says, "I have to take the responsibility for not mobilizing the Protestant groups there to take a cab to the cardinal's house. I think we could have won or worked out a compromise to keep the thing in existence. But it folded just after that."

Jack assesses the cardinal's "power play" as "one of the most drastic actions I have ever seen. Apparently they (at the Chancery Office) felt (IRCUA) had too much influence, or too much power. Kris Ronnow was out of a job right away and there was terrible feeling." Jack Egan believes the cardinal's "unseemly" action affected the work of the churches for years to come. "Ecumenical work was affected very seriously, and also the work of community organization."

Jack feels, "rightly or wrongly," that one of the great tragedies of his going to Notre Dame was that there was no longer a champion in the Roman Catholic Church for community organization. "So you have a period of thirteen years in the Cody regime when there was no pressure for their development. It's also one of the tragedies of Saul Alinsky's death," Jack believes, "and Monsignor Edward Burke's leaving the chancery." Nothing has taken IRCUA's place, as Jack sees it. "We moved into the sixties with a lot of strength and it hasn't been the same since," he said in 1978.

He suggests that this condition obtains into the 1990s. "Cardinal Bernardin, who has not had experience with real mass-based, responsible, responsive, community organizations which are strong enough to affect change in the policy of the city . . . has to take the advice of some of his advisers who believe that community organizations may be too expensive and/or confrontational." Jack believes those advisers "refuse to study the history of community organization since 1972 when Saul Alinsky died."

Three months after the cardinal cut IRCUA's budget in 1968, he had closed down the archdiocesan Office of Urban Affairs. The notice from the Chancery Office announced OUA's absorption by the Office of the Co-ordinator of the Inner City Apostolate and the Commission on Human Relations and Ecumenism of the Archdiocese. By this time the cardinal had gutted the Office of Urban Affairs without garroting it. It was no longer a bully pulpit for Jack Egan. As he could no longer influence the course of the city out of that office, his responsibilities having been transferred to other agencies of the archdiocese, Jack Egan had urged the cardinal to close OAU down. "Either you close that office or I am going public because I have my reputation to protect," Jack Egan told Cardinal Cody. And the cardinal, finally, did.

Sister Ann Ida Gannon, BVM, President of Mundelein College, was on the Office of Urban Affairs board when Cardinal Cody dissolved it. From her perspective, Jack Egan did what he thought was best for the Church at the time. She'd been impressed with the number of persons "in strategic places . . . willing to give their time and insights to providing solutions to the problems (Jack) so clearly identified.

"That made it all the harder to see that you could not obtain freedom to act as, time after time, Cardinal Cody failed to even respond to your initiatives. Most vivid in my mind is the time that you appeared before us with the message that you had finally had a meeting with the cardinal and had discussed our dilemma: much advice, no action."

Jack Egan reported to the board that Cardinal Cody had coolly advised him: "Just continue what you are doing." For Sister Ann Ida and the board members, that translated, "Do nothing." Tom Foran, who had been general counsel in Chicago for the U.S.. Housing and Urban Development Department in charge of urban renewal land acquisition, served on the board of the Office of Urban Affairs. He contrasts the OUA situation under Cardinal Meyer (whom he characterizes as "brilliant, quiet, perceptive, impressive") with that under Cardinal Cody.

Foran tells the story. "To build 221(d)3 housing, you needed a sponsor. When we couldn't find a sponsor in Woodlawn, Jack said, 'Wouldn't it be great to get the archdiocese to sponsor some subsidized housing!'" Tom Foran wrote the proposal which Egan took to Cardinal Meyer. According to Foran, Jack "came back jumping for joy." The cardinal was in favor of the plan. Then Cardinal Meyer died. "We had a good plan," Foran says, "so Jack and I took it to Cardinal Cody. I remember the two of us going to the cardinal's residence. It was like talking to a wall. You could talk yourself blue in the face and he just looked at us like we were out of our skulls. He waved his hand to dismiss us. Cody was afraid to do anything." It followed that the Office of Urban Affairs could do nothing.

Sister Ann Ida recalls for Jack Egan the "general uprising among board members" when OUA folded. They "urged you to 'go public' with your (and our) frustration. It was the time of other headline events and your answer will always remain in my mind, perhaps not verbatim: 'Chicago Catholics can't take another major outbreak at this time; it is better for the Church if I say nothing publicly.' So we disappeared quietly; no headlines. We took with us an abiding respect for your courage in doing what you thought was best for the greater good instead of your own reputation or achievement."

When Monsignor Hillenbrand had fired Jack Egan from his YCW post early in his career, Jack had grieved but also noted, "I had plenty of other things to do." When he was relieved of his duties at the Office of Urban Affairs, Jack Egan still had plenty of things to do. He had more time for his parish and for the Association of Chicago Priests. But he missed the involvement in the wider community.

In his farewell accountability session with the Presentation parish council, Father Egan asked his people to assess his work with them, with a certain confidence that he'd get good marks as a pastor. He got a surprising comeuppance from the people he characterizes, characteristically, as "a great board." The great apostle of listening had not listened to his people as well as they would have liked, his people told Father Egan.

Jack tries to figure out how that could have happened. "Looking back," he says, "I can see me driving out, heading for Presentation for the first time. In my mind, I was bringing God to Lawndale. I soon found out that God was already in Lawndale. In my mind, I was going to bring God to the people at Presentation. I soon found that God was already in those people. I brought in Sisters and priests and seminarians and lay people from city and suburbs to develop programs for the people of Presentation. And what did the people of Presentation tell me about that?"

Jack sets the scene. "A superb parish council. Elected. Representative. Old, young, middle years. I gave each of them a sheet of paper and twenty minutes to write: 1) whether I'd served them well, 2) where I'd made mistakes, and 3) what were the good things about the last four and one-half years." Jack read out the answers to the council as he collected them. Overwhelmingly, the people liked him and what he'd done.

Then they added that he'd worked too hard. "You didn't trust us to take care of the material aspects of the parish." In his defense, Father Egan thought of the garbage story. The first time a neighborhood group asked him to prevail with the powers downtown for twice a week pickup because the neighborhood population—and therefore trash—had multiplied, Father Egan had agreed. "The great white father," as Jack relates the story, went to see Jim Fitzpatrick at the Bureau of Streets and Sanitation. When he'd ascertained that homes in Mayor Daley's neighborhood had twice a week pickup, Father Egan suggested that there might be trouble if the people on Presentation's populous streets didn't get the same service. And so it was done.

However, when an alewife invasion drew the trucks into harvesting millions of tiny fish, the city cut back garbage collection in Lawndale once again. When the people rallied anew, Jack suggested they take steps themselves. And they did, renting a truck, stocking it with fifty gallon drums of garbage for the sidewalk in front of City Hall. It being a slow news day, Monsignor Egan remembers their demonstration getting a big play in the media they had notified. "It solidified a lesson I had been taught for many years: don't do for people what they can do for themselves. It was stupid of me to go down and see Fitzpatrick the first time. The people are responsible."

Evidently, Father Egan had forgot that lesson other times, for now his people lectured him on his role in their lives: "Your job was to give us an understanding of God and the Bible, and what God's will was for us, to develop our spiritual life so that we could better take care of the parish. You did not take enough care of our spiritual needs."

Even when the "Father" was Jack Egan, it seems, the show was still called *Father Knows Best*. Vatican II notwithstanding, Jack Egan had continued to run the parish operation. His people had loved and trusted him enough to warn him, mid-term, that he wasn't priestly enough. He had only half-heard them. "I made a mistake. I hadn't listened to the lay people," Jack admits. "I learned a lesson I hope I never forget."

21

"The Weak Were Not Meant, by Some Divine Decree, to Remain Weak"

Jack Egan can let things go, even things he loves. He presses that useful knack on others. When Nina Polcyn was wooed in post-Vatican II days by a Minnesota widower she'd known in her undergraduate days at Marquette University, she fretted about the fate of St. Benet's Book Store. How could she leave St. Benet's for married life in Sinclair Lewis' hometown? Once he met the warmly human Thomas Eugene Moore, Father Egan counseled against any delay. "I was so impressed with Tom I called Nina the next day after meeting him and said, 'You should marry him.'" Nina wanted to talk about the several loyalties tugging at her. "What about the store?" she asked.

Jack forcefully dismissed the store's importance. "Nina, the store is irrelevant. You got it free. Give it away free. Go out on Wabash Avenue tomorrow morning and hand the key to the first person you see. Say, 'The store is yours.'"

Jack knew Nina would survive and prosper because, while she was giving up a life she loved, she was going to another life that would draw on other parts of her generous nature. She was ready for the next step because she'd readied herself for it. In the same way Jack had worked at marriage education while a curate, worked at community organizing while he was in marriage education, formed close friendships with blacks before he pastored them, and organized a national group of community organizers while he was still at Presentation. He, too, was always ready—and prepared—to move on.

A few weeks after that airport encounter with Father Hesburgh, Jack Egan had received his formal invitation from the Reverend James T.

Burtchaell, C.S.C., chairperson of the Notre Dame Department of Theology. He invited Jack to be a Senior Fellow within his department for one year, starting August 1, 1970. The university was inaugurating a new doctoral program in pastoral theology. "We would particularly like to draw upon the Chicago apostolate's experience in the first days of the program, and know of no better way to do that than to ask your collaboration."

Burtchaell added that Father Louis Putz, Rector of Moreau Seminary, was offering Jack Egan room and board in return for serving as chaplain to the diocesan seminarians at Moreau.

Since 1966, when Peggy Roach had started dealing with all his mail and virtually organizing his life, Jack Egan had thought of their relationship as a co-ministry. He was comfortable in the consultancy and Moreau chaplaincy roles offered him by the University. But comfort did not create satisfaction in Jack Egan. He needed a more demanding, more insistent, challenge. He couldn't manage that without Peggy. Father Hesburgh had understood. "You can bring Peggy along," he'd said when he invited Jack, "so you'll have all your bases covered. Spend a year doing what you want to do."

At some level, Jack Egan already understood that what was billed as his year of reflection and study was going to project him into the national leadership he and Father Gremillion had experienced at Worcester and Hinsdale. This wider role would not be possible without what Republican National Chairman Lee Atwater some years later described to a *New York Times* reporter as the "indispensable" person behind every powerful public figure. The *Times* called those persons behind-the-scenes buffers, alter egos, early warning systems. Peggy Roach was all these for Jack Egan.

It's helpful if the indispensable ally is a jack-of-all-trades as well as aide and confidante, the *Times* reporter noted. The reporter quoted a former press secretary to both Nancy Reagan and George Bush who said, "Trust, that is the key." Another source cited honesty as a *sine qua non*. To a lobbyist, the one hard and fast rule for spear carriers was steering clear of the limelight themselves. "They understand it is their boss who makes the ultimate decisions."

That's how Rabbi Robert Marx came to see Peggy Roach's role in Jack's working life. "I never understood your relationship to Peggy," he confided to Jack. "She always seemed to be in the background."

Eventually, he came to see her as Jack's inspiration, "someone you could trust. You were not out there all alone." Peggy was the maintenance person behind the operation. "You had a diocese," Marx amplifies, "that was not terribly sympathetic to what you were trying to do, a cardinal who certainly didn't appreciate what you were trying to do. You needed somebody you could talk to, somebody who could tell you whether you were full of it or whether you were on the right track. Peggy was your touchstone to bring you back from the clouds, to say, 'This is what you can do, this is what you can't do.' She was as close to being an honest true friend as anyone could have. A prophet needs someone to say, 'You're going in the right direction.'" Or wrong.

Jack Egan's CCUM ally Father Harry Browne (celebrated for harboring Philip Berrigan in his rectory where the FBI found him in a closet) credited Peggy Roach with writing Jack's stuff, keeping him straight, and putting him on the right planes. "Her role and contribution to the American Church, I suppose, is like that of so many great women who will be less honored than the great monsignors."

If Jack was going to contribute to Notre Dame's Institute of Urban Studies and Pastoral Theology program as well as get rest and rejuvenation, he needed the sustaining power of a Peggy Roach. Nor did he intend to fade from the Chicago scene as he took his year-long sabbatical. He would continue to nourish his close ties to the Association of Chicago Priests and to his wide circle of supporters, people like the Friends of Presentation. Jack had mastered the lesson Monsignor Hillenbrand had never learned: touch base to keep your place in the hierarchy. Attend the wakes and funerals. The anniversary dinners and jubilee fetes. Important liturgical functions like Forty Hours Devotion. To preserve his closeness to lay people, Jack Egan burned gasoline royally on the Indiana Toll Road for weddings, baptisms, funerals, and friendly get-togethers of the old John Ryan Forum folks gathered for refreshment, reflection, and re-charging. Additionally, he answered his own phone, and all the mail that came in. Written communication was crucial to him. Like Father Andrew Greeley, he often reflected that his parish was in his mailbox. He needed Peggy for his "apostolate of the short note" as well as the organizing of his multiple enterprises.

While Jack Egan dates his co-ministry with Peggy Roach to 1966, it was at Notre Dame that their combined leadership was legitimized. The way Dick Conklin, university Director of Public Relations, puts it is, "When you think of Jack, you think of Peg. Jack had the titles, Peg did the work. If you wanted to deal with Jack," he adds, "you ended up dealing as much with Peggy as you did with him. I'll say this for Jack: he tried to deflect as much gratitude, thanks, and praise to Peggy as he could in public and private."

Conklin doesn't think co-ministry is a "hyperbolic term to describe the way the two of them went about things. Peggy was the detail person; Jack, the story-teller. He was Mr. Outside, she Ms. Inside. They compliment one another very well. Not long after they came here, Peg won a special presidential award, unusual for someone who had been part of the Notre Dame community for a relatively short period of time."

Holy Cross theologian Jim Burtchaell agrees that when he wants to make arrangements with Jack/Peggy, "it's quite enough to do it with Peggy. She may put me on to talk to Jack, but I do the business with Peggy." He also gets a straighter story from Peggy. "Jack, even in private, can't talk unpolitically. Peggy formulates the truest account of the state of affairs."

Burtchaell assesses the symbiosis Father Hesburgh labeled, finding each of the pair less effective without the other. "Peggy, left to herself, wouldn't have the constant positivity toward people. She would suffer fools less gladly. On the other hand, Jack would fly off into fantasy without her. He would fret about logistics. Now he never frets about them at all."

Father Burtchaell, who was appointed provost of the university the fall that Father Egan arrived, describes Jack Egan seeking his help toward "some refreshment theologically and a rest. As I later came to learn, Jack was so hemmed in by Cardinal Cody's checking him at every point that he was exploring a new base of operations." That explained some of the "tenseness" Father Hesburgh had seen in Jack at O'Hare Airport.

Of that August when Jack Egan and Peggy Roach moved to South Bend, Jack says, "I never questioned the fact that I would go back to Chicago a year later as a parish priest." Peggy rented an apartment, and Jack moved into Moreau. In some ways, Jack was diffident about the move to South Bend. "Your reputation goes before you. I didn't know what to expect or what was expected of me." Jack admitted to Peggy that he was afraid of being chewed up by academia. Would he be able to create a group there like the group he'd created at Presentation, all those marvelous people who had signed the walls in the common room on the second floor?

In spite of flitting misgivings, Jack was in his element. All his life, Jack Egan had harbored an indefatigable awe of the great university founded by Holy Cross Father Edward Sorin in 1842 before Florida was a state, while pioneers were still trundling their hopes across the Oregon Trail. "There is something about the mystique of Notre Dame," Jack says, "which crawls into your soul and spirit and occupies your mind. You love being there. You're proud of being there."

He never lost the thrill of spotting the Golden Dome across the miles as he approached the campus on the Indiana Toll Road, or crossing the campus under the splendid canopy of mature trees, passing the statue of Holy Cross Father William Corby giving general absolution and a blessing to the troops before the Battle of Gettysburg. Jack would often remind an audience that the sturdy yellow-brown bricks in the early buildings like Brownson Hall (where he later moved from Moreau) were shaped "a century ago from the marl of campus lakes." Out of his corner window in Brownson, Jack looked down on a monastery garden seemingly lifted out of an Old World setting where St. Francis would have felt at home.

For Jack Egan, Moreau Seminary in August, 1970, was "an absolutely idyllic place to renew myself intellectually, spiritually, physically, and emotionally after a rigorous twenty-eight years in Chicago." His host, the intense little Holy Cross Father Louis Putz, was a legend in his time. To the wondering new chaplain from Chicago, Putz' heavy German accent, his monumental role in the Catholic Action movements, was linkage and bond to all the European lore and activism Egan had sought in France in 1953. Hadn't the storied Canon Cardijn himself taught Putz those Jocist principles so crucial to Jack Egan's personal development? Putz had come to Notre Dame as a refugee when war forced him out of Europe. Now Putz and Egan, chaplains to the Holy Cross seminarians and the diocesan seminarians, would be in daily contact. Putz would prove to be a good friend to this new priest coming in wide-eyed with newsboy adulation of the great Catholic university and butterfly-stomached before the academic stars on campus.

Jack recalls taking an art class, a Church history class, and a Bible class—"which I needed badly"—that first semester, under "master professors" like Holy Cross Father James Burtchaell (university provost) who developed into a "dear, dear friend," even a "protector." As Father

Burtchaell sized up Jack's position vis-a-vis Burtchaell as provost, "for the only time in his life Jack had perfection." Burtchaell explains that Jack Egan needs "to be in touch with the boss, which he had with (cardinals) Stritch and Meyer." At the university, Jack's "boss" was Father Burtchaell. He had "me day and night," Father Burtchaell says, "and as far as power goes, I had as much as anybody here. Jack was completely protected. If he came to see me and I said something would be done, he never had to fret about it. In Chicago, no one could deliver for sure. And then he had Ted (university president Theodore Hesburgh), not every day and every night, but in a sort of casual and grand way, although not easily scheduled. He had Ted to work with him on the geo-political order out there off campus."

The backup of these two powerful men was extremely important to Jack Egan. Most priests who diverge from the narrow clerical paths stay out of their superiors' way. The freedom they appropriate includes freedom from permission-seeking. Jack Egan, primed by his father to obedient submission, made a lifetime career of clearing every initiative with a superior. At seventy-three he wouldn't write a letter for newspaper publication without consulting Father John Richardson, the president of DePaul University, whom he was serving as assistant. Jack Egan could resolutely push against the Church's restrictions, but he could never breach them.

Jack Egan can describe his first years at Notre Dame as some of the happiest of his life because there he got total support and consummate approval. This was the ratification he had sought all his life. "Jack works hard to keep his relationship with the person in power clear, open, and benevolent," Father Burtchaell says, "but he hardly had to work at it with me. I'd get occasionally annoyed when he'd come at me and obviously had a little plan to work carefully toward the point. I could always call Peggy afterward and say, 'What's going on?' Peggy and I have always had a wonderful relationship."

What Burtchaell and Hesburgh gave Jack Egan was a new freedom, a reversal of his situation in Chicago. Community activist Harry Fagan described Jack's new billet as "an oasis Hesburgh created so Jack could have some independence." In that freedom Jack Egan could concentrate on the community organization that was the love of his life after 1956 because it was a tool for retooling the conditions of the weak. In Jack Hill's words, Egan believed "that the weak were not meant by some divine decree to remain weak." Jack Egan had faith "that through community organization, as through a kind of secular sacrament, the weak can get power to make their lives whole. And that God will not mind at all."

Jack Egan can't pinpoint the moment he realized an individual alone can't change the fabric of society, that individuals have to be organized to hold authority accountable in government—and in the Church. But that understanding is the source of his devotion to community organization. People who don't have money or position have to use their numbers to get what they need. Jack knew which priests across the United States were helping people organize for this kind of change. He would create a refueling station for them at Notre Dame.

The Catholic Committee on Urban Ministry was already in place. Basically, it was a group of Irish priests (with the exception of Geno Baroni) who headed up the few justice and peace offices or diocesan offices of urban affairs there were in the country. According to one of them, New Yorker Father Philip Murnion, these priests "tended to have created their jobs or organization in connection with urban ministry. Very innovative types, very creative types, the first of whatever they were, the first urban ministry office directors, first heads of neighborhood organizations." Jack Egan, as the very first diocesan director of an office of urban affairs, had "godfathered" many of them, "going around to different cities where they were trying to set up such an office and helping them." Once he'd worked with them, according to Murnion, Jack never "felt any reluctance" at pulling them together for a seminar on interracial work or community organization or urban affairs. This is what he'd always done with the people he surrounded himself with.

The Catholic Committee on Urban Ministry had got its start in March 1967. About that time, black activist James Forman was pursuing the Protestant churches, particularly Riverside Church in New York City, for reparations for blacks. Forman made some Protestants and Jews nervous. To relieve the pressure Forman was putting on them, Protestant and Jewish church leaders organized a conduit to funnel money collectively into black community organizations. They invited Jack Egan to join the first board of their Interreligious Foundation for Community Organization. It was clear to Jack that there should be a Catholic on the IFCO board, but each member was expected to contribute a thousand dollars. Where could he find that amount?

When about seventeen of the people whose urban ministries Jack had godfathered met together at a convocation in Evanston, Illinois, in

March 1967, he consulted them about an IFCO presence. Their response was to create the Catholic Committee on Community Organization to raise the money for the IFCO seat. Peggy Roach, also present, agreed to serve as CCCO secretary. Geno Baroni came out of the hotel room, banging his head with his hand, saying, "My God, I can't believe we have started another Catholic organization." Not Monsignor Baroni, nor any of that first seventeen, could have imagined what a sustaining scaffolding this fragile reed would prove to be.

When the group met in the summer of 1967 in conjunction with the National Catholic Conference for Interracial Justice in Kansas City, they changed their name to the Catholic Committee on Urban Ministry. For the first few years their meetings were small, ad hoc, and piggybacked on other meetings these few urban ministers would be attending anyway. In 1970 there simply weren't that many priests in social ministry, although a cadre of veterans of the civil rights movement—people who'd marched at Selma or with the United Farm Workers and Cesar Chavez—had awakened to the necessity for social ministry. However, New York activist Harry Fagan said of them that they had no place to plug in, "no place for support or sharing ideas, nothing like what we have today with the United States Catholic Conference and Catholic Charities and the Roundtable [an association of diocesan social action directors founded by Fagan]." Where they existed in 1970, social action types tended to find toleration, not solid support, in their chanceries.

They needed that place to plug into, some historical perspective, knowledge of wider communities, encouragement, reinforcement, and—as an important part of the package—*joie de vivre*. Now Jack (with Hesburgh's help) could give them place at Notre Dame. Being Jack, he made it his business to put the other desirable elements in place.

Tom Broden, a law professor who directed the Institute of Urban Studies, remembers the first CCUM meeting at Moreau Seminary in the fall of 1970 as "twenty priests, Peggy, and me." Jack challenged the group to have a big party and dissolve, or to make something of CCUM. Those present agreed on their general desire to continue. They were divided on whether they should expand. Some agreed with Jack that membership should be extended to all the community activists in the country, that together they should explore the theological underpinnings of urban ministry.

Others like Texas Father John McCarthy, later bishop of Austin, opposed growth. "Jack Egan, you will ruin CCUM if you open it up to everybody." Jack compromised, consenting to two groups. The original members would constitute the twenty-person board to set policy and organize the agendas for the annual meetings and summer institutes. The larger group would be those who attended the programs.

The board was Jack's construct, highly personal, idiosyncratic. "He played elder statesman," fellow board member Phil Murnion says of Jack Egan, "even when he was a younger statesman." A nun from Houston characterized CCUM types as outcasts. "We're here," she said, "to pat each other on the back and say, 'What a great job you've been doing.'" If there wasn't much outside support for what more traditional church types called rabble-rousers, they would provide support for each other. Jack, of course, was a master at bolstering people's sense of self-esteem.

Jack was ready to recast anyone who felt like an outcast as an out-flanker, outdistancer, outthinker, outsmarter. He would assure individuals that they could outshine, outrun, outspeak, outlast anybody. Weren't these the people he expected to turn the Church around? Wasn't this an historic occasion? Weren't the people in this room the greatest community activists, quite possibly the greatest organizers, in the whole world?

Each person listening to his pitch felt it beamed directly at him or her. Aware as they were that Jack's contacts and zealots ranged from Atlantic to Pacific, each of them construed his or her intimate personal relationship with Jack Egan as unique. Harry Browne (pastor of St. Gregory's Church in New York City until 1970) tagged Jack's mode of making people feel wonderful about themselves and their work, "Eganizing." All CCUM members were Eganized. "The group that became the board," Phil Murnion says, "while fighting and fussing over issues and strategies and stuff like that, had an enormous amount of personal care for each other. That tone was set very early."

Part of Jack's incisive thrust toward a person's psychic jugular was his ability to hone in on need. Father Phil Murnion suggests that Jack Egan picked new board members as much for what CCUM could do for them as for what they could do for CCUM. It was something of a joke with the board that Jack Egan tended to find their new associates at airports. When he'd come back with his suggestions, the board would consider his candidates' merits. According to Murnion, board member Pat Dolan capsulized the necessary qualifications for people joining the board: "The main quality is do they love us?" It was that kind of organization.

Harry Fagan loved them. He was director of the Commission on Catholic Community Action in Cleveland when he got a phone call from Jack Egan about joining the CCUM board. "It was a group of people I immediately felt very close to," Fagan says. "It was odd. They were all where I was on social action, social justice, community organizing, in terms of Church.

"They had a kind of loyalty that was like family. It was okay to criticize because you knew deep down everyone had the same love for the Church." The meetings were loose in the extreme. "No real elections," Fagan says. "No votes, no Robert's Rules." He describes Jack ("I say this lovingly") as the godfather of a "happy Mafia system." When the group came together to plan something like the annual meeting in the fall or the summer institute, he was "the kind of godfather who would get us in a motel room for a couple of nights and we'd plan one of those things. We'd figure what courses, who would teach them."

Jack made a point of mixing the academic intellectuals with the men in the front lines, stimulating both with the interchange. Historian David O'Brien describes how the CCUM experience "transformed my understanding of the intellectual life" after Jack Egan found O'Brien at an airport and put him on the board. O'Brien learned "enormous respect for the shock troops working in the Church's most difficult ministries. I continually learned from them about faith and culture and politics, about power and its uses, and about the tough work of building democracy among real people."

Jack meant the transformation should work both ways, and it did. O'Brien organized conferences (in those motel rooms in the middle of the night), taught in the summer training program, and traveled around the country giving talks and workshops for the eight years he was on the CCUM board. "I was awed by the experience of being told (by activists) they found my work useful and affirming, that they appreciated the critical lens I tried to hold up to their language and symbols as I tried with them to understand how to translate religious meanings and moral values into public practice."

For O'Brien, dialogue with experienced, mature adults made abstract ideas real. He found this especially true when the dialogue was "moderated by the healthy, unromantic Catholic realism of the older generation

. . . people like (Monsignor Jack) Egan and Monsignor George Higgins."

O'Brien wrote in *Cross Currents* in 1990 that the experience awakened in him "a vision of academic intellectuals . . . enriched and empowered by serving the Church, which in turn was serving the human community." Jack's linkage had worked once again.

Another side of Jack at CCUM is revealed in Peggy Roach's story of Sister Marjorie Tuite's irritable reaction to it. Once huge sheets of newsprint listing speakers, times, phone numbers, for the "best annual meeting (or summer institute) the world has ever known" came out of the smoke-filled motel room, it was up to the Peggy Roaches and Jack Egans and Marjorie Tuites to divide up the list and make the calls, checking off carefully each acceptance on the newsprint. This was enough of a routine that Sister Marjorie Tuite was popularly known as "the newsprint lady."

Each acceptance was followed up with a letter. That would seem to settle the matter, but Jack Egan always had an additional agenda. "You've got to find a place for Father Worthy-As-Can-Be."—All right, we'll give him this liturgy. "Sister Never-Gets-Credit would be so disappointed."—Okay, she can chair this session. The list would lengthen and Marjorie Tuite's irritation would grow.

Finally, perhaps when Jack was called to the Morris Inn on a pastoral matter, Marjorie would turn to Peggy, imitating Jack. Pursing her lips, she'd huff, "Can't hurt this one. Can't disappoint that one. Be nice to this nun. Peggy, do you realize we are working for a marshmallow?"

Peggy was well aware, but it amused her enough to repeat the Tuite remark to Jack when he came in from his pastoral luncheon, asking, "How are things going?"

"Jack," she said, "Marjorie says you are a marshmallow. Can't hurt this nun! Mustn't disappoint that priest!"

Laughing, Jack would answer from the high that he experienced when he—and the work—was on a CCUM roll. "Jesus was a marshmallow," he would allow, checking the newsprint sheets to be sure that Father-Must-Be-Included was on the roster. At times like this, Jack couldn't be put down. Jack was happy. He had his new group.

22

"We Had Great People, and a Heck of a Lot of Fun"

At Presentation Jack Egan had been frustrated in his attempts to empower the people. He'd preached at the churches from his Chicago pulpit, suggesting that, "People who came from Eastern Europe and Ireland didn't receive the kind of moral teaching to put the sin of racism into its proper context affecting their lives and the nations." He'd warned the National Federation of Priests' Councils in 1969 that many lay organizations were "far ahead" of the Church "in committing their power and money to the fight against racism and poverty." He had told a lay apostolate convention that parish churches should be using their purchasing power to fight racial discrimination.

He'd even tried to convert Sears Roebuck whose Homan Avenue headquarters was within the boundaries of Presentation Parish. He brought them his vision of how their corporate power together with the generous government programs of the late sixties could turn all of the Lawndale neighborhood around. He thought he had an inside track because Bill Dooley, the president of the Sears bank, had been an active Cana worker. Monsignor Egan did not prevail.

Now the ever-sanguine Jack Egan brought the Catholic Committee on Urban Ministry to the Notre Dame campus as a way of continuing community organizing. CCUM, as he and Peggy often said, was ministry to the ministers, ministry to those empowering the poor. In the process, CCUM people were empowered as individuals. Phil Murnion gets back to the charge that Jack did his recruiting in airports. "That wasn't entirely true, but it wasn't entirely false, either." Murnion says CCUM was, "in language that most of the board members would have rejected, a support group." He agrees it was also "national actions and programmatic stuff."

241

Meetings were like family dinners. Board members fought with each other over actions. "At one point," Murnion says, "when we invited some other people on board and they made a motion, nobody knew what to do with them. A person was scorned for any suggestion that was the way to move the action. You just fought until somebody won." It didn't much matter who won anyway if it was true, as Murnion remembers, that in a sense (another half-truth, he says) "we would fight and make decisions and then go home and Jack and Peggy would do whatever they wanted to do. And that was all right with people. There was enough trust that if Jack and Peggy changed something, it was for a good reason."

After all, "a good bit of CCUM," Murnion says, "was giving Jack and Peggy a base to do what Jack always does whether he's at Notre Dame or Chicago or DePaul, i.e., function as advocate/supporter/confidant/encourager. (People outside normal systems) always have to establish their place because there is no place other than that they establish. In urban ministry, expertise is not the issue. Connectedness is the issue, building enduring relationships."

For Jack Egan, Murnion says, "people are his capital. That's what he draws on. The key question is, 'Who gets the Rolodex?'" Sometimes this backfires as it did when Peggy Roach was sent to Washington with the Rolodex to bring in campaigners for U.S. presidential candidate George McGovern. Monsignor Geno Baroni had told the CCUM board, "Someone has to get George McGovern elected." There was a lot of sympathy for Peggy on that Quixotic crusade because, as Murnion says, "People who care about them care about them both, and care that Peggy be well respected in the process."

Murnion describes the urgency and drama that Jack gave to every CCUM meeting. Every meeting was historic, of course, and every participant full of talent. "The board's reaction," Murnion says, "was affectionate mockery when Jack would tell each of them that he or she was the most important whatever. Jack has probably told a hundred people that he wants them to preach his eulogy." But as hard-nosed an activist as Tom Gaudette agrees that even as people see through Egan's panegyrics, they are grateful to be taken in by them.

Actually, Jack was right about the 1970s being an historic moment in the Church. The whole justice issue was being recognized. It was at their synod in 1971 that the bishops declared that action for justice was constitutive to the preaching of the Gospel. This was taken immediately as a mandate for CCUM. Soon, Jack says, "we saw social action and peace and justice efforts become firmly established in most, if not all, of the dioceses as well as in the religious orders throughout the country." CCUM grew along with this movement, functioning as a network to bring together persons and organizations addressed to human problems and social justice issues.

CCUM trained, in Jack's estimation, "a whole generation of priests, Sisters, and lay people on the depth of the social teaching of the Catholic Church." Participants at the annual meetings and summer institutes learned the theological dimensions of that social teaching, and how to use it in pastoral work.

The week-long annual meeting, and the very intensive four-week summer program were the two conduits to offer "the best of teachers, liturgists, historians to bring participants up-to-date on the teachings of Vatican II, newest developments in pastoral theology, implications of Catholic social teaching, affairs of state, and the possible effects of pending legislation."

As soon as Tom Broden had assigned Jack and Peggy an office in the Knute Rockne building, Jack had begun dialing people like Tom Gaudette. "Tom, I need you now. Could you come down to Moreau Seminary? There's some great people I'd like you to meet."

"[That kind of invitation] was always a trap," Gaudette grins wryly. "After you arrived, Egan would say, 'I didn't tell you why I wanted you to come down here. I'd like you to give a two-hour talk.'" This was part of CCUM's informality and Jack Egan's genius for bringing in people from the field to give an accurate picture of the community organizing scene.

For an ad hoc group, CCUM accomplished a great deal. According to author David Finks, CCUM's brain trust put two members on the U.S. Catholic Conference social action staff in Washington, D.C., and built a lobby to work on church social programming. CCUM developed diocesan urban ministry programs, social action for seminary field education, the National Center for Urban Ethnic Affairs, and the first study conference bringing together social activist CCUM members, the Catholic Theological Society of America, and the U.S. Catholic Conference.

Jack Egan remembers "a few of our people who gathered together in Combermere, Canada, up where the Baroness de Hueck was, after Lyndon Johnson declared the War on Poverty, put together the fundamentals for the Campaign for Human Development. We then met with Cardinal Dearden, president of the American bishops, and sold him on the program. Cardinal Dearden sold the other bishops."

For the first spring CCUM meeting, the twenty-five originals worked out a program attractive enough to bring ninety-two of their peers—now including women religious—to a March 1971 gathering on the Notre Dame campus. Gaudette who found it all marvelously exciting—"great fun"—describes how, typically, Egan would raise the current issues for the assembly. The Berrigans in prison. A Black Catholic office struggling because it was broke. A famous priest in Cairo getting his rectory windows broken. Another priest "getting the hell beat out of him."

"By four-thirty," Gaudette says, "we had everybody pitching in. Egan loved it." And so did Gaudette. "It was a ball. The atmosphere was fun. Peggy was the creator of the whole thing. Egan was up front; he took the credit. This is where you met everybody, the unions, the gays, the women who wanted to be cardinals—this is twenty years ago when women were just beginning to want to be cardinals—the poets, the workers, the prisoners. This was real Church, working Church. Everybody used their skills. We never went to bed. You could be serious. You could be silly. It was marriage between the Church and the real world."

Jack Egan worked to keep CCUM within bounds. He agrees with Gaudette that "we had great, great people, and a heck of a lot of fun." He stresses the lifelong relationships established, and the social development. "Peggy and I brought to the Notre Dame campus extraordinary people, the best of the thinkers in the U.S. and European Church." He was also careful to keep CCUM respectable. "There was no dancing at Mass, nothing experimental, no consecrating pancakes," Father Murnion recalls.

Jack Egan could see that the action people were beginning to look at Notre Dame as a mecca. "What we were doing was developing a consciousness in the university that there was a world outside Notre Dame, and opening the university to the needs of the people in the world."

Dick Conklin, Director of the Department of Information Services, watched Jack Egan become "an important part of Notre Dame" as he carried out Father Hesburgh's mandate to put the resources of the university at the service of the Church. As the "linkage between Notre

Dame and urban ministry," Jack succeeded, according to Conklin, in developing a sensitivity to social issues on the campus as well as that campus connection with the wider Church. Conklin admits there was tension. "Academics sometimes view advocate people with suspicion." But he recalls Jack succeeding "well in establishing credibility with faculty people. I think you can look at certain things happening today (that testify to Jack's influence). For instance, Notre Dame has put $400,000 in a homeless shelter in South Bend in cooperation with the city and volunteer communities. That is a departure."

Additionally, Conklin suggests that through "Jack Egan and other people like (Father) Don McNeil (who developed the Urban Plunge program with Father Egan), we have got the thread of justice and peace issues woven into the community in a way they simply were not ten years ago, twenty years ago . . . Jack Egan was a very important agent of change in terms of the way the university views its education mission vis-a-vis social justice issues." Conklin says the "university is more likely to look at (social ministry and urban problems) for Jack Egan's having been there."

Jack Egan reached out from Notre Dame to Harry Browne, longtime activist pastor of St. Gregory's church in the Strykers Bay area of Manhattan. "I wasn't much for going to national Catholic meetings," this colorful (later resigned) priest reflected as he looked back on his life when he was terminally ill with leukemia in 1980, "but Jack seduced me out to them. Of course, he had the skills of organizing. He knew if you gave Browne a chance to talk, he'd crawl across the country."

By that time Browne had done enough work in the Strykers Bay neighborhood that, "I could pontificate on schools, poverty programs, health care systems, and varieties of housing," Browne says. He describes Jack Egan's jaunty hyperbole. "It didn't take long for me to appreciate Jack's rhetoric and his little old manipulating ways leading you down the primrose path."

Harry Browne, who christened "Eganizing," admitted to being Eganized. It was another term for what Father John Fitzsimons characterized as "good" manipulation. However expressed, this was the power behind the success of the Catholic Committee on Urban Ministry. At first, Harry Browne reacted by thinking there was some pertinent content not being mentioned. "But then it all becomes a blur of Jack's presence like a great sun over the shoulder of my ministry."

Browne could laugh at himself. "I know it is extreme," he conceded, "to compare anybody in your life with sunshine, making yourself the heliotrope. But the sun was constant and taken for granted. Jack's warming glow on your efforts, his continual presence . . . when he knew you were into something he'd be there with an encouraging call or a note." Harry Browne left his pastorate at St. Gregory's in 1970. "(Jack's) offer to come and be of any help came as a kind of pleasant shock to me. I didn't know what he could do, so I did nothing, but just the thought that he was there and would call just to check in was comforting. He has never missed a chance to back a faltering brother or sister."

As an activist, Browne was a guy who thought he needed no support. "I was too busy browbeating everybody in the field. I had no need to be loved by the bishop or else go into a purple funk." What he learned from Father Philip Murnion (who lived in Browne's rectory while a student at Columbia and succeeded Jack Egan as CCUM chairperson) was that, whether Browne acknowledged it or not, he was getting constant support from his reference group, "the people with whom I could compare my successes and failures, and exchange ideas. I never went to a CCUM board meeting or conference without coming back in a high—in a physical and liver low, but a high intellectually and spiritually."

Peggy Roach remembers Harry Browne greeting Jack Egan with a hearty kiss on his bald pate at every CCUM gathering. That tied into the story she often repeats about Harry Browne's perennial answer to questions about his concern for the attitude of the New York Archdiocesan Chancery Office toward his social action. "I don't care what they think," was Browne's fixed rejoinder. "It's what that little bald-headed guy in Chicago thinks that I care about." Browne guessed that he had referred to Jack Egan hundreds of times as the "Underground Eminence of the American Church." For Browne, Jack demonstrated that position "in his many ways of connecting the boondock and love-bureaucracy social justice caring ones around the country."

By the fall of 1975, seven hundred CCUM "change-agents" gathered at Notre Dame for a five-day conference on "Coalition Building: A Strategy for Justice." By now, CCUM membership was over three thousand. Sixties activists who'd burned out were regrouping. As one religious leader told Father Egan, "Jack, I've got my second wind. I'm ready to go again."

However, the newly formed program of pastoral theology to which Jack had been invited as a Senior Fellow "never got off the ground," in Jack's words. Jack Egan had suffered another setback in the area of pastoral theology before Father Hesburgh singled him out to add some heft to Notre Dame's experimental pastoral theology program. That assignment came from his friend, Archbishop Paul Hallinan of Atlanta. Jack was to organize a study of the pastoral aspects in the priesthood in the spirit of the *Pastoral Constitution on the Church in the Modern World*. That constitution states that "the Church stands forth as a sign of that brotherliness which allows honest dialogue and invigorates it." Seemingly, the Church was going to indulge in some honest dialogue of its own.

Other research groups would dig into clerical psychology (headed by author/psychologist Eugene Kennedy), sociology (headed by University of Chicago-trained Father Andrew Greeley), ecumenism (headed by the future William Cardinal Baum), history (headed by church historian Father Robert Trisco of Catholic University of America), and liturgy (Father Fred McManus).

Jack assembled what he considered a "competent team of (Protestant and Catholic) theologians, sociologists, and pastoral ministers" to formulate a questionnaire on pastoral considerations to be sent to priests' senates and associations. In addition, they compiled a mailing list of seventy-five major superiors of religious orders, male and female, approximately fifty theologians, seventy-five Catholic lay men and women, and one hundred Protestant clergy and theologians. Thirty-two of the fifty superiors of female religious groups returned reports, according to the study. Because most of them conducted group sessions, the number of individuals who actually influenced the final tabulation was over three hundred.

The team billed their report to the bishops as descriptive, not scholarly. Jack thought it was a good, even prophetic, piece of work. Unfortunately, he couldn't deliver it to Archbishop Hallinan who died during the study. As had happened before when Jack had lost a sponsor during a controversial project, he was now bare to the winds. And he felt their chill. First, from fellow research chairperson Andrew Greeley who denounced the pastoral ministry study. In what Jack remembers as a scathing letter to John Cardinal Krol, General Chairman, and Bishop Joseph Bernardin, at that time Secretary of the National Conference of

Catholic Bishops, Greeley called the Egan study superficial and an interference with his own sociological paper.

Jack was also excoriated for his expense account. Having been given the responsibility to study in depth the life and ministry of the priests of the United States, Father Egan confidently spent what he considered a modest $10,000. He knew Father Greeley's study was billed at $250,000. The comparison did not save him. He had not gotten prior clearance. When he presented his budget, he was roundly criticized. While Father Greeley's study was widely circulated, Jack's study was ignored because Greeley had put it down. Again, as when he'd testified alone against the University of Chicago's urban renewal, Jack was chilled by cold shoulders from his fellow clerics.

However, this time there was a difference. Father Hesburgh continued to be impressed by Jack and Peggy's abilities. After their first year, he'd called Jack into his cluttered, unpretentious office under Notre Dame's golden dome where he worked to a great hour every night. He was gratified by the caliber of people CCUM had brought on the campus. "It'd be a shame if you and Peggy should leave now when what you have started is so good. So helpful for the university." To Father Hesburgh, Jack Egan was an valuable asset. Nationally, "Jack was in touch with anyone doing anything," Father Hesburgh recalls. On campus, "being gregarious, Jack knew everybody in five minutes. Everybody liked him very much. He found something good in everyone." For Hesburgh, inviting Jack to Notre Dame was a suggestion that had worked out. "They don't all."

Hesburgh and Egan shared a common vision of their use to the world, and the university's use to the world. "A university is a place where the Church can face problems in full freedom," Father Hesburgh says. "Everybody around here talks when they feel like it, I think in a responsible way. Freedom is the lifeblood of a university." Talking to Eugene Kennedy for his book *Believing*, Father Hesburgh described his life as "on the fringes of the Church. Most of the things that I have been a part of, I have not only been the only priest but also the only Catholic present. And my value to these people on commissions and committees came from trying to bring some deeper dimension of faith."

Like Father Hesburgh, Jack Egan saw himself on the fringes of the Church, bringing "deeper dimensions" to committees and boards. Like Father Hesburgh, he professed a faith with a horizontal dimension. Jack shared Father Hesburgh's notion that, "If you really believe in the Incarnation, you understand that the vertical dimension (person to God) is only meaningful if it is expressed horizontally (person to person)," and, "You have to have faith in what man can be if he is cared for."

This faith undergirded Jack's work to make Notre Dame the center for Catholic social thinking in the United States from CCUM's March meeting in 1971 until 1978. Holy Cross Father Jim Burtchaell says that, "Actually, for the activist part of the post-Vatican II Church there was no place like here (Notre Dame), and Jack had a lot to do with that." He adds that Jack Egan's ambassadorial work for Father Hesburgh "greatly improved our relationship with the clerical Church. He gave the place credibility." Father Hesburgh's reputation achieved the same goal, "but no one ever saw Ted."

Father Hesburgh put the period at the end of that sentence when he called Jack about eleven one night in the spring of 1976. "I'd like to talk to you about something." This was another of those command appearances, arranged by phone, with pivotal consequences in Jack's life. In this case, the consequences would extend to the Catholic Committee on Urban Ministry. How would Father Egan have replied to the university president's offer if he had known how the decision he was about to make would affect his beloved CCUM? That CCUM would be a only a memory in ten years?

23

"What Registers With Jack Is Possibility"

A certain stiff academic element resisted the fresh winds of change coming from some of the new centers like CCUM taking up residence on the South Bend campus. Some academics deemed the centers a threat to the purity of the university's mission.

President Hesburgh welcomed the new centers, as he did the winds of change. Experience on many boards, and in positions like the chairmanship of the U.S. Civil Rights Commission, fostered Father Hesburgh's easy acceptance of societal shifts. His generous view was, "What is genuinely human can't be faulted."

That wider view played into Pope John XXIII's expansive notion of a Vatican Council in 1961. Hesburgh suggested, in an interview with author Eugene Kennedy, that Pope John called that council "to do something about the crime of four hundred and fifty years without any change." Father Hesburgh further observed that, once the council had done its work, church people tried to "cram all that change into ten years, and it's been pretty hard," displaying a patience that hangs well on the president of a great university. For Father Hesburgh, the centers he was bringing on campus could be experimental channels to fine tune the changes. Hesburgh's "big dream," according to Peggy Roach, was Notre Dame in service to the Church.

Hesburgh meant the centers to be a vehicle of that service. (After his retirement as president of the university, after Father Egan had gone back to Chicago, Father Hesburgh himself would move into the role of connector between the university and the universe. Having made the decision to spend the rest of his life working for peace, he would chair the institutes that relate to that purpose. As chairperson, he would interface between them and the fifty-plus international bodies of which he was a member. "To keep our institutes from reinventing the wheel," he says.)

In 1976, looking for ways to strengthen the centers then on campus, Hesburgh fixed on Father Egan to be liaison between academe and the main stream. That decision prompted his postprandial call. Working late as he most often did, Father Hesburgh, along with Father James Burtchaell, the university provost, awaited Father Egan. They meant to ask Egan to integrate the five centers now operating on the campus into one new entity. Jack was already directing the Catholic Committee on Urban Ministry. Centralization would add the Murphy Center for Liturgical Research (later named Center for Pastoral Liturgy), the Notre Dame Institute for Clergy Education, the Center for Human Development, and the Religious Leaders Program to his portfolio. Later, Retreats International would be integrated into the entity.

When Jack walked in, the two educators eagerly presented their proposal. Would Jack agree to organize the five centers Father Hesburgh admitted were "all over the place" in their programs as well as their geography? "I'm getting some criticism on how they relate to the university. They all relate in different ways. I'd like you as the director of a Center for Pastoral and Social Ministry to pull them all together," Father Hesburgh said. (Later, the title would be changed to Institute for Pastoral and Social Ministry.)

Jack's internal monitor started bleeping. He shook his head, backing off from the offer. "You're making a serious mistake," he told the president and the provost, both his good friends by 1976. Jack Egan had been at Notre Dame long enough to remind them that an advanced degree—which he did not have—was the only legitimate calling card at their university. "My second objection," he told his friends, "is that I'm not a Holy Cross priest." That identity would have been another potential source of legitimacy.

Father Hesburgh was not easily deflected. "I want a diocesan priest," he insisted. "I want someone known by the bishops and known by the Sisters, priests, and lay people in the social action field. I want you to do it. I've worked with you. I trust you." Jack reworded his objections. "This will never be recognized on the campus because I'm not degreed."

Father Hesburgh knew how to confer legitimacy. "I'll make you my special assistant," he announced. "I've only done that once before, with

Dr. George Shuster. He's dead now. I'm entitled to an assistant." With presidential assurance, Father Hesburgh added, "That should open doors to you." That did open doors, Jack admits. "Nobody knew if I had any power, or how much power I had, and nobody was going to test it." Nevertheless, it was at Father Hesburgh's request he acceded, and not without misgivings. Jack had put in his thumb and pulled out a plum, but it wasn't a plum without blemish. A blemish that would in time threaten the fruitfulness of his work at Notre Dame.

"Father Hesburgh was the last person in the world who needed an assistant," according to Jack. "There was nothing you could assist him on. Well, maybe to appear on his behalf. Like going over to Belfast for him or to a particular meeting or to give an invocation or to substitute before what might be an important group but wouldn't be a substantive talk." Jack edged into the role of aide-de-camp and confidant. "I'd see Father Hesburgh frequently at his office or at dinner and he'd talk to me about any number of things. He used me the way Mayor Daley used Judge Lynch, as a friend outside the Democratic machine whom he could trust."

That's precisely how Father Hesburgh saw the relationship: "When you're president here, you are constantly being called on for a wide variety of things. You really need a second opinion, someone to talk things over with. Jack was perfect in that role because he knows everybody out around the country in these areas. He has a sense of the Church that's very deep. He's an apostolic priest. He doesn't butter you up. He tells you what he thinks is right so he's a very good counselor. We all miss him."

Supported by the president and the provost, Jack Egan could probably have survived the several battles that broke out after the consolidation of the centers. But soon after Jack moved in as director, a new provost—a man decidedly less sympathetic to the centers—was installed. "A book man, a scholar, he ran the university like a book. He had an entirely different personality from mine," Jack says. "There was always a battle with him as to the place of these centers. He didn't think they belonged on a university campus." Soon the new provost was quoted in the Faculty Senate Journal as saying the role the centers had played in the larger educational endeavors of the university had been disappointing and that new initiatives in this area were unlikely.

There were other continuing irritations within the institute concerning fees for lodging at conferences, financial arrangements, and accountability. Jack surmises it was his fronting for the university that induced a personal antipathy in several center heads. "I made life difficult for them. And, in time, they made life intolerable for me." Those difficulties would influence the Egan/Roach move back to Chicago in 1983. Meantime, Jack knew an opportunity when he saw one.

At Presentation he'd had few resources with which to make do. He was always contacting his friends on the outside for some kind of assistance, stretching a little money to do the work of a lot of money. Now at the University of Notre Dame he was sitting on a cornucopia, a cache of learning, an intellectual bowl brimming with subtle arts, scientific acumen, spiritual gifts, and housing space. As Father Hesburgh's special assistant, Jack Egan could maximize his already seasoned connecting skills to bring together groups who could profit from linkage and from the university's abundance. That's what Peggy and he thought they were all about. That's what they thought the centers were for. At Presentation they'd scrambled for resources. At the university they dispensed largesse. All this good stuff, bed and breakfast, lore and learning, theological enterprise, and liturgical innovation.

They plied their nifty tools of post and telephone to their limits, summoning groups to come and partake. Father Hesburgh observed early that to Jack Egan a phone line was a life line. Like Kay Fox back at St. Justin Martyr where Jack began his priestly life and his daily dialing, Father Hesburgh was indulgently unbegrudging as Jack succumbed to what Hesburgh wryly calls "the temptation of the telephone." Hesburgh recognized this as Jack's means of keeping his network together. Aware that Jack writes hundreds of letters most weeks, Hesburgh still estimates Jack "must make two or three phone calls for every letter."

Illustrating how a phone can put Jack on hold, Hesburgh describes his arrival with Jack Egan at a Wisconsin lodge for a meeting with the nation's bishops. "We walked into this big room with a fireplace and a porch beyond it, looking out on a lake." All Jack saw was one of the two phones in the place, sitting on a table. "He came to a shuddering halt," Father Hesburgh recalls, "grabbed the phone and called our friend Gene Boyle (a CCUM board member) in San Francisco. Maybe Gene was on his mind," he adds tolerantly.

Jack had profited enormously from his sabbatical year at Notre Dame. Together with Peggy, he replicated his personal program for others. First for religious leaders. "After the first year, I felt there must be lots of priests and religious who were going through the same experience I had. After years of ministry, they needed time off, particularly if they were changing to another arena of work." He cites, for an example, a provincial of a religious order stepping back into teaching or hospital work after a term as leader.

"Peggy and I devised a Religious Leaders Program. It still exists. The first year we had four people. We were very strict. We made sure the participants lived on campus, the women at the new dormitories, the men at Brownson where I lived. We insisted they take classes, but no more than two. We wanted them to have time to sleep, pray, relax, attend lectures and art demonstrations." Most of them took Father Burtchaell's theology class as Jack had done.

Organizing the program was a chore the first year. After that, Jack claims the succeeding programs were "sheer fun." Peggy, who served as director one year, saw that the participants were invited to liturgies, that they got football tickets, that their courses were individually tailored. During the South Bend years, she was their Perle Mesta. As she had done in Washington, Peggy entertained any time anyone of note came to town. Jack didn't know how she could afford it, in spite of the fact that Tom Broden had arranged that she be compensated as Jack's associate, not his secretary. "Peggy's home was a mecca," Jack says. "Hers was one of the few homes Father Hesburgh came to. He seldom visited homes, trying to spend the time he was in South Bend with the Holy Cross Fathers."

Jack and Peggy brought Sisters on campus to talk to canon lawyers about changes in their rules prompted by Vatican II. "The finest of the Canon Law Society came there at our invitation." Later, Jack and Peggy invited a large group of laity, priests and women religious to analyze the whole question of pastoral ministry in a parochial setting. They hosted a group of international theologians come to bring Vatican II up to date at a conference called *Toward Vatican III*. They brought bishops ordained to the episcopacy during the preceding two years to the campus for a ten-day seminar designed for them. Shortly after the invitation went out under Father Hesburgh's signature, thirty-two of the forty-one bishops invited responded enthusiastically. "A man placed in a position of high responsibility needs certain skills immediately, skills in finance, personal relationships, conflict resolution, listening, organizing," Jack says.

To work up the bishops' program, Jack and Peggy recruited a team of four, including Evelyn and Jim Whitehead whom Jack was instrumental in bringing on campus as freshly minted Ph.D.s to direct field work for seminarians and teach in the theology department. For the Whiteheads their time at Notre Dame was "incredibly formative." They credit Jack for giving them, at the time, a research psychologist and a scholar of Chinese culture, a mutual vocation in ministry education. "He was mentor for both of us," Evelyn Whitehead says. "He championed us in that way where you feel so special, sponsored us, loved us, encouraged us. We always felt there were no strings attached." As trained observers, the Whiteheads note how often mentors shape people in their own image. "But Jack empowered us to do what we do. He didn't make us do what he did." Evelyn Whitehead never has the sense "that he will take something back if we don't toe the line, because he doesn't give you a line to toe."

As a mark of Jack's faith, they describe the circumstances of his invitation to design the ten-day workshop for new bishops. "We were absolute nobodies. Who else would have given us the opportunity? Anyone else would have ridden herd on us. Jack never raised a doubt in a way that would undermine our faith in what we were doing. None of the insinuating sort of thing that depletes you. He really does build up the Body of Christ."

They remember those bishops' workshops in 1980 and 1981 as "absolutely wonderful events," the culmination of their involvement at Notre Dame. The next year the bishops themselves organized a similar event at Collegeville. For the Whiteheads, it was a "sign of Jack's genius" that he knew how to produce the result desired. "On the one hand, he wanted a beautiful design because he knew the bishops wouldn't come unless the workshop looked worthwhile. But his real goal (as it is in most of life) was to get people to talk to one another." In their work on ministry, the Whiteheads had observed how often pastors "really think they have to go it alone. It's awful for them, devastating for the Church. Let nobody into your heart. Let nobody into your plans."

Father Egan, a virtuoso at finding tutelary geniuses for himself at crucial junctures, was by now figuring as a tutelary genius in the life of others. To the Whiteheads, he was "for decades a shining light." He was ahead of his time because he understood that "partnership is essential. That's what Christian community demands." He never sees religious leadership "as a prima donna event, a solo. He's not tempted by being an eminence." According to the Whiteheads, that's his "saving grace." Jim Whitehead perceives in Father Egan "a genuine sense of his own incompleteness, his own inadequacy. He knows he needs people but I've never seen anybody recruit people the way he does."

Regretfully, they note that Jack could be intimidated, that he was more impressed with university people than he needed to be. The Whiteheads class Jack Egan as an intellectual, "a man of ideas, with a broad range of interests, and a deep respect for knowledge." Jim remembers a faculty member saying at a campus gathering he wished there were more people like Jack Egan "who was an intellectual but not an academic."

The Whiteheads always relied on Father Egan as a sign of hope. "The facts aren't always hopeful, but he keeps hoping." They describe "marvelous Monday morning meetings at Notre Dame when we were all on the pastoral theology team." Jack was traveling widely and came back each week with stories from the field. To the Whiteheads these were often "tales of ecclesiastical horror," but Jack always discerned "a glimmer of hope or fidelity or courage or community" in any disaster. "What registers with him is possibility."

To church historian David O'Brien, that ability to look at reality and bring hope to it is prophetic. He told CCUM people in 1983 that recovering a sense of Church in terms of the prophets was needed. He explained that a community must bring the presence of God to the place where they are, and cultivate a sense of the Church as an organized people bound by experience. A community can be neither despairing nor triumphal.

O'Brien knows it's difficult to look at the world as it really is—at the situation of the poor, the handicapped, women, farm workers, parish priests, Sisters—and not despair. "It requires those who uphold that view to develop a more articulate and compelling rationale, to communicate with one another and gain influence in appropriate institutions like colleges and universities, learned societies, seminaries, publications," all the time being careful to avoid elitism "by maintaining close ties with the people and pastoral workers on one side and with the bishops on the other."

O'Brien cites Jack Egan as part of a company that wants "Church in the Catholic sense, community in the grass roots voluntarism sense, and the social gospel as it has developed since Vatican II." This special company isn't exclusively right, left, or center. Because they think Church is possible, they simply appropriate the best of right, left and center views.

Jack and Peggy ran CCUM their first seven years at the university, living on possibility. "We were bridge-builders, enablers, connectors. We thought connecting was our task. We spent a lot of time on the phone, a lot of time with the mail. In 1972, Don Thorman, managing editor of the *National Catholic Reporter*, asked Peggy and me to write a four-page biweekly newsletter called *Link*," Jack recalls. Under the auspices of the *National Catholic Reporter*, Peggy and Jack used *Link* as another tool to connect people in similar work across the country. Those interested in housing in San Antonio, for instance, would get to know of people doing the same work in Seattle. In 1974, when NCR gave up on the *Link*, Jack and Peggy published their own monthly version called *Connector*. It had 5,300 subscribers.

CCUM was truly the area where Peggy and Jack's mutual gifts were best utilized. They gladly poured themselves into this vessel of service, assured that urban ministers they enabled were enabling urban communities. Once Jack was director of the Institute for Pastoral and Social Ministry, however, and Peggy his assistant in that capacity, they thought it inappropriate to hang on to the CCUM leadership.

Father Phil Murnion, activist priest/sociologist from New York, came on as CCUM Board Chairperson, and Presentation Sister Margaret Cafferty as Executive Director. Cafferty brought in a new agenda: implementing directives from the 1976 A Call to Action meeting in Detroit. (Many CCUM members had done yeoman work for that gathering.) Sensing a split in the CCUM board over support for her program, Cafferty brought it to a vote. She resigned when the vote showed inadequate support. "From that moment," Jack recalls sadly, "CCUM started going down." Looking back, Jack thinks that Peggy and he should have absented themselves from what looked like a loyalty vote. "If I had it to do over again, I would have abstained. In retrospect, I think we were wrong."

It's not surprising that A Call to Action forces split CCUM. In 1976, the Church worldwide was sitting on a fault created by those four centuries of stagnation Father Hesburgh talks about, the fault cracked open by Vatican II. Everywhere the rift between the conservatives and the liberals threatened to erupt into conflict. A Call to Action, an effort to further Vatican II initiatives, menaced the status quo. The bishops were afraid of getting burned. In Rome, they knew, change was frowned upon—even if it seemed to stem directly from Vatican II.

A Call to Action started innocently enough. Propelled by a heady— and short-lived—Vatican II audacity, American bishops conceived the notion of a country-wide "town meeting" on the theme of justice in the world. This was to mark the country's bicentennial in 1976. (Historian David O'Brien says that Father Brian Hehir, director of the United States Catholic Conference division of International Justice and Peace, hoped the event would be comparable to the Medellin, Colombia, conference in 1968.)

For two years prior to 1976, the bishops solicited responses to Vatican II initiatives at local and regional hearings in almost half the nation's dioceses (but not in Cardinal Cody's Chicago). Feedback sheets showed that as many as 800,000 Catholics participated. John Cardinal Dearden, archbishop of Detroit from 1959 to 1980, remembers "the unrehearsed plaint of a farmer who lived on the land he and his parents before him had tilled . . . the testimonies of blacks caught up in the seemingly hopeless cycle of metropolitan poverty . . . the simple narratives of migrant workers telling of the bleak anguish of rootlessness." He found what he heard "poignant and moving."

In October 1976, 1351 delegate Catholics—many elected, the majority appointed by the bishops—gathered in Detroit's Cobo Hall. There, the people's representatives in general congress assembled were meant to disclose to their bishops "the mind of the Church" by voting on the proposals synthesized from the many testimonies. It would be up to the bishops to implement the directives as they saw fit. Whatever changes they made after this colloquy would be from an informed and supported position.

The process was headed by Cardinal Dearden, and directed by Sister Margaret Cafferty, the Presentation sister who later moved into the CCUM executive directorship. "A brilliant woman, a hard worker," Jack says, "a good choice" for this effort to empower the laity and parish priests, to grasp the "sensus fidelium," as Vatican II had decreed. Early on, it looked as if the assembly was going to succeed in its mission. The apostolic delegate attended. Five cardinals. Fifty bishops. The delegates and alternates represented the wide spectrum of American Catholic thought from the very conservative to the very liberal. Cardinal Dearden told them the goal "of this extraordinary assembly" was to "translate their sincere commitment to liberty and justice into concrete programs of action."

Jack Egan felt very much at the heart of this assembly at Cobo Hall because Margaret Cafferty had asked him to serve as one of two chairpersons to bring the issues to the floor and direct the proceeding. He vibrated with anticipation. It was his sort of affair. "All nationalities were represented. All mindsets, the far right, the far left. A Call to Action was based on the teachings of the Church, American notions of religious liberty, and the democratic principles in the Constitution and the Bill of Rights." Jack Egan's great hopes matched Cardinal Dearden's. Their euphoria was not general. After his first session on the podium, Jack met Bishop Bernard Law (later, cardinal of Boston). "Jack," Law urged vehemently, "we have to adjourn this meeting right away."

"Pardon me?" Jack asked.

"We have to adjourn," the bishop insisted. "Certain resolutions are coming before the floor that Rome is not going to like."

"Bernie," Jack patiently maintained, "the people here have a right to express their mind on these resolutions. The bishops can accept the recommendations or turn them down. And they don't have to think what Rome will think of them one way or another. Let me go to the washroom. You go back and sit down. We are not going to adjourn this meeting."

It was the judgment of co-chair Jack Egan that delegates voted "very intelligently" between Friday evening and Saturday night. Jack was impressed with conference resolutions on racism, neighborhood development, housing, employment, family life, and religious vocations. Jack didn't agree with critics who claimed that dissidents had a disproportionate role. From his point of view, press coverage that headlined such provocative issues as birth control, clerical celibacy, women's ordination, and homosexuality obscured the conference's solid achievement.

But Jack Egan was coming from a different corner than the bishops. He was ready, had been ready for a long time, to share the governance of the Church with the laity. The American bishops were more diffident. According to Church historian David O'Brien, who participated in A Call to Action, the National Conference of Catholic Bishops was at that time "unclear about its relationship with Rome and with its own local dioceses." The organization's capacity to respond to a large reform agenda was strictly limited. Even ten years after A Call to Action, according to O'Brien, the "bishops (were) still far from being ready to accept the degree of collaboration involved in A Call to Action, while the need for building structures of shared responsibility remain(ed) clear to all who care(d) to look."

Jack Egan found it hard to suppress his disappointment as the Church moved at an elephant's pace without taking an elephant's long steps. Through his association with lay people, he'd come to admire and rely on their expertise. He could never have looked at the participants—sixty-four percent of whom were employed by the Church—as a "ragtag assembly of kooks, crazies, flakes, militants, lesbians, homosexuals, ex-priests, incompetents, castrating witches, would-be messiahs, sickies, and other assorted malcontents," as Father Andrew Greeley did.

In a long article in the *Chicago Tribune* Jack took issue with Bishop Joseph Bernardin's view that "too much was attempted at the meeting." But a bishop speaks louder than a monsignor in the American press, as in the Church. The impulse that was A Call to Action quickly decelerated. It was not a North American Medellin Conference. Nevertheless, Jack Egan suggests, within a decade maybe eighty-five percent of A Call to Action resolutions were implemented by the bishops. They did not ratify the controversial stands on optional celibacy and the ordination of women that upset participants like Cardinal Law. However, there was a positive aftereffect: the use of widespread hearings for the bishops' letters on peace and the economy published within the next decade. Many of the concerns that surfaced at A Call to Action resurfaced in the bishops' pastoral letters on racism, cultural diversity, Hispanic concerns, and nuclear weapons.

Meanwhile, back at the university, the change in provosts that altered the Institute for Pastoral and Social Ministry equation also affected the make-up of the team set to mount a $180 million fund raising campaign for Notre Dame. It left one of the three teams without a leader. Father Hesburgh was heading a group, Holy Cross Father Ned Joyce a second. Father Hesburgh cast around for a fill-in with the enthusiasm for the university and the exuberant personality necessary to rouse generous impulses in alumni with the resources to support their alma mater. What about his assistant, a priest awed by the university since he was a Irish Catholic newsboy in Ravenswood identifying with the Four Horsemen of Notre Dame?

Father Egan got another of the president's late night "Can-you-come-over?" phone calls. Father Hesburgh explained the fix he was in. After all the months of planning, all the advance work, one of his teams was leaderless. So much depended on the front man who presented the picture of the university to graduates and friends. Father Hesburgh wanted Jack Egan to fill in for the former provost. "At Notre Dame," says Jack Egan, "that was comparable to getting the Nobel prize."

Again, he pleaded that Hesburgh was making a serious mistake since he, Jack, was neither Notre Dame alumnus nor Holy Cross priest. Again, Father Hesburgh cited Jack's enthusiasm, his ability to put across a story, and his devotion to the university. Overwhelmed with gratitude, Jack finally assented. "My heavens, I'd be honored to do it." He joined the team going to thirty-six cities to raise money and raven on broccoli. "I haven't had broccoli since."

In each city, at a home or a club, Jack would pitch the dreams being developed for the university at South Bend. Teams from the development office followed up, pitching for funds. The effort raised $230 million. Jack discounts his contribution. He thought he owed it to the university. Father Hesburgh has never forgot it. "He has never stopped talking about how I stepped into the breach and saved the day."

Returned from his fund-raising trip, Father Egan heard murmurings at the Institute for Pastoral and Social Ministry. Jack's operational mode was to assess up front his possibilities of success at any enterprise. He knew his skills involved engaging people in significant enterprises, motivating them, supporting them in subsequent difficulties, reassuring them, making contacts, offering a sympathetic ear and ready assistance. If these were the skills necessary for a potential task, he had a good chance of succeeding. When his associates were proof against his charm and in no need of his support, they would have different expectations of a director. They would expect rules of order CCUM members, for instance, would dismiss as inconsequential.

By the spring of 1982, Jack's managerial style was not working with the directors of the individual IPSM centers. The management style acceptable to the CCUM group was experienced as hierarchical at IPSM.

Center directors let it be known they'd prefer a more communitarian management style. Center directors, bound together now into the Institute for Pastoral and Social Ministry, felt they were thrashing through a thicket of financial and administrative hazards. They knew about that $400,000 Jack had raised for CCUM. Between 1976 and 1981, Jack Egan raised $1,335,642 from 152 donors to divide among programs of the component centers. There were those who felt Jack used "imperial power" to distribute university monies without any accountability. Monday morning staff meetings became tense, painful.

Meanwhile, Jack was doing double duty, serving simultaneously as institute director and Father Hesburgh's assistant. Part of the latter role was representing the president of the university at conferences. In 1980 Hesburgh asked Jack to attend a British/Irish conference at Oxford. Free for a couple of days after the conference finale, Jack decided to case the territory of Northern Ireland to assess whether some of the information he'd heard at the conference was "a lot of nonsense," as he suspected. He set off for Belfast. His first indication that he was not well was a terrible chill at the bus station. "I looked like a person with a terrible palsy. My whole body began to grow cold." Once he boarded the plane for Northern Ireland, Jack knew something was very wrong. His body burned with fever.

When he met his priest hosts, he begged off on an afternoon meeting they'd planned. He was shown to a room on the third floor of the rectory, a room without a phone. There he collapsed. "I can never remember being so wet from perspiration. I yelled for help. I tried to get out of bed. I felt myself growing weaker and weaker. I knew I was dying and subsequent events proved I was very close to death. I felt a tremendous peace and knew I was going to meet the Lord."

Jack retained enough of his faculties to know that he shouldn't just lie there and die without trying to keep himself alive. "I rolled off the bed and crawled to the door." With his last energy, he reached up, turned the handle of the door, opened it—and with all the strength left in his body—yelped, "Help."

The doctor called by the rectory cook admitted "in a typically Irish way," as Jack says, "'you have a touch of difficulty with your heart.'"

"What the hell is a touch of difficulty?" Jack demanded in a typically American way.

"God damn it, you're having a heart attack," came the answer. The Belfast doctor was more explicit with the paramedics he ran down the hall to phone. "Dammit to hell, it's 123 Springhill. Can't you understand me? Hurry over here, the man is dying." The Malaysian doctor who accompanied the medics couldn't find a vein competent enough for a pain-killing injection. Time was passing. He placed a fibrillator directly on Father Egan's chest and discharged an enormous shock through his body. "I have never in my life had a pain like that," Jack recalls. But it regulated the ventricular fibrillation, making it possible for Jack to be removed to the Royal Victoria Hospital and to live long enough to come back to Rush-Presbyterian/St Luke's in Chicago for surgery on his arteries, on a valve, and on the aneurysm behind his heart which could have exploded at any moment.

Father Hesburgh had appointed Peggy Roach acting director at the institute during the time of Jack's surgery and recovery. The appointment did not sit well with the center directors. Advances were made to the provost about replacing Jack if he weren't soon well enough to return. "It was almost a palace coup against Peggy," from Jack's point of view. "That was a very distasteful period in our lives." It was equally painful for those directors who, according to an observer at the time, felt they were treated with less respect than they deserved.

To Jack and Peggy, Chicago looked better and better. Jack, who had always kept the priests' personnel board up to date on his activities, reporting in each year, advised them that he and Peggy were thinking of coming back to Chicago. Giving Father Hesburgh six months notice, they fixed on April 16 as the day they'd leave the university.

Summing up, Jack calls their thirteen years at South Bend, "excellent, the people we met, the contacts we made, the contributions we made." Thus, in his usual ebullient style, he blanks out any negative aspects of their Indiana sojourn. He'd been right. He had suffered for being neither Holy Cross nor PhD. But as Satchel Paige once advised, "Don't look back. Something may be gaining on you." Overall, the years at South Bend were among the best in Jack and Peggy's lives in service to the Church, in personal development and satisfaction, in widening their grasp and their grip on reality. In many ways, they had had the time of their lives.

Eschewing any jarring memories, Jack tots up the aggregate projects and people he and Peggy brought to the university and gives them a good review. "We came back to Chicago in 1983 with heads held high." Once again they'd followed the Joe DiMaggio principle that it's better to leave a year too early than five minutes too late.

24

"You Just Don't Say No to the Call of the Lord"

In certain circles, Jack Egan came back to Chicago in 1983 more a symbol than a person. He'd tried to fend off the notion that he was in exile at the University of Notre Dame. "That's why I tell the story of Cardinal Cody giving me his reluctant permission to leave in such detail." But the myth—as Jack Hill says, "myth takes over when history deteriorates"—persisted. To much of the city Monsignor John Egan had been exiled, and the exile was returning. "Jack's Back," the *Chicago Sun-Times* trumpeted.

The headline in the *National Catholic Reporter* on a story linking Jack's return to his 40th anniversary Mass and party at Sauer's Restaurant on Chicago's near South Side read: "Monsignor Jack Egan—home at last!" The *Chicago Tribune* called him a maverick returning from exile and described him shaking his head over racism in the current mayoral campaign. "In a certain sense," he said of those manifesting hatred toward black mayoral candidate Harold Washington, "you can cry for those people. It's sad, because they're rejecting the very fundamental basis of what their religion is. They're rejecting the meaning of Easter; they're rejecting the meaning of the Crucifixion. Their religion becomes hypocritical, self-serving." Jack was back. Jack was speaking out.

For many, Jack returned from the exile-that-never-was as the grand old networker of the halcyon ecumenical days, the inveterate tilter at windmills who stirred the imagination of the young and the stumps of the lethargic. The first to organize a welcoming dinner were members of the American Jewish Committee. To many Jews, as Judge Abraham Lincoln Marovitz said repeatedly, Monsignor Egan was the best friend they had in Chicago.

265

Not everyone was equally enthusiastic at the exile's return. Some saw him as less than untarnished hero. Jack's friend and classmate Bishop Timothy Lyne offered him a berth at Holy Name Cathedral rectory (where Lyne was rector) in hopes that the cathedral parish's "certain amount of prestige" would help Jack "over a hump that wouldn't be that easy somewhere else." Lyne was aware of pastors who felt they'd suffered the daily heat of the "battle when Jack had fought and run away." Lyne adds mildly that "there were years when (pastoring) was a tough business. It was hard. So I think there was . . . I don't know if resentment is the right word as much as questioning . . . that it's one thing to take a position somewhere else."

Lyne was one of those consulted "in numerous conversations with Archbishop Joseph Bernardin and other people" about a post tailored for Jack. On July 23, 1982, when Jack first talked to the Archdiocesan Personnel Board about a return to the Windy City, Archbishop Bernardin was newly appointed. He had yet to be installed. Two months after his August installation, Bernardin talked to Jack Egan about returning to the archdiocese. Jack immediately wrote Father Hesburgh about his desire to "go back to Chicago where my roots are . . . I wish to assist the new archbishop in his quest to make Chicago the finest archdiocese in the country. The problems there are overwhelming, and he knows full well that he will need all the help that can be offered to him."

On March 16, 1983, Jack Egan was appointed Director of the Archdiocesan Office of Human Relations and Ecumenism. He and Peggy moved to Chicago permanently on April 17, and went to work the next day. To Bishop Lyne, his friend Jack Egan was an "outstandingly good organization person." That skill plus "a lot of connections with various other churches" made him a natural for the human relations/ecumenism post. When Archbishop Bernardin offered Father Egan the post, Jack was unhesitating. "I'd like it very much," Monsignor Egan told his ordinary, "so long as you don't expect me to be an ecumenical theologian."

Under the human relations and ecumenism mantle, Jack Egan could pick up the threads of his earlier activities and reclaim the friendships and alliances he had carefully nurtured. As he says of his South Bend days, "There was never a week I wasn't in Chicago." Bishop Lyne ascribes much of Jack's accomplishment to his energy. He says Jack went to "so many affairs at black and non-Catholic churches that he developed a very fine relationship with a lot of ministers and leaders in those communities. Even when he was at Notre Dame, he kept up a great deal of that. So he had national exposure and a good relationship over a lot of years. When he came back and took this job, he did an outstandingly good job of cultivating these people."

If that office seemed a natural spot for Jack to archdiocesan brass, it still intimidated Father Egan some. As always in times of change, Jack's natural eagerness (he'd once been parodied as "Father Eager" at a Cana gala) was undercut by his residual craving for approval. That need for approval was mitigated, in part, by his willingness to see "life steadily and (see) it whole." In some ways coming back to Chicago scared Jack. But he was scared by the reality of the currently tense situation in the city as well as by his perception that much was expected of someone billed—perhaps overbilled—as a returning prophet.

By the time he moved into the Holy Name rectory, Chicago had experienced an election that raised problems of race in unacceptable ways. An angry crowd had jeered Harold Washington, the black mayoral candidate, and Walter Mondale, the presidential candidate, on the steps of a Catholic church in the city.

Jack had witnessed the coverage of the troubling scene on South Bend television a few days before he took leave of Notre Dame. He was haunted by the sight. As he told Arthur Jones, religious affairs writer for the *National Catholic Reporter*, he lay in bed that grim night, asking himself: "What can the Church do? Have we completely failed? Or, in the last twenty years since Martin Luther King's death, have we just taken it for granted that the educational work and formational job were being done?"

He told Jones, "It would be abnormal not to be scared. If there's anything I've learned over the last thirty years, it's that this thing (racial animosity) is one of the most intractable of problems." Back in Chicago, he would have to heft some of the responsibility because, as Jack saw it, "This has to be looked at on a diocesan basis. Plus, it transcends the Catholic Church—it's a citywide issue in a political campaign. It's a challenge to all the churches; particularly the Roman Catholic churches where, it seems to me, the key people are the parish priests."

Realistically, what could Jack do? Those who felt the city was in a holding pattern vis-a-vis church-to-church-to-synagogue relations, advocacy for the underclass, and community organizing, were heartened by his return. Also expectant. They expected that Jack would reach out to them as the archdiocese was reaching out to him.

"If Cardinal Bernardin had appointed a committee of my dearest friends and said, 'How can we make Jack Egan's return to Chicago most pleasant?' they couldn't have devised a finer plan," Jack says of his welcome back to his hometown.

He breakfasted with aldermen, lunched with community activists, and dined with church people. He probed for insight. What important things were going on in the city? Who was spearheading laudable endeavors? How could he expedite the good work going on from his position in the archdiocese? He was seen back in the kitchen in Florence Scala's Taylor Street restaurant, celebrating their jousting against the University of Illinois at Chicago during the early sixties. Scala had headed the Harrison-Halsted Community Group pledged to prevent the leveling of entire blocks filled with old families and solid homes on the near West Side.

To witnesses like John Johnson, the most successful black businessman in American history, who founded *Ebony* magazine and built a multimillion-dollar cosmetics and insurance empire on $500 he borrowed using his mother's furniture as collateral, "Jack Egan is everywhere. He's like the sun, the moon, and the stars. I give a commencement talk at Roosevelt University. He's there. I appear for the National Conference of Christians and Jews. He's there. I'm at the Economics Club. He's there." Jack dubs his social suffusion the sacrament of presence. He cites Woody Allen as his oracle in this regard: "Eighty percent of success in life is just showing up." Jack Egan wants to show up for the people of Chicago. Evidently, they want him to.

No life is without its special ironies. Jack Egan experienced one of those unexpected turns of events when he and Peggy Roach arrived at the Chancery Office on April 16, 1983, to work out the details of their move. They were nervous. Maybe, Jack suggests, because those offices had put the fear of God in people during Cardinal Cody's tenancy. Jack had written down his twenty or so questions in case he might be intimidated by those memories and forget something important. There was no need. Monsignor Francis Brackin, instructed by Cardinal Bernardin that Jack and Peggy were to be treated royally, dealt with most of their concerns with no prompting. Jack decided not to ask his last question: "What about moving costs?"

The office they were assigned was one of the finest in the Chancery Office on East Superior, Jack recalls. "Roomy, well-lighted, and in an advantageous location on the friendly third floor." Father Larry Gorman had already told Peggy and Jack that the third floor was the fun floor: nice people and away from officialdom. The splendid new quarters had "great space, many windows, and good closet room."

Monsignor Brackin could see they were pleased. "Is everything okay?" he asked, poised at the door. Jack assured him they were completely satisfied. More relaxed now, he made bold to ask one more question. With his eye for the handsome artifact, Jack had observed that the commodious desk set across the side of the commodious room was an unusually handsome piece of cabinetry. He'd accepted a passel of hand-me-down furniture in his day and learned to make do. He'd expected furnishings of a higher order in the Chancery Office. But this was truly special. He asked Monsignor Brackin the origin of the "mighty large" and beautiful desk.

Monsignor Brackin's expression did not change. He answered coolly as he stepped out into the "friendly" third floor corridor, "That was Cardinal Cody's desk."

Jack matched the official equability. Only when Monsignor Brackin was gone—and in succeeding days as he had the time—did he explore the secret doors in that wonderful desk. And allow himself to marvel at this twist of fate. "Someday I shall know how Cardinal Cody felt about my getting his desk," he says. For himself, newly returned to an as yet untried slot in the Chicago Church's sanctum sanctorum, that he should inherit Cardinal Cody's desk was a certain sign of a new order. However the legacy might have affected his late ordinary, Jack Egan knew how he reacted to inheriting this piece of Codiana: "I felt delighted."

He couldn't preen, however, because he and Peggy also found old files from Monsignor Ed Egan's days in the office. "I found them discouraging," Jack admits. The exchanges between Cardinal Cody and Ed Egan in the files were very critical of Jack Egan and his work with the Association of Chicago Priests. "It looks like Jack Egan is up to his old tricks again, something like that," he quotes loosely. The past wasn't quite buried.

Nonetheless, the priest who sought social contact as assiduously as Cardinal Cody had avoided it set out immediately to use the phone on Cody's desk to plug into the city. "We hit the ground running," Jack says of himself and Peggy Roach. "I look around. I smell around. I find something very interesting." The newly elected mayor of the city, Harold Washington, "didn't know the Catholic Church. Neither did the people around him understand its structure: the Church's 443 parishes, each with a school. We were educating 150,000 youngsters, most of them black or Hispanic. Our sixty-three high schools. Our Catholic Charities bigger than all other charity operations put together."

Jack Egan determined to get to know the new mayor through their mutual friend Bill Berry, who had worked on Mayor Washington's campaign. Soon Jack could say, "I was the only Catholic priest in the city with a warm personal relationship with the mayor." Jack had the mayor's home phone number. "I would call him on Christmas, Easter and Thanksgiving." He also arranged breakfasts between the mayor and Cardinal Bernardin at the cardinal's mansion on north State Street.

"I think the Lord gave me the talent to encourage people, to help them, to walk with them. I think that's a ministry," Father Egan says. "And it's the same in the political order. I become friends with politicians not because I want anything from them. I want to know movers and shakers to help solve the problems of the city."

The mayor began to trust the guidance of the archdiocese's human relations intermediary in such matters as attendance at public functions. Father Egan spoke firmly to the mayor about his by-passing an ordination of four bishops that included Wilton Gregory, Chicago's first black bishop. Mayor Washington found Egan's nudging so valuable he invited him to join his kitchen cabinet. Both Cardinal Bernardin and Father Egan considered that an inappropriate role for an archdiocesan official. But the rotund mayor and the little monsignor grew close enough that Father Egan could press the mayor on his health when they met at the Palmer House Hotel only three days before Mayor Washington's untimely death.

The Father Egan/mayor of Chicago relationship continued into Mayor Eugene Sawyer's term. By now, Father Egan had the confidence to advise the mayor to fire an employee giving virulent anti-Semitic and anti-Christian speeches. "I've asked him to tone down his rhetoric," Mayor Sawyer told Jack. Jack replied firmly, "I'm asking you to fire him. He is a blight and he's going to cause you a great deal of trouble if you don't fire him now. He's causing great distress, especially among the Jews of this city."

As reaction against Steve Cokely's diatribes spread, Ann Marie Lipinski, Pulitzer Prize writer at the *Chicago Tribune*, called Monsignor Egan (by now at DePaul University) for comment on Cokely tapes the *Trib* had secured. Jack listened for ten minutes and found Cokely's sentiments as "truly anti-Semitic" as any he had ever heard. The four paragraph response he typed out (and cleared with Peggy Roach and DePaul president Father John Richardson) appeared at 10 a.m. Saturday morning in the first Sunday edition of the *Tribune*. "It was a big story on the front page," Jack recalls. When the paper hit the newsstands, "all hell broke loose. I was the only clergyman quoted in the story."

By 11 a.m. the *Chicago Sun-Times* had called for a statement for its Sunday edition. Popular columnist Irv Kupcinet phoned for an inclusion in his Monday column in the *Sun-Times*. Television Channel 7 was at the cathedral Sunday at noon for a statement for their six and ten o'clock news shows. "I was all over the place," Jack recalls, "and now whenever I meet anyone concerned about Jewish relations or anti-Semitism, they thank me for speaking out. 'I'll never forget you.'"

The practice of making himself available to reporters, as to the rest of the city, was by now as natural to Jack as the daily walk to work down Wabash Avenue recommended by his doctor for cardiac health. In contrast, the Council of Religious Leaders issued what Jack Egan considered a fine statement about the Cokely matter. However, it had to be cleared in so many places that it was ignored when it was finally issued. The city had moved on.

Jack Egan was not simply plinking at flying targets like Cokely. In his mind, he was living what his friend David Ramage, president of McCormick Seminary on Chicago's South Side, calls "a lonely witness." Ramage's career in the city paralleled Jack Egan's in many respects. In the early fifties they were both working on the near South Side, Ramage as a detached worker with teenage gangs in the Pilsen area. Frustrated in his dealings with an "old Bohemian priest at St. Procopius who thought that any Roman Catholic kid involved in a Protestant settlement house should be excommunicated," Ramage sought help. "Someone said, 'Go see Egan,'" he recalls.

That first meeting was replicated often, for their lives corresponded in interesting ways. Both were ecumenical pioneers in a Protestant/Catholic clerical discussion group Father Tom McDonough hosted Saturday afternoons once a month at the Calvert House at the University of Chicago in the late 1950s. "We couldn't talk about it," Ramage says. This sub rosa support group "was not a public event." The separation between churches was so absolute, the degree so extraordinary, the insularity so total, Ramage says, that pastors with churches on the same block did not know each other as human beings in those pre-Vatican II days.

Egan and Ramage worked together subsequently at the Urban Training Center and the Organization for the Southwest Community. By this time, Ramage was pastor of the Emerald Avenue Presbyterian Church in Englewood, a parish going from white to black. When Jack Egan headed the Office of Urban Affairs for the archdiocese, Ramage held the corresponding office for the city's Presbyterians. "We were exactly equivalent counterparts," Ramage recalls. Both men left Chicago about the same time. "Jack did not leave until he was essentially forced," Ramage says, "which stands to reason because of the nature of his commitment to the city."

To Ramage, that commitment was to "carry the whole Roman Catholic Church with him" to the city. Jack Egan saw himself as a vessel, a means, in Ramage's words, "to allow people today to have a sense that there is a continuing truth that the Church in resecularized society can act in such a way as to do justice, love mercy, and walk humbly . . ." Ramage's voice trails off.

Ramage understands the ambiguity in having two concepts of Church "living uncomfortably in the same use of language." One is the Church sacred: the Body of Christ. The second is the Church human, sinful, and fallible, the pilgrim Church defined by Vatican II. "Some see the church," Ramage says, "as an institution to be controlled, managed, and used for their purposes." Jack Egan meant the Church to serve the people in whatever way they needed service. His willingness, Ramage says, to be the "token Roman Catholic invocation-giver in the city" links in here with his understanding of himself "as a public Roman Catholic presence at these important value-defining structures and events."

In his official capacity in the archdiocese (before he "retired" to DePaul University), Father Egan had suggested to Cardinal Bernardin that he invite the judicatory heads of Chicago's faith communities to form with him a Council of Religious Leaders of Metropolitan Chicago. "I thought it was important that they should know one another," Jack says. Experience had taught Jack Egan that such entities flourish only when each religious leader agrees to participate personally. When

Father Egan suggested that no substitute should take his superior's seat in his or her absence, Cardinal Bernardin agreed to attend each meeting. "To his credit," Father Egan says, "he's kept that pledge except on the occasions he's been in Rome. And he served as chairperson that first year."

Buoyed by post-Vatican II empowerment, Father Egan and Peggy Roach planned signal events to bring to life the decrees Vatican II bishops had brought to paper. They used those decrees the way Monsignor Hillenbrand had used the social encyclicals, pressing them to the extreme. With their ecumenical partners they planned a celebration of the 500th anniversary of Martin Luther's birth. People came to Holy Name Cathedral from city and suburb. They came from Roman Catholic church and Lutheran. People young and old, but particularly the old who had lived with Protestant/Catholic division to their sorrow, all came "walking in the air of glory," in poet Henry Vaughn's words, the fresh blameless air of mutual interfaith respect and regard.

Chicago artist Franklin McMahon caught the moment in an impressive rendering: Dr. Martin Marty, esteemed Lutheran minister and historian, preaching from the pulpit of Catholic Holy Name Cathedral, embracing each worshipper with word and gesture. Many of them had known when it was a sin for Protestant and Catholic sisters and brothers to share church pews. Now they could sing together their great hymns as fit benedictions. They could share their great awe that this moment—unbelievable in a world so recently divided into Catholics and "publics"—should come to pass.

Mundelein College on the North Side where Sheridan Road turns west at the lake, where young Jewish women had been welcome from its earliest days, hosted the Jewish/Catholic exploration of the 1965 Vatican II document *Nostra Aetate*. "The Church repudiates all persecutions against any man," the Council Fathers had written in their declaration on the relationship of the Church to non-Christian religions. "Moreover, mindful of her common patrimony with the Jews, and motivated by the gospel's spiritual love and by no political consideration, she deplores the hatred, persecution and displays of anti-Semitism directed against the Jews at any time and from any source." However beg-pardon-come-lately this declaration may have seemed to some, no muttering could muffle the general exultation as Christians and Jews mingled at Mundelein in general gratitude for the declaration they celebrated.

"We did four programs in those four years we were at the chancery," Father Egan recalls with gratitude and satisfaction. "Besides the celebration of Luther's anniversary and the Jewish/Catholic event, we completed the Episcopalian/Catholic covenant, marked the twentieth anniversary of the Vatican II decree on ecumenism, and started the process for the Lutheran/Catholic document."

By Christmas, 1986, Jack had talked to Father John T. Richardson, president of DePaul University, about "retiring" to DePaul as Father Richardson's Assistant for Community Affairs. Jack was seventy. His brother had died that spring from a heart condition strikingly similar to his. Jack knew that the stress of developing archdiocesan programs and the staff work for the Council of Religious Leaders of Metropolitan Chicago was telling on him. He wrote Cardinal Bernardin about a June 30, 1987, retirement. Father Richardson's offer to Jack Egan was intriguing. "We'd look at you as an ambassador from DePaul to the city of Chicago."

Mentally adding his small pension benefits to the amount he was receiving from Social Security, Jack's response to Richardson was a counter-offer. "How would you like two for the price of one?" he asked Father Richardson. "If you compensate Peggy Roach adequately for her services, you can have me free." Jack welcomed the association with DePaul which he admired for its generous policies, its administration open to new ideas for helping the city and the Church as well as the university. "Here I am at one of the great universities of our land," he said after moving into the offices at 243 S. Wabash. "It wasn't (great) when I was here in 1935, but it is today. It has no religion test for anybody—faculty or student—and it never did. It admitted women in the early part of the century when other Catholic universities did not. Some great universities had quotas for Jews. This university never did. It has educated some of the finest lawyers, Christian and Jewish, in the city. It has taught the poor and the city's working men and women."

At his last meeting with the Council of Religious Leaders of Metropolitan Chicago before he left the Office of Human Relations and Ecumenism, Jack made two suggestions born of his years of organizing: 1) hire an executive director, and 2) reach out to members of all religious faiths with large contingents in Chicago: Buddhists, Hindus, Bahais, Moslems, and American Indians.

Reach out, reach out! Jack Egan had been reaching out since the day he was ordained, since before his ordination. Reaching out to his friends, his fellow priests, to Sisters who wanted to organize, to laborers and labor organizers, to the poor, to young marrieds and old marrieds, to blacks, to seminarians, to Jews, to Protestants, to young working women and old faltering priests. Always as a priest.

Always and everywhere, Jack Egan is first and foremost priest: *Father* Egan. When his friends asked what to call the new Monsignor in those days before priests went by their first names, Jack suggested that "Father Egan" would still do very well. He displays a touching eagerness when he tells stories of functioning as a priest, particularly when he can describe bringing the gentleness of Jesus to a sick bed or the side of a dying friend. He lingers reflectively over his accounts of special people who have called for him in their extremity. "Have I told you this story before?" he asks, eager to tell again how he achieved closure in some of the most important relationships in his life. Jack Egan is able to live with certain inevitable break-offs of friendships as the condition of this pilgrim existence. He is constitutionally unable to let a person once dear to him die alienated from him.

From Jack Egan's point of view, Father James Voss had turned on him after Cardinal Stritch and Monsignors Burke and Hillenbrand died, because "I was the recipient of the largesse." Years before, in 1947, Jack Egan had got the Cana appointment that Jim Voss had every reason to expect. Jack would hear reports of badmouthing: "Boy, what did you do to Father Voss?" fellow priests would ask after visiting Voss' rectory. "Apparently Jim had it so much in his gut," Egan says, "and it hurt so much that he had to tell everybody about it."

Yet when Jack Egan heard that Jim Voss was dying of cancer, he wrote him a long letter "telling him that if there was anything I had ever done that hurt him in any way, I was deeply sorry for it. I regretted the day he was not appointed."

Two days later Egan got a phone call from Voss: "Jack, this is the letter I wish I had written." When Jack asked if he could visit, a meeting was arranged for nine o'clock the next morning. "Jim," Jack said, "let's begin at the beginning." As Jim told his story and Jack told his, they realized that they were both wrong and should have talked years before. "I really didn't know the depth of his hurt until that day," Jack says, although, "I suspected it. If we had only talked to each other thirty years before, maybe we would have cleared it up. But maybe we wouldn't have been able to talk at the time. Here, Jim was facing death and we were very honest with one another."

The two priests prayed together. They rehashed their backlog of old stories. Then Jack Egan prepared to leave for the last time. "I knelt down and he blessed me. I blessed him. We hugged one another for a long time. It was one of the better days of my life." Jack Egan got one last letter from the man who'd lost out to him thirty years before. "He died with that bitterness removed."

There are others, like Joe Matthews of the Ecumenical Institute, a neighbor of Jack's in Lawndale, who simply want to check in with Jack Egan before they die. In Joe's case, Jack got a request—"it is such a humbling request," Jack says—from Joe's wife Lyn. "Joe doesn't want to die until he sees you." What Joe Matthews wanted to entrust to his cherished friend was his vision of the Church for the future, his patrimony to the world, the results of his lifelong search for a unifying principle.

"We've tried to get the established Church to see that it's not about peddling abstract dogma but about awakening men into life and significant engagement in the historical process so that they might truly experience the glory of life through intensification of consciousness, and intensification of engagement," Joe urgently capsulized his belief for Jack as an attentive Sister in the corner took down his urgent message.

As he had with Father Voss, Jack prayed with his friend Joe Matthews, blessed him, and knelt for the blessing "of this very beautiful and bright man." At Matthews' funeral at the Ecumenical Institute headquarters at 4750 N. Sheridan Road, celebrated by Joe's brother, the Methodist Bishop of Washington, D.C., Jack placed the cross of Jesus Christ on the oak box holding Joe Matthews' ashes. It was October 1977. "I was the only outsider participating," Jack says. "If this had happened before Vatican II, I never would have been allowed to so participate. And to this day I am a member of the Ecumenical Institute's Board of Directors."

Jack describes his calling to be present as people are dying: "I think there is a certain kind of judicious instinct which will help a person to know when they must give time to the need of another." But how do people know that the person they need is Jack Egan? How did Father Charles Curran, "the finest counselor" Jack Egan ever encountered, know? Jack was at Notre Dame when he got a call from Jenny Rardin, Curran's faithful associate. Charles Curran's cancer was spreading, she told Jack. He wanted to see Jack Egan before he died. The doctor thought that Father Curran, who was a relatively young sixty-two, had perhaps about three months. But three days after first alert came a summons: "Father is slipping and the doctor says he's going to go fast. You better come. He is asking for you." Jack cancelled his appointments and got on the road to Dubuque.

Charles Curran "was totally jaundiced, but that mind was clear and lucid. I sat at the side of his bed, and we went over everything. I thanked him for what he had done for me, which was considerable. Then he thanked me for all I had done for him which was also considerable." After the old war stories, ritual prayers, and the mutual blessings, Jack remembers looking down at the failing body that still harbored Curran's indomitable spirit. "Charlie, is there anything that you want to tell me that you would like me to remember? We will not see one another again in this life."

"Yes, Jack," said the dying man, counselor to the end, "you are Irish and probably feel guilty about all you have not done. Please never forget all the good you have done. It was God's work and grace, but *you* did it." His last kindness was to absolve Jack from the might-have-beens, an impossible task as Peggy Roach could have told Curran, but a necessary and valiant effort. Jack Egan, in turn, used Curran's last words to absolve many others in after years. To this unusual rite of absolution, Jack Egan often adds the story of the eighty-five year old woman asked why she didn't rest. To "Haven't you done enough?" she routinely answered, as Jack would answer, "How do you know when you have done enough?"

How could he have ever done enough for Father Curran or for Monsignor Reinhold Hillenbrand, the most profound single influence in his life? When Jack Egan got the word that Monsignor Hillenbrand was dying in May 1979 he called Hillenbrand's rectory immediately. "Peggy," he said as he hung up, "I'm going to try to see the great man, perhaps for the last time." He began the familiar route from South Bend through Chicago and north to Sacred Heart Church in Winnetka, where Monsignor Hillenbrand was pastor for thirty years.

Monsignor Hillenbrand was sitting in a chair, erect, rigidly neat as always. His flat, lined face was expressionless, his hands empty although his breviary and rosary were beside him. Fans could be heard shouting, Cubs could be seen whacking balls, on the television set up by the deacon who got the revered monsignor up each morning and settled the monsignor each evening as he returned from work.

As his old teacher flipped off the ball game and looked up at him, Jack Egan felt their mutual surge of joy. "It could not have been otherwise since we had shared so much of life together. We talked about old times, old friends." Jack felt a satisfying contentment in their ease with one another. But here were tears misting the monsignor's fading eyes. What could be disturbing him? Jack was wholly startled when his idol, always so sure of his preeminence, began uncharacteristically questioning his own achievement. "Johnny," he wavered plaintively, "have I wasted my life? People tell me I wasted my life working with small groups, with the Young Christian Students, the Young Christian Workers, and the Christian Family Movement."

The old roles were reversed. Once Monsignor Hillenbrand had been Jack's mentor. Now Jack was the monsignor's mentor, a "father" talking to a "son." He gathered his resources, the skills he had learned at other bedsides, with others who had looked to him for the guidance, the wisdom, the help, the solace he wanted to give. To Jack, Monsignor Hillenbrand asking if his life had meaning was the voice of the Lord. "The call of the Lord comes to you through the needs of other people," Father Egan says. "You just don't say no to the call of the Lord." Jack had become a priest to answer the needs of those who needed him, and now—bless God—he was there for this old priest who needed him as much as anyone ever had.

Jack Egan brought to this task of reconciliation all the poetry and compassion of his Irish soul. "I recounted his life for Monsignor Hillenbrand, the influence he had in Catholic Action, the liturgical movement, the social action endeavors in the United States, his influence in the labor movement, the renewal of the seminary system." Then, as he would in a few days for the reporter at the *Sun-Times*, Jack assured the dying priest that he was one of those rare persons who truly made a difference in the American Church, that he had "anticipated and helped prepare the total American Church for Vatican II."

Jack Egan listed for Monsignor Hillenbrand the roster of those whose lives he had directly influenced. "I mentioned them all by name. The tears streamed down his tired cheeks."

Then Jack generously recalled the influence that his beloved teacher had had in his own life. Monsignor Hillenbrand listened with exquisite attention, finally bringing himself to sigh, "Then, Johnny, I didn't waste my life?" Jack Egan assured him that his "was one of the finest priestly lives that had ever been lived."

They prayed together. Jack knelt for the blessing of this great old man from whom he had been so long estranged. Then he blessed his friend, "both of us knowing that we would never see each other again." The monsignor died the following week.

The deacon who cared for Monsignor Hillenbrand stopped Jack in the parking lot after the funeral Mass celebrated by Cardinal Cody. He described how restless Monsignor Hillenbrand had been in his last weeks, "until you came, Monsignor Egan. After your visit a great peace settled over him that lingered until he died." Jack was grateful to have played a final part in Monsignor Hillenbrand's life. He remembers that last visit as "the rarest of privileges."

25

"He Deserves the Honor He Needs"

In some extravagant metaphorical sense, Jack Egan became a man of the Church because it not only made him a Father, it made him a Father Christmas. If there's one thing he likes better than Nina Polcyn Moore's fresh file in a fresh folder in a fresh filing cabinet, it is putting his hand to the big bag on his back and drawing out a wonderful gift for someone in terrible need. It may be solace for a Monsignor Hillenbrand needing to be eased into his next life. It may be, and often has been, a bundle of money for some young woman who needs her teeth fixed. Jack knows young women need to feel pretty. It can be a woman needing guidance in annulment proceedings. It can be that legitimacy that people get from Jack's presence because he brings the presence of the Church to the spot where he is operating. It can be his last twenty dollar bill to a person who knocks against him in an El station.

Jack's response to need can be seen in Jack Hill's story of Jack Egan, Jack Hill's mother-in-law, and Jack Hill's mother-in-law's sore toe. Years after Jack Hill had left Presentation Parish and resigned from the priesthood, after he was married and working to build low-income housing with RENEW in South Bend, the Hills invited Jack Egan to a family party on the Fourth of July at their Michigan farm about thirty miles from the University of Notre Dame. "A cook-out," Hill says. "A lot of people."

Jack Egan was at his gladhanding best, circulating through the gathering, punctuating the conversational hum with short bursts of gentle repartee. Always alert to the out-of-the-way, he noted that Jack Hill's mother-in-law was having trouble walking, "hobbling just a little bit," as Hill tells it. Matching his pace to hers, Jack Egan said, "You're limping." When she explained, Jack Egan was immediately concerned about her disorder. He described a friend with the same problem. They talked at some length about the friend's toe and the mother-in-law's toe.

Jack made it clear he knew how irritating such an ailment could be. The mother-in-law listened wonderingly, thinking, "He noticed, someone noticed."

She's never forgotten Jack Egan, according to Hill, although it was eleven years later when he was telling the story and she'd never seen Jack Egan again. "When it was all over, Jack had got through to her through the sore toe. To this day, she thinks the world of him. 'Oh, that wonderful man.'" Hill notes that Jack Egan "didn't sit down and talk with her about the social needs of the world. He met her on a personal level when he asked about her toe. Her toe was what was bothering her."

That hankering in the psyche that Jack Egan observed in himself, marked in the people at St. Justin Martyr, acted on in Hyde Park-Kenwood, dealt with in the Office of Urban Affairs, and studied at the University of Notre Dame is the universal need to have one's sore toe recognized. Jack Egan learned to attend the sore toes of the world. He discovered early that it was through those sore toes he could enter into the heart of life.

Monsignor Hillenbrand made Jack see that he could never stop with individuals' sore toes, an easy thing to do because there are so many of them. Hillenbrand fixed Jack's focus on the sore toes of society—racism, homelessness, poverty, illiteracy, prejudice. It was by continuing to function as parish priest that Jack balanced individual needs against society's needs. Just as he kept one foot firmly in the Church and one outside, so Jack had wall eyes, one fixed on the individual and the other trained on the community.

Jack credits all the "great people" in his life (whom he will list *at length* at the drop of a biretta) for any insights he has. It was they who brought Jack Egan early to his ministry as enabler of the laity, servant of the needy, and minister to the wider Church and the wider society. They helped him eschew triumphalism before most people in the Church knew they suffered from it. Looking at Jack's ministry in the Church, columnist Father Richard McBrien, chairperson of the theology department at the University of Notre Dame, suggests that Jack Egan, who saw himself as a mouse at the Vatican Council, was actually one of its props.

In a column he wrote when Jack Egan left Notre Dame, Father McBrien told of "the valiant men and women who prepared the way for

Vatican II, often at the cost of their health, their reputations, their peace of mind, and their standing in the Church." Vatican II did not invent critical biblical scholarship, McBrien reminded his readers. There were great biblical scholars who "paid a high personal price for their pioneering achievements" long before the council.

Vatican II did not invent the concept of religious liberty. "There were scholars and ecumenists who were way ahead of their time in this apostolate, and working always under a cloud—people like Fathers John Courtney Murray and Yves Congar, both of whom were forbidden for a while to publish and even to teach."

"And Vatican II did not invent the profile of the priest as enabler of the laity, servant of the needy, and minister to the wider Church and the wider society," McBrien continues. "Twenty years *before* the council there were priests exactly like that, preparing the way for Vatican II and for the Catholic church we all now take for granted: Monsignors Reynold Hillenbrand, George Higgins, Daniel Cantwell, and one who holds a very special place in my heart, John J. Egan."

McBrien calls Jack "a pioneer in the marriage and family apostolate, a pioneer in the urban ministry apostolate, a pioneer in the lay apostolate, a pioneer in the building of priests' associations, a pioneer in inner-city ministry, a pioneer in community organization, a pioneer in priestly ministry as a ministry to the whole Church and to the whole of society."

In McBrien's view, the Church was playing catch-up at the Vatican Council. One of the people it was catching up to was Jack Egan. Only now are theologians formalizing the concepts Jack Egan lived. Joseph Nangle, O.F.M., director since 1982 of the Justice and Peace Office of the Conference of Major Superiors of Men, tells today's superiors of men's religious orders that the beginning point for a spirituality of social justice is not the Church's traditional inward orientation. Rather, Nangle suggests, "it's an outward orientation to reality—the world, current history. The source of life in God for those who take seriously the call to engage in 'the transformation of the world' is the parade of countless issues and events which affect that transformation." Put in Jack Hill's terms, God is encountered in reality, in mothers-in-law, in the sore toes of the world.

Theologian Karl Rahner advises modern Christians to "pray with the Scriptures in one hand and the daily newspaper in the other." Rahner couldn't have described better a Jack Egan who turns daily from the news of the day to his daily writing stint, the sheaf of short notes that carry his sympathy, his encouragement, his commentary on life and his explication of motive, his warm congratulations and hot tips, his fellow-feeling, his deferential admiration, and his pleas for understanding to all those who feel they have a special tie to Father Jack. His newspaper and his mail are his daily agenda for action.

Nangle specifies a corollary: the social minister increasingly finds his or her center of gravity outside the self. That's how Jack Hill describes Jack Egan. "At rock bottom, Jack is a very selfless person." Jack Egan has kept the vow he made on his ordination day that he would never say no to a person who came to him in need.

That's not to say that many people don't remain ambivalent about Father Egan. "There's a certain amount of resentment," the former Father Hill admits, slowly trying to analyze the special nature of Egan's effect on people. "You almost have to come to peace with Jack and your relationship with him. A person doesn't become a friend of Jack's. He comes to know him. Then he comes to hate him. Then he comes to respect him. Then hates him again. Then he comes to appreciate him and comes to love him."

Perhaps the ambivalence in that off-hand, but thoughtful, analysis settles in the ambiguity of Jack Egan's tremendous need to be liked. His father set him up when he refused his son the approval that would have saved Jack Egan the torment of seeking approval all his life. But, in making friends with his own hunger, Jack learned to respond to the hunger he found all around him. He found ways to show people how much he approved of them. He learned to notice other people's sore toes. "He knows how to do it with a word," Jack Hill says. "That's why a large number of people at Presentation (where Hill served with Egan) felt they each had a personal relationship with Jack," Hill says. "And they still do, I'm sure."

For Jack Egan's friends, as for Jack Hill, their "special tie" to Jack is nourishment for them. According to Hill, "This is also nourishment to Jack. He needs to be liked. He needs to be honored. He's paid his dues. He deserves the honor he needs."

Through the years two forces have played off each other within Jack Egan. In one area he harbors this charism for special friendship. In another, he's done the work Nangle says is necessary for social justice.

He's allowed himself to be formed by "the joys and the hopes, the griefs and the anxieties of the people of this age, especially those who are poor or in any way afflicted," as the bishops wrote in the Vatican II document about the church in the modern world, *Gaudium et Spes.*

In his *CMSM Forum* article, Father Nangle explained why such an orientation sometimes looks like less than whole-hearted loyalty to the Church. For Nangle, "The interests of the Church, important as they are, must be at the service of the New Creation." He suggests that for one working at the transformation of the world, criticism of a Church which at times abdicates its service to the Kingdom is a supreme act of loyalty and love. It is the same love, Nangle says, which impelled God to chastise his chosen people: "You may multiply your prayers, I shall not listen . . . search for justice, help the oppressed, be just to the orphan, plead for the widow."

Many times Jack Egan's political skills have been criticized. Years after the Sunday night group at Annunciation had broken up, long after the "Egan heresy trial," those priests imprinted by their master rector at Mundelein Seminary got together with Monsignor Reynold Hillenbrand one last time. For one last mutual purpose. Jake Killgallon. Gerry Weber. Dan Cantwell. Larry Kelly. John Hill. John Egan. Walter Imbiorski. William Quinn. John Hayes. These men were not comfortable with their mission. They shrank from the dark, dark, dark. Were they all going into the dark?

In talking over the future of the movements at that moment in the 1960s, they had agreed that Monsignor Reynold Hillenbrand's growing rigidity and controlling presence were hindering the Catholic Action movements from evolving and maturing as they might with another national chairperson. No one of them brave enough to bell the cat, they'd gathered as a group of loving associates to suggest to their long-time mentor that he step down. They meant to broach the subject delicately. However, no matter how carefully they worded their conviction, there was no disguising its import. Monsignor Hillenbrand listened patiently, according to Jack Hill.

Finally, stonily, eyeing the circle of earnest, uncertain faces, he gave his reply to their suggestion he step down. It was in character: "Hell, no." Who were they to be judging his effectiveness? Then he cannily worked his way around the circle of those who had thrown the first stones, piercing each of them in his most vulnerable aspect. "John Hill, your criticism comes from you with ill grace," Jack Hill remembers clearly Hillenbrand's felicitous phrasing of his criticism of Hill's current counseling efforts. Then Monsignor Hillenbrand turned to Jack Egan. "Who are you to criticize me, Johnny? You who are nothing but a politician."

Jack Hill agrees that Jack Egan has political gifts, but "Jack never considered them dirty which, of course, they're not. They're very necessary. But we were living in a world where we all thought they were (dirty) at some repressed level of our being." Jack Egan used his political gifts, knowing they worked. But other people didn't understand a political sense like Peter Finley Dunne's or like "the sort of thing talked about in *The Last Hurrah*," Jack Hill says. They couldn't understand how Jack could combine political pragmatism with idealism. Didn't he have to be one or the other, pragmatic or idealistic?

Jack Hill describes how Egan used his political gifts in a typical week at Presentation. First of the week, Father Egan would call Streets and Sanitation for a tot-lot clean-up. Next day he'd be consulting with Jack Macnamara about local organizers putting garbage cans on the City Hall sidewalk as a protest. Sunday, Father Egan would baptize the child of Mayor Daley's administrative assistant. On Tuesday, he'd be back with the local organizers to plan another action to get some desired movement from the city administration. Jack Egan found no contradiction here. But the typical liberal priests of the 1960s, according to Jack Hill, "had pure consciences by definition. They were always on the side of the angels, wouldn't want to tarnish their consciences by sitting down with the other side and checking out what could be done."

Hill suggests that in this area, as in many, Jack Egan moved ahead of history. "Jack was prescient. He felt things before they were here. He fought the widespread demolition of brownstones in Hyde Park which would never be allowed today. Same way with ecumenism." Like Father Hesburgh who wrote his thesis on the role of the laity, Jack acknowledged early the importance of the laity.

And finally he was ahead on what Joseph Nangle calls "this new spirituality of social justice which has the power to serve as an antidote to the pallid and deadening religiosity practiced in much of the affluent world." Nangle traces the beginnings of the spirituality of social justice to that first social encyclical which Monsignor Hillenbrand taught his boys, Rynie's boys, at Mundelein Seminary in the 1940s. Its principles were carried into the present by Pope Paul VI who said it is not enough to recall principles. "These words will lack real weight unless they are accompanied by a livelier awareness of personal responsibility and by effective action."

It has not been easy for Jack Egan to be in the vanguard, whether it was setting up one of the first pastoral teams, the first office of urban affairs, directing the first diocesan-wide marriage education program, heading the first national organization of social activists. Misunderstanding pains him, and innovation breeds misunderstanding. He has gone to bed many nights wondering how he could smooth out some faltering relationship.

Yet he goes on trying to blend the principles Monsignor Hillenbrand taught him with that "livelier awareness of personal responsibility" and effective action Pope Paul VI advised. Jack thinks of that responsibility in the words of his friend and fellow student Monsignor George Higgins who told Jack in his seminary days, "You have to learn to fight injustice wherever you find it, Jack."

Jack accepted what he calls "that terrible responsibility" when he was ordained. "Don't be afraid to stand up against injustices, whether it be in government, industry, in labor, throughout the world, the injustices you find within yourself, and also within the Church," he says. "Injustice weighs heavily upon personhood and denies the magnificence of the creation of Almighty God."

"One of the difficulties of getting older," Father Egan admits, "is that you feel tired. I've done my part. I've fought against this and not much came out of it. I developed these programs and nobody seems to care. Whatever the ennui that sets in, or the laziness, or the frustration, it is a temptation."

Then he adds, reflectively, "What I think I am learning as I grow older is that maybe your task, your responsibility, is changing, that you may not have to be the one to develop the programs to fight against injustice.

"What you have to do is find the people and encourage them, inspire them, educate them, mentor for them, train them, build bridges for them, so they will do the job. You have to pass the torch, to use a trite expression. But the torch has to be passed. You cannot just throw it out. You can't say the fight's over. It's never over."

Jack realizes he has to moderate that remark. He's summing up a life that ties himself as a newsboy-fresh seminarian to himself as a young priest standing up against forceful Chicago powers to himself as a middle-aged pastor of a struggling parish. What energized his spirit for almost fifty years? "You fight injustice wherever you find it and for as long as you find it. Because you never, never can stop loving, right until the very, very end."

Then, characteristically sanguine, Jack Egan looks toward that moment expectantly, reassured that he cannot have strayed much from the goal he set himself on his "marriage day," his ordination on May 1, 1943. "You can never stop loving until the very end," Monsignor Jack Egan sums up his core belief, "because your last breath may be your best act of love."

Afterword

"How can your Gospel be so interesting, and you who speak it so G— D— dull?"[1] A poet who teaches preaching told a group of us that that was how she began a course on preaching after having heard homilies by her students. Merely to quote that question here, so out of place at the end of a biography of an unfailingly *interesting* servant of the interesting Gospel, is to remind the reader of an experience we have just had together. Rare it is to run across such a life in the late 20th century American church. One envies Margery Frisbie the hours she spent interviewing, digging, observing, and writing.

Not long ago I brought to a ministerial-professorial colleague the biography of a Protestant pastor who flourished a half century ago. He glanced at the Table of Contents and the index, noted all the events generated by the subject of the book, all the people whose lives the minister had touched, and said: "What a signal of how times have changed; which one of us would merit a biography, and whose biography would hold the attention of readers?" As I read *An Alley in Chicago,* the most obvious feature kept coming to mind: Jack Egan has been on the scene, shaping events in Chicago, being where trouble needed to be stirred up, comforting where that act was in place. Where were the rest of us? We need a book such as this to keep up the jabbing and prodding. Where were we?

On the sidelines. Reading about Egan's doings. Checking up with Father Hesburgh or Cardinal Bernardin: "How's Jack Egan doing these days?" Being in the suburbs. That, at least, is where I was between 1956 and 1963 when the priest was taking on the University of Chicago, where I had studied and was eventually to teach. (Lucky for me that I was not on the scene, I thought as I read: whose side would I have been on, had I been where it would have been necessary to choose?)

---

1. I use dashes instead of letters because I am a Protestant who does not want to jar the sensitivities of Protestant readers, of whom I hope there may be many, and to provide an excuse for this footnote, because I thought this book needed a footnote.

Karl Marx famously commented in a thesis on Ludwig Feuerbach: "Hitherto the philosophers have only interpreted the world. The point is to change it." On the sidelines, reading, checking up, being elsewhere, were places and acts which positioned so many of us to interpret the world. Egan, however, has been changing it, by dint of personality, a delicious squandering of his unmatched energies, learning from experiences—such as being felled by illness and untrue friends, being lifted by the Christian Good News and people he helped—and by embodying so much of what a "city priest" is called and ordained to do.

One note at the very end struck me as less than true, out of place, but not unanticipatable. Author Frisbie must have slowed Egan down long enough to get him to reminisce. He speaks of the effects of aging, his tiredness, his feeling that "not much came" out of his efforts, that "nobody seems to care." The positive consequence of such thinking is Egan's awareness that a day comes when one does get to pass the work on to a new generation. The sad corollary is the haunting thought that maybe Egan thinks that what he here said is true, that "not much" resulted and that "nobody seems to care."

Of course, never does as much come from efforts as one might have wished. Many achievements turn to ashes, get covered with dust, stop being acknowledged. For almost a generation the nation has been learning the lesson that it is fashionable not to care about the city, about social justice, about the Church's being called and ordained to seek results and stimulate care where injustice reigns. One should also note that most people whose circumstances and lives are changed for the better never do know who were the agents of change. God knows.

Father Hesburgh and I, while providing the bookends for this biography, are both drawn to commenting on Monsignor John Egan, who would protest that since this is not a life but a story of a life, we should also note the book and the author. To those who have read it, who have been carried along by lively prose written by someone whose genre captures the pace and verve of its subject, Margery Frisbie's writing needs no commending. But I do want to lift out what might be overlooked: the fact that this is a book of theology.

Classifying it thus is not a design somehow to elevate it, to make it sound more important than a mere biography—or, for those who are unmoved by theology, to damn the book with misplaced praises. My intention is to suggest how we can keep on seeing "how much comes out of" Egan's life, how we can extend the reasons for "somebody to care."

The point can become clearer if we compare. Colleague Langdon Gilkey has written a shelfful of duly footnoted, referenced, profound works of systematic and constructive theology. But a generation from now people are likely to continue taking most from Gilkey's narrative *Shantung Compound*, a reflection born of his own experience as he tried to make sense of Gospel, human nature, and human purpose while a prisoner of the Japanese in China during World War II.

Here Frisbie generously quotes Egan doing something similar about God and humans, not in a prison camp but in a city of magnificent vistas, great extremes, soul-imprisoning injustices, and occasional breakthroughs by a Catholic church and Christian people. Not a few of them are sinners who let Egan stir them up, "manipulate" them, as Frisbie finds some of them noticing that he is allowed to do. *An Alley in Chicago* is narrative theology. Egan becomes a paradigm—to use the postmodern word—or an exemplum, to retrieve the medieval and thus more expressive one. He embodies and exemplifies that *interesting* mix of gifts and cicumstances, shortcomings and slight stabs of saintliness, fallibilities and occasions for eucharist, which God must enjoy in priests and other sinners, having made them so evident in the ones who get to do some changing of the world, who provide reasons for others to keep on caring.

My poet friend when reading this life will be experiencing "narrative theology," which means talking about God by telling stories of humans. She will not find it necessary in this case to contrast the interestingness of the Gospel with the damn dullness of those who profess and speak it. By keeping the story central and the interpretation minimal, Margery Frisbie has stayed out of the way, and thus served narrative theology well, while keeping all of us interested. For those who have been looking for exempla, models and molds, *An Alley in Chicago* will have turned out to be right down their alley. Pass it on.

—Martin E. Marty
The University of Chicago

Index